The Joy of HORSES

A Beginner's Guide to Safe and Responsible Horsemanship

Joy Roberts

CONTEMPORARY BOOKS

Library of Congress Cataloging-in-Publication Data

Roberts, Joy, 1962–
    The joy of horses : a beginner's guide to safe and responsible
horsemanship / Joy Roberts.
        p.   cm.
    Includes index.
    ISBN 0-8092-3065-8
    1. Horses.   2. Horsemanship.   I. Title.
SF285.R645   1997
798.2—dc21   97-30269
                                             CIP

Cover design by Monica Baziuk
Cover photograph copyright © John Terence Turner/FPG International
Interior design and production by Susan H. Hartman
Photographs on pages 111, 114, 119, 120, 126, and 199 courtesy of the author
All other interior photographs © Kit Houghton

Published by Contemporary Books
An imprint of NTC/Contemporary Publishing Company
4255 West Touhy Avenue, Lincolnwood (Chicago), Illinois 60646-1975 U.S.A.
Copyright © 1998 by Joy Roberts
Printed in the United States of America
International Standard Book Number: 0-8092-3065-8

18   17   16   15   14   13   12   11   10   9   8   7   6   5   4   3   2

1998
Merry Christmas
to
Hannah —
All our love to you
The Hiltons

Contents

Introduction

The Essential Ingredients for a Rewarding Relationship with Horses

In our enthusiasm to get involved in a new activity, some of us have a tendency to plunge straight into the deep end and wind up floundering, gasping, and paddling desperately for the safety of firm ground. This happens in the realm of horses, where riding is often thought to be the focal point—the goal of horsemanship—and a beginner's first experience may be setting a foot in the stirrup. Such a ride may be an unforgettably magical experience; more often than not it will leave the new rider laden with memories of fear, lack of control, and awkwardness, not to mention a sore bottom and chafed legs.

It's not difficult to find literature on riding techniques or instructors for riding lessons. Although this book will cover riding, my goal is not to make you look dazzling in the show ring or to turn your horse into a performance machine. I aim to teach you the basics of smart horsemanship, thus eliminating the fear, insecurity, negligence, and abuse associated with lack of knowledge. What you don't know or understand can not only hurt you but can affect the well-being of the horse and others around you.

I have been hanging out with horses all my life. I've worked with everything from mongrel ponies to racehorses. I've spent enough time around horses and horsepeople to recognize that ignorance is dangerous and even the sharpest professional horsepeople can be downright hazardous if they forget, ignore, or believe themselves to be above the rules of basic horsemanship.

In the belief that it is easier to teach good habits in the first place than it is to break bad habits, I have designed this book to address the person that has not necessarily ever laid a hand on a horse. I hope to teach the beginner sensibility and confidence in all aspects of horsemanship and to help restore lost confidence in those who have had bad experiences around horses due to lack of knowledge, help, and understanding.

Beyond knowledge there are characteristic traits I've found common in the best of horsepeople—traits helpful in forming and maintaining a rewarding relationship with horses. Among these traits are patience and the ability to control your temper. If you are lacking here you will find yourself in constant battle and may even learn to hate horses. The ability to empathize is vital. You must be able to get inside your horse's head, to some extent, to understand what it is going through, what will motivate it, and what will not. Hand in hand with empathy is kindness. Being kind does not mean you must spoil or pamper a horse, it simply means you must act with the intention of causing no harm. Finally, you must have a positive attitude. You must actually like horses and enjoy being around them. You must accept the work, the expenditures, and the occasional mishaps without constantly grumbling or begrudging the horse. You must be willing to measure progress in inches rather than miles. With these simple ingredients you will find the keys to successful horsemanship.

There is a huge amount of responsibility necessary for the proper care and handling of horses. There is also an enormous amount of pleasure to be had, not just for you but for the horse you choose to devote yourself to. Your conscientious attempt to gain skills and knowledge and to develop good habits will be rewarded with a horse that learns to accept and welcome your presence, that performs without hesitation, confident you will lead it to no harm, and that will in turn not think to deliberately harm you.

Horses have been an ongoing source of joy throughout my life. I believe with the right sort of instruction and a proper frame of mind you will also find great pleasure with horses. This is my hope and my motivation in writing this book.

1

Getting Acquainted
An Introduction to the Horse

*I*n order to write this book I had to break down and learn how to use a computer, something I'd avoided successfully for years. Because I lack the patience to take a class, my computer-whiz brother-in-law sat down with me one evening to give me a crash course at the keyboard. He was spewing all sorts of bewildering terms at me that were to him just basic language and common knowledge. When he referred to "clicking the mouse" and "booting it up" some odd pictures ran through my mind, none of which had much to do with keyboards or monitors. As a beginning horseperson, you may have experienced just these sensations when listening to horse jargon, and I hope to clear up some of the confusion in this chapter. I'll provide a review of basic horse terms and an understanding of what a horse really is and the many ways it can be described. This information will help you get through the rest of this book and get by in the real-life world of horses.

Basic Makeup

Horses first became of use to man as a source of meat and skins. Hunting horses was soon replaced by raising and keeping them domestically in herds to help with harvesting, and from there it was a matter of time before the more valuable uses of horses were discovered.

About five or six thousand years ago, horses began to be used for riding, pulling carts or carriages, and performing various other chores. The horse's size, strength, and horizontal spine made it ideal for these duties. Obviously these traits are not unique to the horse—cows, elks, ostriches, zebras, and pigs are also capable of carrying a rider or pulling a cart. What sets the horse apart from the pack is its comfortable gait, its reliable stamina, and most important, its complacency. The horse, compared to the above-mentioned animals, is trainable. It is surprisingly sensitive to a light touch, making it highly responsive. It is smart enough to learn quickly and retain knowledge and pliable enough to give in to commands. It is a comparatively timid, trusting creature that tends to cooperate rather than fight, given reasonable demands.

As mentioned previously, the horse is a powerful creature, capable of carrying weight and pulling heavy loads. A horse has muscle mass from the head to the knees and hocks, but below the knees and hocks there is relatively no muscle or fat. This accounts for the spindly look of the lower leg and the prevalence of bone and tendon injuries in this area.

The hoof is hard, composed of keratin rather than skin and hair. This characteristic keeps a horse from suffering frostbite, burns, or easy bruising at the hoof. The hoof is not an infallible structure, however. The wall of the hoof grows continuously, similar to a fingernail. To prevent the formation of cracks, it needs frequent trimming and shaping, hoof dressings to keep the walls and sole pliable, and the protection of horseshoes.

Parts of a horse

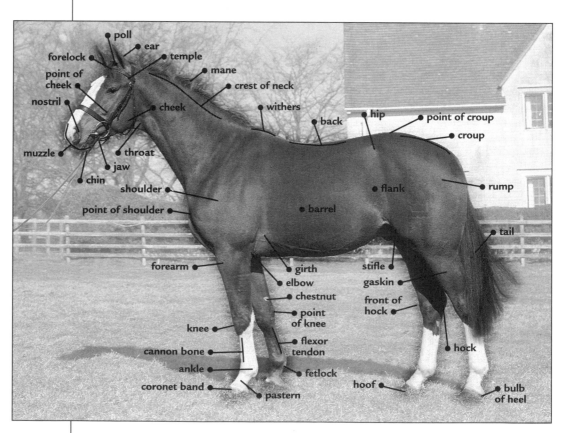

Mare and foal

The aged horse does not differ much in appearance from a young, mature horse.

A horse is adaptable, given time, to whatever environment it lives in and will grow a coat of hair accordingly. Some breeds have shaggier coats than others, but any horse left to its own in a cold environment will develop a thick coat of long hairs that shed in warmer seasons to a short, glossy finish. The mane and tail of a horse are more than decorative accessories; they are used to ward off flies in the warm months and offer a slight amount of protection from the elements during cold or wet spells.

Growth Cycle

The horse is a mammal that carries its offspring full term, about eleven months, and gives birth to a foal that, if healthy, can stand within minutes and run within hours. This natural design has enabled foals to survive by allowing them to follow their mothers, which cannot carry them, and by allowing them to run from predators. Around the age of two most foals will be physically mature enough to carry a rider. They will usually reach full height by age three but will continue to develop physically until age five. Sexual maturity occurs by age two for most horses but can come as early as one year or as late as three years. Sexual maturity is recognized in females when they begin their heat cycles. This cycle lasts one to eight days every month . . . but longer, more regular periods occur in the spring, during which the female horse can be impregnated. During a heat cycle the mare is either termed *in heat*, *in season*, or *horsing*.

The life span of a healthy horse is about twenty-eight years, but there are horses known to live past forty. A horse remains relatively unchanged during the aging process. The spine might weaken and become swayed, muzzle hairs will often whiten, coat hairs tend to shed later or incompletely, and the eyes become somewhat sunken. The most apparent age change is in the teeth. A knowledgeable person can accurately determine a horse's age by examining the dental caps and length of the teeth, but even an amateur can distinguish young from middle-aged from aged—the older the horse gets, the longer, yellower, and more protruding the teeth become.

Eating Habits

Horses are vegetarians. When they are born they will suckle mare's milk, but will almost immediately supplement this diet with grasses and grains. After weaning, a horse can survive on grasses and grains alone, which provide the necessary proteins and other nutrients. Horses enjoy many other vegetables such as carrots and lettuce, and many savor sweets such as apples, cherries, sugar cubes, and even cookies and candy. Horses need salt in their diets and usually must get it from supplements because there are inadequate amounts in most hay and grass sources. Vitamin, mineral, and bran supplements are also popularly added to the domestic horse's diet, but many horses thrive without supplementation.

Horses that derive their primary food source from grass will spend many hours a day grazing to get enough to survive. When prevented from grazing, they may chew wood or eat bedding materials. Horses can and do overeat, which can endanger their health. One particular hazard, unique to the horse, donkey, and mule, is foundering (laminitis). Caused primarily by overeating rich green grass, foundering causes permanent crippling and disfigurement of the hooves and crest of the neck.

Rest and Exercise

The resting period of a horse is broken into short intervals. Some people never actually see their horses sleeping. A horse will frequently sleep standing up, but it can lie down to sleep. Young horses tend to lie down more often and for longer periods than older horses because the massive weight of a mature horse puts pressure on the horse's lungs in the prone position and makes breathing uncomfortable. Sitting is an unnatural, but not impossible, position for a horse; you will rarely see a horse sit on its own and will never see it sit for extended periods of time.

Horses have a good deal of stamina but do not tend to keep themselves at an adequate level of fitness for human use. When left on its own to exercise, a horse will run and play in spurts broken up by resting and eating periods. In order for a horse to perform well under saddle or in harness without suffering stress or undue fatigue, the horse must be conditioned gradually, just as you would expect for any other athlete in training.

Defense Methods

Horses in the wild were handy prey to many animals. In order to protect themselves, horses developed methods of defense. Defense has also been necessary for the horse in the herd setting to establish hierarchy, to ward off unwanted company, and to ensure an adequate food supply. The domestic horse oftentimes considers the human an adversary and will use methods of defense during training sessions and other human encounters.

The first and most popular method of defense a horse will attempt is escape. Horses are fast, strong runners and have a good chance of eluding capture. A startled or frightened horse can explode into motion and may run "blind and brainless," actually putting itself into more danger. A stampede can occur when a number of horses panic as a group.

If the horse cannot run away, it may cower and press itself into the furthest space from its threat. It may try to jump or break through whatever barrier prevents its escape. This method of escape is not particularly effective and can cause the horse more harm than the original threat.

If a horse is forced or chooses to face a threat, it will defend itself in several ways. A fairly passive horse might turn away and keep turning away so as to present its backside as a threat to kick and to protect its more vulnerable head and neck area. Another method is to push against or crush the threat.

More common methods of defense are kicking and biting. These range from threats without real intent to make contact to aggressive attacks. A horse need not wait for a threat to approach—it may lunge forward, swing sideways, or back into its victim. Similar to kicking is striking with a forefoot. Horses typically rear to strike but can also strike from a standing position.

Although bucking is often a form of play, it is also a pretty effective method of defense. The horse can buck to rid itself of something—often a rider but perhaps a biting insect or an uncomfortable or unfamiliar piece of tack.

Measurements

The height of a horse is measured in hands, from ground to the topmost point of the shoulders, a hand being four linear inches (about ten centimeters). This measurement originated from the method of "walking" up a horse with the flat of the hand, which averages about four inches in width. A small pony might be nine hands tall; a draft horse can stand eighteen-plus hands. The average horse is fourteen to sixteen hands. If the height is between one hand and the next, it is termed the lowest hand plus point one, two, or three. For instance, a horse standing three inches taller than fifteen hands would be 15.3 hands tall, or 15.3 hh (horse hands).

The length of a horse is measured in inches, from the point of the shoulder to the end of the rump below the tail base. This measurement is used mainly to fit a horse for a blanket.

Horses are also measured by weight, in the United States still commonly in pounds. An average horse weighs one thousand pounds, and weights may vary from two hundred pounds for a small pony or newborn foal to twenty-five hundred pounds for a draft horse. The rare draft horse will weigh more than three thousand pounds.

Gaits and Motion

Horses move in gaits. The slowest gait is the walk, followed by the trot, then canter, then the fastest pace, the gallop. The trot is characterized by diagonal movement, two opposing hooves hitting the ground simultaneously while two hooves are raised. For instance, the left hind and right front land while the

The walk

The gallop, a horse's fastest pace

The trot

right hind and left front are raised. A slow trot is a jog, and a variation of the trot is the pace, a lateral movement wherein the two hooves set down are on the same side of the horse's body. The right front and hind will be raised when the left front and hind land. Only certain breeds can pace; most horses trot.

The canter, also known as the lope, is a four-beat gait. A pattern might start out with the right hind landing first, then left hind, then right front, then left front. The last hoof to land (always a front hoof) in a stride is the most heavily emphasized and furthest extended. When a horse finishes its stride on the left front, it is termed to be cantering in the left lead. If it finishes the stride on a right front hoof, the horse is in its right lead. Cross-leading, or cross-firing, is when a horse is in one lead behind and an opposite lead in front. For instance, the right hind begins the stride, followed by the left, then the left front hits the ground, and the stride finishes with the right lead. This is an unnatural, awkward gait and very uncomfortable to ride.

Some horses do not trot or pace but have a unique gait called a rack, amble, or running walk. This is specific to certain breeds, such as Tennessee Walkers and American Saddlebreds. When a horse is racking at a fast pace, it appears to be trotting with the hind legs and cantering in front. A very slow rack looks like a shuffle and is commonly called an amble. This is a very smooth gait to ride. Another silky smooth gait is the fox-trot, unique to the Missouri Fox Trotter. This gait is a brisk walk in front and a trot on the hind end, the hind legs actually gliding along and overtaking the front hoof steps.

A horse has other characteristic movements that are not considered gaits. It can back up, but only at a walking pace. It can jump, rear, or pivot on the front or rear legs, and can (regrettably) buck using a variety of techniques and actions.

Gender

Horses are either *hes* or *shes* when spoken of, but you will notice throughout this text that I refer to horses as *its;* this is merely to simplify. I will also refer mainly to horses, again for simplicity, although the information given will generally be inclusive of ponies or mules and sometimes donkeys.

A mature horse of either gender is generally more than fourteen hands tall. A pony is commonly less than fourteen hands tall, but both horses and ponies are truly categorized by specific breeds, and a horse may stand shorter or a pony taller than the height listed. A good example is the Miniature Horse, which is smaller than any pony but is not a pony by official standards.

An immature horse or pony of either sex is termed a foal until it is about six months old, then it is called a weanling, whether or not it is actually weaned. At a year the weanling becomes a yearling, and at the age of two it is either referred to as a two-year-old, a colt or filly, or incorrectly but commonly by its mature gender term.

There are specific terms for the gender of a horse. A male horse can be a colt, gelding, or stallion, and a stallion can be referred to as a colt, stud, stud horse, or horse. A colt is officially any male horse under the age of five years. Unofficially, a colt will commonly be called a gelding or stallion at the age of two or three when it no longer looks immature. Some people refer to a colt as a gelding the moment it is castrated, no matter what the age; castration is what defines a gelding. A stallion, then, is an uncastrated male horse of mature age. A foal stallion is rarely called such—it is more likely to be called a colt. A stud or stud horse is just another term for stallion but is usually reserved for stallions that are used for breeding purposes. The term *horse*, as mentioned earlier, is also sometimes used to describe a stallion.

The female horse is called either a filly or mare, a filly being officially under five years old and a mare of

Terms for Age and Gender

	FEMALE	MALE
	DAM *mother* *of foal*	SIRE *father* *of foal*
The Foal *newborn to six months*	filly	colt
The Weanling *six months to one year*	filly	colt
The Yearling *one to two years*	filly	colt *or* **gelding** *(castrated)*
Two to Four Years Old	filly	colt* *or* **gelding**
The Mature Horse *five years old and up*	mare	stallion** *or* **gelding**

* *may be called* **stud colt** *until mature*
** *other terms for* **stallion: stud, stud horse, horse**

mature age. Again, if a filly looks mature, even at the age of two, she might be referred to as a mare. A brood mare is a mare used for breeding purposes. When a brood mare is pregnant, she is termed *in foal*. When she gives birth, she is said to have *foaled*. A sire is the father and a dam is the mother. A horse is born *by* a sire and *out of* a dam.

Mules and donkeys are referred to as jacks for males and jennies for females. The donkey is a species of its own, but the jack donkey can breed compatibly with a mare to produce a mule. All mules are born sterile and cannot be bred, therefore a mule is always a female-horse (or pony)–male-donkey hybrid. A male horse can also breed with a female donkey to produce a hinny, but this is far more rare for two reasons: one, the hinny most resembles the donkey so does not benefit the breeder by an increase of size, strength, or other valuable properties; two, only about one out of eight breedings actually produces an offspring.

Many horses cannot be differentiated by gender just by looking at them, unless of course you look at their genitalia. The gelding and mare will be similar in build and features, as will all immature animals. The mature stallion or a gelding castrated after full maturity are the exceptions. The strong hormonal influence during growth often creates a mature horse with a thickened neck and exaggerated shoulder and hindquarter muscles. The jowls, or cheek bones, are commonly enlarged and the throat more pronounced.

Identification

Unofficially, a horse is identified by its breed, gender, color, and age, but there are some specific means of identifying a horse to prove its lineage, age, sex, and ownership.

Breed registration is the most common, reliable form of identifying a horse. A horse that is registered, or papered, has an official document, held by both the owner of the horse and the breed registry, that states its lineage, place of birth, and date of birth. The registration document includes precise details of the horse's markings, hair-growth patterns, and color to prevent falsification or swapping horses and papers.

This Mustang can be legally identified by the freeze brand on its neck.

In addition to registration papers, a person can have a horse freeze branded with identification symbols. This type of branding whitens the hairs in the shape of designated numbers and letters and is usually placed inconspicuously, for example, under the horse's mane line.

Racehorses in the United States must be tattooed with an assigned registration number. The tattoo is permanently stamped under the horse's top lip.

The oldest form of identification, less common today but by no means obsolete, is the fire brand. Large ranches or horse establishments sometimes use a hot branding iron with an identifying logo or initials to create a permanent scar pattern, usually placed in plain view on the horse's hindquarters or shoulder.

Coat Color

Horses come in a variety of colors, and the color of a horse's coat is often a main descriptive. Unless you are hopelessly color-blind you can usually blunder through with some sort of description for color, but there are specifics that are good to know. Bear in mind that in most cases being close in color description is quite adequate; only if you are being judged or tested would you need to worry about the official color specifics.

Black
The true black horse is much less common than one would think. Many horses considered black are actually brown. A black horse has no brown hairs whatsoever on its coat or in its mane or tail. The body coat, tail, and mane are solid black, but the legs and face are allowed white markings. If the horse has white spots of any sort on its body it is considered a colored horse, either a Pinto, Paint, or Appaloosa.

Brown
You will see many shades of brown among horses. An actual brown horse, in human terms, would be a brunette color. It is a dark, seal brown with a black or dark-brown mane and tail. Some brown horses are so dark as to appear black, and you can call a horse like this black without feeling foolish, but if the horse has any brown hairs at all, such as around its muzzle, it is officially brown.

Bay
A brown horse can have a black mane and tail, providing the coat is a dark, seal brown, but some believe any brown- or red-coated horse with a black mane and tail is officially a bay. Therefore, a brown with black mane and tail would be called a dark bay. The bay has black legs from the knees down but can also have white leg markings over the black. Some bays sport a dorsal line, a dark or black line running the length of the spine, but many do not. The most common shade of bay is a milk chocolate brown, but again, any shade of brown with a truly black mane and tail and black legs is a bay.

If differentiating between bays and browns still seems confusing to you, try this. Look at a horse that is brown with a black mane and tail. If the horse is coffee-colored, it is brown. If it is the color of a mocha, the horse is a dark bay. A horse the color of a cup of hot chocolate would be a bay.

Chestnut
An off shade of brown is the chestnut, or sorrel in Western terms. Many people simply refer to chestnuts as red horses. A chestnut is like a redheaded human, ranging from deep auburn to bright orange-red to almost blonde. A liver chest-

nut is the darkest shade of chestnut. A flaxen chestnut, most commonly seen in the Shetland Pony and Belgian Draft Horse, is a dull shade of chestnut with a pale cream or blonde mane and tail.

Palomino

A Palomino is a dramatic form of the flaxen chestnut, but is *not* a chestnut. Its coat ranges from copper to golden to pale blonde and is characterized by a true white mane and tail.

Buckskin and Dun

Additional off-browns include buckskin and dun. The buckskin is a tawny or beige color with a black mane, tail, and legs. The legs may or may not have white markings. A line-back buckskin has a black or dark line running the length of its spine; this line is known as a dorsal line.

The dun is generally tan or cream-colored but can also be a blue-gray or mouse-brown and has either a matching or lighter-shaded mane and tail. The dun might also sport a dorsal line but it will not be as dramatically dark as the buckskin's.

Gray

The gray is pretty self-explanatory, but there are many shades of gray. A true gray has only black, white, and gray hairs. If there are brown or chestnut hairs mixed in, it is considered a roan. A dappled gray is characterized by, well, dapples—darker or lighter roundish spots over the coat. A flea-bitten gray looks speckled or peppered. A steel gray is very dark and can sometimes look black. A very light gray will look, and often be called, white, but a true white horse has no black or gray hairs whatsoever. A good example is the Lipizzaner, which is commonly referred to as white but is by definition gray, albeit very light-colored. The only truly white horse is the Albino, which is a term used for horses born with no pigment. The skin of an Albino is pink and the eyes commonly blue or hazel, a very rare color for a horse.

Here's a bit of trivia on grays: Most horses are born their permanent color, or an off shade of their adult coloring, but grays are never born gray. They are either born black, bay, or brown, and turn gray after they shed their first baby coat. In addition, many grays lighten considerably with age.

Roan

A roan can be any of the previously mentioned colors except the golden

A gray is never born gray. This foal will likely resemble its dam in color by maturity.

color of a Palomino or Albino white, but it is characterized by white hairs interspersed in the coat of any chestnut- or brown-based horse, or chestnut or brown hairs in a gray-based coat. A roan is usually specified by the main coat color, such as blue (gray) roan or strawberry (chestnut) roan. Some chestnuts and bays have white hairs around the base of the tail, in the flank area, or on the face. This does not qualify them as roans. The white hairs must be mixed throughout the majority of body hairs and are generally included in the mane and tail hairs.

Grulla

The grulla is a rather rare color but unique enough to have developed into a registered breed. These are pewter or mousy solid-colored horses that can change shades by the season. They can look almost black in the winter, then turn to a dull, dun-gray in the summer. Many grullas have a black or dark line down the spine like the bay, buckskin, and dun.

Appaloosa

Colored horses are horses with spots of some sort; they can be bi- or tricolored and always include some white coloring. The Appaloosa is a breed of horse based on the spots it sports, although some registered Appaloosas are born without spots. The Appaloosa's coat ranges from all-over speckles or leopard spots to a solid coat with a smattering of spots on a white background blanketing the horse's rump. In an unspotted Appaloosa, you should see at least some spotted skin color around the eyes, if nowhere else.

Pinto and Paint

Another horse with a spotted coat is the Paint, or Pinto. This coat is not really spotted but consists of large patches of color on a white background (tobiano), or white patches on a darker background (overo). Paints and Pintos can be any base color, from black (skewbald) to chestnut or bay (piebald) to the rarer Palomino color, buckskin, and gray.

Skin Color

The skin color of a horse coincides somewhat with its coat color. White hairs generally cover pink skin. Colored hairs, even light gray, generally cover black or very dark skin. The hoof color is also coincidental to the hair and skin color. A white (yellowish, really) hoof almost always indicates pink skin, and a black or dark gray hoof indicates dark skin. A horse with one white leg (the white hairs must reach to the hoof) will have three black hooves and one white hoof. Appaloosas are characterized by the striped color of their hooves; this is due to the mottling of the skin common to the breed.

White Markings

There are names for the white markings on the legs and face of a horse. These can be very specific but provide simple descriptives. A stocking is a white marking on the leg that runs from the hoof to or above the knee or hock. A sock is a shorter marking and never extends to the knee or hock. If the white

Pony with four white stockings. A stocking must reach to the knee or hock; anything shorter is a sock.

Star (forehead) and snip (muzzle)

Palomino with a blaze running from forehead to muzzle

coloring covers only the ankle or below, you can get away with calling it a white foot.

A star is a white spot of any shape between the horse's eyes. A blaze is a wide white strip and a stripe is a narrow white strip running down the center of the horse's face. A snip is a small white spot or line on, near, or between the horse's nostrils. A horse with a blaze extending in width past the eyes is termed either white-faced or bald-faced.

∩ ∩

Again, keep in mind that you don't have to use official terms at all times to get your point across. If you point to a light gray horse and call it white, most people will know what you're talking about. I often call very dark browns black because that's what they really look like. Whether or not you use the terms, it is vital to understand them so that when you hear about some fantastic bay gelding for sale you know they're talking about a color and not a horse that comes from the seaside.

Dressage horse

Descriptions

Many terms used to describe a horse are self-explanatory. Besides color and gender, a horse is commonly identified by its breed, which we will cover shortly. Other

English-style show jumper

descriptive terms are based on what the horse does or what type horse it is. For instance, a light horse is what most would consider a regular horse, large enough to carry an adult. A heavy horse is a draft-type horse. These terms are not used all that much today but were popular when draft horses were common work animals. Bear in mind that these terms only describe what a horse does; they are not official terms set in stone. If a horse has multiple functions, it may be called by different terms at different times, and if a horse is extremely versatile, it will probably be termed an all-around horse or performer.

Performance horses are often described by the way they are trained and used. A horse that jumps can be called a hunter, show jumper, steeplechaser, or cross-country jumper. Hunters ideally are used outdoors for long treks over fields, fences, walls, and streams to chase a pack of hounds that are in turn chasing a fox. Show jumpers jump through set courses inside arenas. Steeplechasers race over courses set with jumps. The cross-country jumper is similar to the hunter; it will cover a great distance over a variety of fences, walls, ditches, and water barriers, though it is not chasing anything.

Generally, jumpers of any kind are ridden English style. Other English-ridden horses are also described by what they do. A dressage horse is one that performs precision maneuvers on cue. An equitation horse is one that is judged

Stock horse performing a reining drill

This Morgan is a show-harness performer.

Polo "pony"

by its ability to make the rider look good. A gaited horse displays its unusual stepping action in the show ring.

Western-ridden horses, sometimes called stock horses, are also described by performance. A barrel racer is a horse that races around a set course of barrels. There are many speed events like this, performed in an arena, and they are called gymkhana or game events. Likewise, a horse that performs in such will be a gymkhana horse or game eventer. A horse that chases calves in rodeos while its rider is attempting to rope them is simply called a roping horse but can be specified as a header or tailer, depending on whether its rider ropes the calf by the neck or leg. A cutting horse is trained to cut one calf out of a herd, either for sport or on a cattle ranch. A ranch horse is trained to do ranch work, from roping to cutting to riding fences to leading strings of other horses. There is also the Western equitation horse; both English and Western horses can be called pleasure or trail horses if that is their primary use.

There are also: carriage and cart horses that pull carriages or carts; trotters and pacers, also known as harness racers—horses that race at these gaits while pulling a light one-seater cart called a sulky; plow horses (though not many work these days); pony horses—saddle horses trained to escort racehorses to the starting gate or for exercise; pack horses that carry packs on long trail rides or other treks; halter horses that are shown without a rider and judged for their conformation attributes.

Polo ponies (horses actually) are used as mounts for the sport of polo. Therapeutic horses are used as mounts for physical and mental therapy programs. School horses are used for riding lessons. Circus horses perform tricks and act as mounts for trick riders. A teaser is a stallion, sometimes a hormone-enhanced gelding, used to excite and encourage a mare to breed though the teaser is not actually used for breeding. There are many more types, but I am confident you will learn the terms you need as you become interested in a specific niche of horsemanship.

Breed Profiles

There are more than 150 different breeds throughout the world. About sixty are recognized through registries, but all horse breeds derive from three foundation breeds: the Arabian, the Barb, and the Andalusian (Spanish). It is suspected that the Barb and the Spanish were derived from Arabian blood, making the Arabian the true foundation breed for the modern horse.

Today's horse types are said to be derived from four foundation lines present at the time horses were first domesticated. There is the Pony Type 1, a small European pony resistant to damp, mild climates. Pony Type 2 was a bit larger and originated in northern Eurasia, a very cold climate. Pony Type 3, of central Asia, developed resistance to heat and drought. Horse Type 4 is another desert-climatized horse, originating in western Asia and smaller in size than Pony Type 3.

Today's horses share more than the Arabian and Type 1, 2, 3, or 4 lines; many modern breeds are mixtures of other modern and existing breeds. Breeds are changing constantly, although the official registration of breeds has limited creative breeding by setting strict guidelines as to each breed's ideals and specifications.

A complete description of all existing breeds would fill a volume of its own; I have no intention of spending a thousand pages describing all breeds. Nevertheless, it's highly useful to be able to recognize the most prevalent breeds and to acknowledge their primary use and common characteristics. I will list all these things, including some personality or temperamental traits, but I want you to remain open-minded and considerate of the fact that all breeds have all levels of temperament among their members. In any breed, you will find nervous members, those who won't learn trust, members who are aggressive or flighty, horses that are gentle, sweet as a lap dog, lazy, or hyperactive, etc. You simply cannot stereotype personality and temperament by breed.

Light Horses

Albino

The Albino Horse is a registered breed based on color. It is characterized by a pure white coat caused by lack of pigmentation. The skin is pink, the hooves white, and the eyes most commonly blue or hazel, but sometimes brown. Any breed of horse can produce an Albino-colored offspring, but a true Albino is bred from an Albino mare and stallion. The foundation breed, originated in the 1930s, is of a Morgan-Arabian cross.

Andalusian (Spanish)

This is one of the three foundation breeds mentioned earlier. The Andalusian was developed in Spain around 700 A.D. from blood of the Barb and Spanish ponies. It is a large horse of fifteen to sixteen hands, with a heavy frame. The predominant colors of the breed are gray and bay.

The Andalusian has a lofty, collected action, smooth to sit and beautiful to watch, making the horse ideal for festival and parade events. The Andalusian is known for its courage, strength, and docile nature, and these characteristics have created an outstanding performer in the bullrings of Spain. Spanish conquistadors brought the Andalusian to the New World in the sixteenth century, thus providing one of the first, and most prevalent, influences on the North American breeds present today.

Appaloosa

The Appaloosa is another breed based on color. The Appaloosa can have dominant blood from any breed, most commonly Quarter Horse or Thoroughbred, but it must meet color specifications to be registered. At least one hoof must be striped, there must be mottled skin present on the face, and the scleras, or whites of the eyes, must be visible. With these minimum standards, an Appaloosa can be registered with a solid-colored coat, but most Appaloosas have spots of some sort, ranging from a spotted white blanket covering the rump to all-over leopard spots or speckles.

American Quarter Horse

The Quarter Horse is one of the most popular and versatile horses in the United States. It is an American original, but carries the blood of both Spanish and English Thoroughbred lines.

The Quarter Horse ranges from fourteen to sixteen hands and has a square, stocky frame. The ideal Quarter Horse has strongly muscled hindquarters and shoulders, giving the horse compact strength and quick, fiery speed, but not exceptional long-distance endurance at faster gaits.

The Quarter Horse was named for its outstanding speed at short distances of about a quarter mile, and it shares a spot in the racing industry today. The Quarter Horse is also a popular ranch and cattle-working horse. It excels at gymkhana events, but this breed can perform in just about any event, from jumping to packing to pulling a carriage. The Quarter Horse comes in all colors, but is most commonly a chestnut, bay, or brown.

American Saddlebred

The Saddlebred is a tall (sixteen hands or better) breed known for its elegant carriage and movement. It carries the blood of the Morgan, Standardbred, and Canadian Pacer. This breed is popular in the show ring, both under saddle and in harness, because of its ability to high step and perform the dramatic gait of racking. The Saddlebred also makes a pleasurable trail mount due to its smooth motion.

The Saddlebred has a long, high neck, a high tail carriage and is fairly straight backed to the tail base. It is commonly seen as a solid-colored chestnut or brown but also appears in black or Pinto coloring. The horse's natural high-stepping action and tail carriage are often enhanced artificially for the show ring.

Arabian

The Arabian is the oldest recognized breed of horse, with the purest of bloodlines. Records of the presence of the Arabian can be traced back to 3000 B.C. The blood of the Arabian has helped develop many of the existing breeds of horses and has been a notable contributor to the development of the Thoroughbred.

Due to the purity of its bloodline, the Arabian carries some of the most consistent physical characteristics. It is very beautiful to look at, with an elegant, rather feminine appearance. The head is short and finely outlined, the muzzle small, cup shaped, and very soft skinned. The eyes are large and well-defined, and the face dishes from the broad forehead to the petite muzzle.

The body shape of the Arabian is smooth and rounded. This breed has a fewer number of vertebrae and bones in its ribs than any other breed, giving the Arabian a shorter back and higher tail base. The croup is often straight rather than sloping downward to the tail. Arabians come in all colors and can be bred to carry the spots of an Appaloosa or Pinto. The Arabian is not large, averaging fourteen to fifteen-plus hands, but is deceptively strong.

The Arabian is famous for its stamina and hardiness. Desert bred, it can withstand severe heat and famine conditions. The Arabian today is popular in all phases of showing, including jumping. But this versatile breed will be seen in almost any role, including harness competition, endurance trail riding, and racing.

Barb
The Barb can be traced to the Ice Age. Originating in North Africa, this is one of the three foundation breeds and presently carries the blood of the Arabian. The Barb is average size, about fifteen hands, with a long, convex head (Roman nose), spare muscle build, and very hard, tough bones and hooves. The horse is desert bred and desert toughened, with incredible stamina, resistance to heat and drought, and the ability to sustain itself on meager portions. Originally, the Barb was seen as a black, brown, or dark bay, but the introduction of Arabian blood created a popular line of gray Barbs.

Dutch Warmblood
The Dutch Warmblood originated in Holland, a product of crossing two native breeds, the Groningen and the Gelderlander. Today's Dutch Warmblood also shares the blood and many of the characteristics of the Thoroughbred. This horse was bred specifically to produce a competitive show animal. Strict breeding guidelines in the Netherlands have helped the Dutch Warmblood develop into an athletically competitive horse with an exceptionally unflappable temperament.

The Dutch Warmblood is a large horse, generally standing more than sixteen hands. The horse has a heavy frame, deep girth, long back, and well-defined muscles. It is most commonly seen as a bay or brown, and increasingly, a chestnut. The breed excels in jumping and dressage competition.

Lipizzaner
The Lipizzaner originated in Austria from six foundation sires and carries the blood of the Andalusian, the Neopolitan, and the Arabian. The Lipizzaner is a medium-size, strongly built horse predominantly bred to be gray (commonly thought to be white), but it can appear in any color. The Lipizzaner is an extremely intelligent and highly trainable horse; this breed has become an integral member of the famous Spanish Riding School of Vienna.

As a student of the Vienna School, the Lipizzaner will undergo four to six years of training to perform athletic dressage maneuvers and leaps called airs. The ability to perform airs is unique to this breed. A group of Lipizzaner stallions is toured internationally for public performance. The stallions consistently awe crowds with their dazzling "white" color, skills, and obedience. Lipizzaners are not limited to public entertainment; they make excellent riding and harness horses and are popularly shown under sidesaddle.

Missouri Fox Trotter

The Missouri Fox Trotter was bred in the United States from a mixture of Thoroughbred, Morgan, Arabian, and Saddlebred blood. The infusion of the Saddlebred led to a gaited animal, noted for its ability to cover long distances without fatiguing either itself or the rider. This ability is due to its unique fox-trot, a gait consisting of a fast walk on the front end and simultaneously a gliding trot behind. The fox-trot is a silky smooth gait, easy on the rider and attractive to watch. Missouri Fox Trotters are respected for their natural looks and ability, and unlike the Saddlebred and Tennessee Walker, are not artificially altered by tail sets, weighted shoes, or other devices for the show ring.

The Missouri Fox Trotter is a medium-built horse, fourteen to sixteen hands. The horse has well-boned legs and large feet, which aid in its ability to cover long distances. The horse is most popularly seen as chestnut but is not uncommon as a brown or black.

Morgan

The foundation sire of the Morgan breed was a little stallion by the name of Figure, later renamed after its owner, Justin Morgan. This led to the name of the breed, another North American product originated in the late eighteenth century. No one knows for sure what the breeding of Figure was—there is possibly a cross of Arabian, Welsh Pony, and Friesian blood.

The Morgan is rather small and short coupled, thirteen to fifteen hands tall, but is powerfully muscled and noted for its ability to pull massive weight. This breed is also a popular pleasure mount and show horse and can perform in many athletic endeavors such as jumping. For a time, the Morgan was the chosen mount of the U.S. Army.

The Morgan has been a major foundation line for other American breeds such as the American Saddlebred (a gaited breed) and the Standardbred (a trotting or pacing breed).

Mustang

The Mustang is descended from Spanish and Barb horses brought to the New World by conquistadors. Basically, this breed developed from Spanish stock that escaped or were turned loose and formed herds of wild horses. Thus, the Mustang we see today is a compact, hardy breed resistant to harsh elements. Presently very few Mustangs exist in the wild; they have either been killed (they are now protected by wildlife laws) or captured and domesticated. Mustangs, with careful training, make good pleasure and trail mounts and perform well at ranch work but have not yet become popular in the show ring as a distinct class breed.

Due to the variety of wild strains, the Mustang has no definitive characteristics. Careful breeding has developed some guidelines, however. The most common Mustang will be about fourteen hands tall, short backed, low withered, and with a small, straight head. The colors most commonly seen are roan, buckskin, dun, or grulla.

Paint or Pinto

The Paint and the Pinto are essentially the same breed, a breed based primarily on color, but the American Paint Horse Association registers only Paints of stock-type foundation, such as Quarter Horses and Thoroughbreds. The Pinto Horse Association of America accepts any Pinto-colored animal, dividing the types into categories. A Pinto can be a light horse, heavy (draft) horse, or a pony.

The Pinto or Paint is characterized by patches of white over a colored coat, known as overo, or patches of color on a white coat, called tobiano. A black-and-white Pinto or Paint is termed a piebald; a chestnut-, bay-, or brown-and-white Pinto is a skewbald. A Paint or Pinto can also be gray, Palomino-colored, dun, or roan, but these are not as common.

Palomino

The Palomino is another breed based strictly on color; it can be of any breed, size, or shape. To be registered, a Palomino must have a solid golden-colored coat, which can range from almost copper to pale blonde. The mane and tail must be a true white, with no more than 15 percent off-colored hairs. The legs can have no white markings higher than the knees or hocks and the spine can show no sign whatsoever of a darker dorsal line.

Paso Fino

The American Paso Fino is derived from the Peruvian Paso, carrying the blood of Barb and Andalusian horses. The Paso Fino is small and strong, with a unique front-end structure that gives it a smooth-gaited motion. When in action, the Paso Fino's back slopes slightly down toward its tail. It steps high in front and glides behind, overstepping the front hooves. The easy, swift motion has made this little breed very popular for showing, parade exhibitions, and pleasure riding.

Standardbred

The Standardbred was originally bred in the United States in the late eighteenth century from Thoroughbred, Morgan, and Hackney lines. The Standardbred is the most noted, and talented, harness-racing breed and was bred almost exclusively for this sport. The breed has a unique ability to either trot (a diagonal-patterned gait) or pace (a lateral gait) at very fast speeds. Today there are show classifications in both riding and harness designed specifically for the Standardbred. The breed is also well suited for pleasure and trail riding.

The Standardbred is similar in appearance to a Thoroughbred, but generally a bit shorter legged. The Standardbred stands fifteen to seventeen hands and has solid bone structure, medium muscle build, and a large, straight head. The breed is predominantly bay or brown, but can be seen in chestnut, black, or gray.

Tennessee Walker

The Tennessee Walker was founded in the late nineteenth century from a mixture of Thoroughbred, Saddlebred, Morgan, and Narragansett Pacer blood. Sometimes called a Plantation Horse, this breed's original use was to provide an elegant, comfortable mount for the inspection of vast plantations by their owners.

The Tennessee Walker has a unique gait called a running walk. The gait is characterized by a high-stepping canter with the front legs while the hind legs trot in a gliding motion. The running walk is smooth, swift, and stylish and has become popular in show rings. In order to enunciate the high-stepping motion and elegant raised-tail carriage of the Tennessee Walker, trainers have put into use artificial devices such as ankle chains, thick shoe pads, and tail sets. These devices can be cruel to the animal and are now regulated within the show industry.

The Tennessee Walker is generally tall, fifteen to seventeen hands, with a smooth muscle build and good frame. The neck is long and thick, the head large and straight, and the tail high. Tennessee Walkers are predominantly black or chestnut, but can be almost any color. Pinto coloring is becoming quite popular in this breed.

As with the other gaited breeds, the Tennessee Walker's elegant, smooth gaits make it ideal for the show ring or for pleasure or trail riding.

Thoroughbred

The Thoroughbred is derived from three distinct Arabian bloodlines—the Godolphin, the Darley, and the Byerley Turk. It was first recognized for registration in Great Britain in the late eighteenth century. Originally bred for racing purposes, the Thoroughbred's size, strength, and athletic ability have made this breed exceedingly popular for hunting, jumping, and dressage endeavors.

Despite its Arabian ancestry, the Thoroughbred shares little resemblance to its parent breed. The Thoroughbred is large, fifteen to seventeen-plus hands. It has good bones, well-accentuated muscles in the shoulders and hindquarters, a long back, and deep barrel. The head is long and straight with a square muzzle. The Thoroughbred can be of any color but is very rarely seen in Palomino, Pinto, or Appaloosa colors, dun, or buckskin.

Trakehner

The Trakehner dates back to the thirteenth century. Developed in East Prussia, the breed relocated to the West during wartime strife. Of unknown origins, the Trakehner bloodlines were carefully interspersed with top-quality Thoroughbred and Arabian blood around the nineteenth century to produce a performance animal of exceptional quality. The Trakehner has excelled in dressage, jumping, hunting, and steeplechase events and is a popular Olympic Games mount.

The Trakehner is quite similar in appearance and build to the Thoroughbred but is not used for flat racing. Many believe the Trakehner shares the Thoroughbred's highest physical qualities but exceeds it with a more even, tranquil temperament.

Heavy (Draft) Horses

Belgian Draft (Brabant)

The Belgian Draft or Brabant was developed in Belgium in the Middle Ages. This breed has contributed its bloodlines to the Clydesdale, Shire, and Suffolk Punch. The Belgian is one of the earliest and most famous of the European draft breeds and became enormously popular in the United States for its abilities as a work animal.

The Belgian is the heaviest draft breed, commonly weighing more than two thousand pounds. The world's heftiest recognized horse in history was a Belgian stallion by the name of Supreme, which weighed in at thirty-two hundred pounds. The Belgian stands as much as eighteen hands tall and is thickly muscled with short, heavy-boned legs. The mane and tail are thick and wavy, and the legs feathered with long hairs at the fetlock area. Most Belgians, as well as other draft breeds, are seen with short, stubby tails not more than twelve inches in length. This is not a natural trait—the tailbone is docked for aesthetic purposes and to prevent entanglement in harness lines. The most common color seen today on the Belgian is a flaxen chestnut, but the Belgian can also be red roan, dun, brown, or gray.

In medieval times, the Belgian was used as a battle mount, large enough to carry a knight in full armor. The horse also proved invaluable as a farm laborer, capable of pulling massive weights and working long hours. Today the horse is a popular carriage horse and is exhibited in driving competitions. The Belgian is a gentle giant and can be ridden, but due to its broad back and galumphing gait it has not been considered an ideal mount.

Clydesdale

The Clydesdale was developed in Scotland about 150 years ago from the infusion of Flemish Horse blood with local draft stock. The Shire bloodline was added soon after to increase the horse's strength. Obviously successful, this draft breed is considered the strongest breed of horse.

The Clydesdale is known for its usefulness as a workhorse, and was exported worldwide. This breed's labor was a major factor in the development of Australia. In the United States, the Clydesdale is best known as the horse in the Budweiser beer advertisements and in promotional tours for Anheuser-Busch. The Clydesdale is also used for pulling competitions and parade and festival exhibitions.

The Clydesdale stands about seventeen hands, but has been known to reach twenty hands in height. It is bay, brown, gray, or black with white markings on the face and legs. The legs are feathered at the back from the knees or hocks down and the hooves are capped with long, feathered hairs. The Clydesdale is fairly long strided and a high stepper, giving it the distinction of the most elegant mover of the draft breeds.

Percheron

The Percheron's origins date back to the Normandy region of France more than one thousand years ago. The Percheron carries the blood of the Barb and the Arabian, giving this draft breed a more refined and elegant appearance than most. The breed has been used in battle, on farms, and in the forest, and is considered suitably smooth gaited for riding purposes.

The Percheron breed boasts the tallest horse known, Dr. Le Gear, who was measured in 1908 at twenty-one hands. The average Percheron is not nearly this large, standing sixteen to seventeen hands. The Arabian influence has given the Percheron a rather pretty head, often with the characteristic Arabian-dished face. The Percheron has the typical thick, heavy build and short, stocky legs of all draft breeds, but has little feathering on the lower legs. It is almost exclusively seen as gray, usually with dazzling dapples, but can also be found as a black, bay, brown, or chestnut.

Shire

Descended from the English Great Horse, a medium-size cob used for battle, the Shire appeared in late sixteenth-century Great Britain. The Shire, much larger than its parent breed, missed the days of packing heavily armored knights about, but showed up in time to do farm labor and pull heavy coaches and carts over nasty, rutted roads. The Shire gained its size and strength from the Flanders Horse and a bit of refinement from the Friesian. It is best known for its ability to pull heavy weights and is still in use as a working horse as well as a contender in pulling or driving competitions.

The Shire is thought to be the all-around largest draft breed. A Shire must be 16.2 hands or better to be registered, and is commonly eighteen hands tall and well over two thousand pounds in weight. The Shire has the characteristic heavy, rounded body with short, thick legs. The legs and hooves are well feathered and the neck is unusually long for a draft breed. The Shire is commonly bay, dark brown, black, or gray and typically sports four white stockings.

Suffolk Punch

The Suffolk Punch can be traced directly to the founding sire, Thomas Crisp's Horse of Ufford, born in 1768 in Suffolk, England. The Suffolk Punch was developed exclusively as a farm worker and was favored for its strength and ability to work long hours for many years. The Suffolk Punch is an active farm laborer today and competes in agricultural shows. The breed is known to get down on its knees in order to increase its pulling ability.

The Suffolk Punch is a bit short for a draft breed, sixteen to seventeen hands, but very stout and rounded and tends to fatten easily. The legs are feathered lightly only on the fetlocks. The Suffolk Punch is valued for being easy to keep, requiring less food and less frequent feedings than the other draft breeds. This breed is exclusively chestnut in color but can vary in shade from blonde to liver chestnut.

Ponies

Chincoteague

Today's Chincoteague Pony is thought to have originated from the bloodlines of horses such as the Barb. These ponies developed exclusively on two islands off Virginia, Assateague and Chincoteague, and are rumored to have found their way to the islands after surviving a shipwreck. However they arrived, the ponies were originally wild, hardy horses, inbred and ill fed to the point of stunted growth and conformational defects such as narrow shoulders and crooked legs. The introduction of Welsh and Shetland pony stock by breeders in the 1920s has created the true breed of pony currently recognized—more desirable in conformation and typical of features.

There remains a wild herd of about two hundred Chincoteague ponies on the island of Assateague, but an annual roundup and sale of foals and yearlings has created a domesticated population. This roundup has been vital in controlling the population on the island and preventing inbreeding.

The Chincoteague Pony averages twelve hands in height. It is commonly Pinto-colored but can be solid as well. It continues to show its poor foundation lines with narrow shoulders, weak hindquarters, and poorly developed joints, but is improving with careful breeding practices.

Connemara

The Connemara Pony is an Irish native that at one time carried Celtic warriors. This pony's size and style were enhanced with the blood of Arabian, Barb, and Andalusian horses, and its strength and durability was increased with the bloodlines of the Welsh Cob.

The Connemara is a stylish mover with an athletic affinity for jumping. At thirteen- to fourteen-plus hands, it makes a desirable mount for large children or small adults. The Connemara is crossed frequently with Thoroughbreds or Arabians to increase its size and create an outstanding cross-country performer.

The Connemara is well muscled with a long, graceful neck. Its well-formed bones and hooves keep this pony sound under hard usage. These ponies live long lives and can produce foals into their thirties. Originally dun, the most popular color today is gray.

Hackney

The Hackney Pony was developed in Great Britain from the blood of trotting horses of the eighteenth and nineteenth centuries. The breed today carries the bloodlines of trotters, Arabians, Thoroughbreds, and a mixture of pony breeds.

The Hackney is primarily a carriage pony and is used almost exclusively for show. The pony has the refined physical qualities of a horse but is never taller than fourteen hands. The pony has a high, proud tail carriage, a long, elegant neck, and a natural high-stepping action. It is most commonly seen as a bay, brown, or black.

Pony of the Americas (POA)

The first Pony of the Americas was produced as recently as 1956 from a founding Shetland Pony stallion and Appaloosa Horse mare. This North American breed has since been crossed with Arabians and Quarter Horses to produce a breed standard of a miniature Arabian-Quarter Horse–featured pony with the coloring of an Appaloosa.

The POA stands eleven to fourteen hands tall and always carries the spots and other characteristics of an Appaloosa, such as striped hooves and conspicuous scleras. The breed is fairly refined and is used as an all-purpose child's mount, performing in events from jumping to gymkhana.

Shetland

The Shetland originated in Scotland more than two thousand years ago, a probable mixture of Tundra and Scandinavia Pony stock. The most popular breed of pony, it has been exported worldwide. An offshoot of the Shetland is the American Shetland Pony, a cross between the classic Shetland and the Hackney Pony. The American Shetland was developed to increase its size and enhance its gait.

The classic Shetland is a tiny pony, averaging ten hands tall. It is close coupled, round bodied, and short legged, with flexible joints that give it a pleasant, springy step. The mane and tail of the Shetland is very thick and often wavy, its fetlocks and hooves commonly feathered. Common coloring is flaxen chestnut or black, and many Pinto-colored Shetlands are seen today.

The Shetland is an extremely powerful creature for its size and can pull a sizable cart. The pony can also carry a full-size adult (though the adult's legs may drag on the ground) and can be used as a pack animal. The Shetland has become a favorite starter mount for small children and is used for harness and pleasure riding.

Over the years, the Shetland Pony has developed a reputation for being ill-tempered and uncooperative. This reputation is likely the result of handling by very young, very inexperienced riders and is not a real measure of the pony's temperament. Proper handling and training has proved the average Shetland Pony as docile and pleasant natured as other breeds.

Welsh Mountain

The Welsh Mountain Pony is derived from prehistoric British origins, and has helped found several other Welsh breeds. Today the Welsh Mountain Pony carries the influence of Arabian and Thoroughbred bloodlines.

The Welsh Mountain is slightly larger than the Shetland, topping out at 12.2 hh. This breed shares the pretty head—large eyes, tiny ears, small muzzle—of the Arabian. The Welsh Pony is well proportioned with a deep barrel and stocky legs. It comes in all colors and is especially popular as a gray.

The Welsh Mountain Pony is an ideal mount for children. Its size gives it greater longevity as a mount than the Shetland. The pony's athletic ability, natural soundness, pretty looks, and even temperament make it popular in the show ring.

What's Its

This category includes breeds that don't fit other classifications: mules, donkeys, and horses that have the characteristics of ponies.

Falabella (Miniature Horse)

The Falabella originated in Argentina with the crossing of a tiny Shetland Pony mare and a small Thoroughbred stallion. Subsequent inbreeding of the smallest offspring created the pygmy horse seen today. The Falabella is the original Miniature Horse, but many breeders are presently developing their own strains of miniature horses.

The Falabella is considered a horse because of its Thoroughbred line and its physical resemblance to a horse. More and more frequently, the Miniature Horse resembles a poor Shetland Pony. The head is abnormally large, the body rounded, the hindquarters weak, and the shoulders straight. The Falabella stands less than 8.2 hands and is generally considered unsuitable for riding, but it can pull a small cart. The Falabella is most commonly used as a pet, a halter show animal, or a novelty collector's item.

Icelandic Horse

Developed in Iceland more than one thousand years ago, this breed stands twelve to fourteen hands tall but is adamantly termed a horse by its Icelandic breeders. The Icelandic Horse is a hardy, thick-coated, stocky breed, resistant to harsh weather conditions and capable of surviving on meager rations. This breed is strong and can carry a large man and pull heavy loads. In its native region, this horse was, and remains, invaluable as transportation on icy, muddy, and deeply rutted roads.

The Icelandic Horse has a long, free action at the walk that makes it a pleasant mount for long treks. It is a five-gaited animal, with a pace and running-walk (tolt) in addition to the typical walk, trot, and canter. The Icelandic Horse is a slow developer—not considered mature enough for riding purposes until the age of five—but makes up for this slow start by typically living a long life, well into its thirties. The Icelandic Horse comes in a variety of colors but is most commonly seen as a dun or flaxen chestnut.

Donkey (Ass)

The donkey, originated in North Africa, has been recorded in existence as a domestic animal as early as 4000 B.C. The donkey has been used as a riding and pack animal and can pull a cart.

The donkey is generally around eleven hands tall, but dwarf strains are as small as six hands and the American Mammoth Donkey measures up to sixteen hands tall. This breed, not a horse or pony but a species of its own, is sparse in frame, spindly legged, with a short, low neck and large head. The mane and tail are short and scant. The donkey's hooves are very hard, narrow, and have a steeper slope and more heel than a horse's. It is best known for its enormous, long ears. The donkey is generally gray or dun, and almost always has a dorsal line and a black line running down its shoulders.

Mule

The mule is a hybrid donkey-horse. The sire is always a donkey, the dam is always a horse or pony. The mule is recognized for superior strength over a horse of similar size. It has been traditionally used as a farm laborer and has proved a valuable transportation animal capable of packing or pulling an amazing amount of weight. The mule is extremely sure footed and has a good bone structure that keeps it sound under heavy work conditions.

The mule is generally fourteen to sixteen hands but if produced from a pony or draft mare can be much smaller or larger. It has the basic body shape of a horse, with rounded, smooth muscles. The head is large and convex and sports the long ears of its donkey sire. The mane and tail are usually sparse but occasionally are the longer, thicker type of the horse. The hooves are very hard and are narrow and high walled like the donkey's. The mule is most commonly seen as a dark brown but can also be chestnut, bay, gray, roan, or Appaloosa- or Pinto-colored.

Hinny
The hinny is another horse-donkey hybrid. The hinny is produced from a horse sire and a donkey dam. The hinny is much rarer and does not share the popularity of the mule. The hinny is difficult to produce; only one in eight breedings results in a live offspring.

The hinny most resembles its donkey parentage. It is small, donkey shaped, and not particularly strong or durable. The hinny is generally gray, but can be found in any color.

Both the mule and the hinny are born sterile and cannot reproduce themselves. These animals are not true breeds but are strictly considered hybrids of compatible species.

Horse Breeds Photo Gallery

See pages 14–26 for breed profiles.

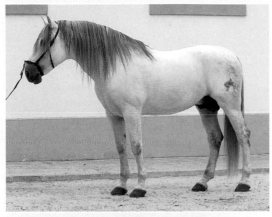

The Albino, a non-pigmented color breed

The Andalusian (Spanish) Horse, an ancient foundation breed

Appaloosa, a color breed

American Quarter Horse

American Saddlebred, a gaited breed

Arabian, the true foundation breed for all horses

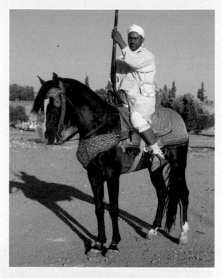

Barb, an ancient foundation breed

Dutch Warmblood

Lipizzaner

Missouri Fox Trotter, a gaited breed

Morgan

Mustang

Paint Horse

Palomino (Quarter Horse)

Peruvian Paso, foundation breed for the Paso Fino

Standardbred, the only breed used for harness racing

Tennessee Walker, a gaited breed

Thoroughbred

Trakehner

Belgian Draft Horse (Brabant), the heaviest breed

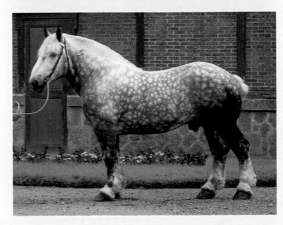

Clydesdale, the strongest breed

Percheron

Shire, the tallest breed

Suffolk Punch, exclusively chestnut in color

Connemara Pony

Shetland Pony

Welsh Mountain Pony

Falabella (Miniature Horse)

Icelandic Horse

Donkey (Ass)

2

The Natural Reaction

Behavior Patterns of the Horse

𝓘t's vital to understand a little about what makes horses tick if you expect to have some sort of successful interaction with them. It's just as important to understand that each individual horse has its own personality, temperament, emotions, and physical limitations, and these factors must be taken into account when dealing with any horse.

Horses originated as nondomesticated herd animals and served as prey for a variety of carnivores. The basic instincts developed in horses to help them survive in the wild all those years ago have persisted and show up strongly in the inherent behavior of today's domestically raised horses, providing a basis for understanding the motivation behind certain characteristic behaviors.

Need for Companionship

In order to protect themselves from predators, horses moved and lived in groups called herds. An isolated horse was an easy target for other animals, especially carnivores that hunted in packs. Not only was the force in numbers of a herd a deterrent to predators, but the greater numbers lowered the chances that a particular horse would be singled out for attack, thus giving each individual horse a heightened sense of security. Horses today still prefer the company of other horses and generally are not content or at ease when isolated, whether kept in a stall, paddock, or large range area. The weaker and younger a horse, the more it relies upon the company of others. A weak or immature animal receives better protection and sense of security by surrounding itself with others, especially if the herd it joins has stronger and more experienced members. Being on the bottom rung of a herd's pecking order is often preferable to a horse than trying to fend for itself alone.

Although there's no doubt that a horse prefers the company of its own kind, when not allowed to be with other horses it will seek out the company of just about any living creature, from goats to chickens, and yes, even humans.

Horses quickly become attached to their companions, especially if they are paired with only one. Separation after bonding has occurred can be very stressful for all involved whether the separation is permanent or short-term, as when one horse is removed to be ridden or treated for a medical problem. A separated horse will often experience immediate anxiety and fear. The horse left behind may react by whinnying, running the fence or stall, or trying to break free. If the separation is prolonged or permanent, the horse may become depressed and refuse to eat. The one taken away often shows a less immediate or volatile reaction, but may act "mate-spoiled"; that is, the horse may attempt to return to its mate or refuse to cooperate and perform because of its distracted, distressed state. The larger the herd the fewer problems that occur from separation since there is less dependence on a single, constant companion. In addition, a substitute companion provided when a pair is broken up will often minimize the separated horse's reaction.

A horse kept alone on a permanent basis often picks up habits such as pacing the fence or stall or acting vicious in an attempt to get attention when someone comes around. This is especially true for horses that are not on a regular exercise routine or are not handled daily. Depression or boredom caused by isolation can also cause a horse to lose its appetite or grossly overeat. In addition, if a horse spends a prolonged period living alone it will not have the chance to develop social skills necessary for herd life and will have a difficult time adjusting when integrated into a herd.

Many horses simply are not allowed to live with other horses because of their performance duties. A racehorse prospect or a show horse is often separated deliberately to prevent the horse from developing a dependency on another horse and to keep the horse's mind on business. These horses are moved around often—from show to training center to another show, or from racetrack to layup farm to training facility to racetrack, perhaps to several racetracks. There is no chance that a mate other than a pony or goat would be able to match the individual performer's schedule or accompany the horse. By never allowing bonding to occur, a trainer need never deal with separation anxiety.

Lacking dependency or the opportunity to bond with a particular horse or herd does not make a horse completely independent. Most horses are followers to some degree and still prefer to be around or follow another horse when possible. This is readily seen in the greenbroke horse that has yet to build full confidence in its rider. I have frequently observed the enhanced performance of the greenbroke horse when it is allowed to train or exercise in the company of others, whether that horse is familiar with its company or not. The green horse will often move forward more willingly and spook less often. A green trail horse that would normally refuse to cross a wooden bridge will commonly follow a veteran trail horse across without hesitation. It is very common when training racing prospects to send them out on their gallops in the company of others. This not only raises the juvenile's confidence, it also adds a little excitement and pleasure to the experience and helps the green horse learn what is expected of it by demonstrating the actions of other, more experienced horses.

Herd Class System

As herd animals, horses developed their own societal system, apparent in most groups of horses living together today. They have what is commonly known as a pecking order, or status hierarchy. As in the days of wild herds when there was one dominant stallion ruling over the herd, there is always a dominant leader in any established domestic herd today, though not necessarily a stallion or even a gelding. The dominant horse in a domesticated setting does not spend a great deal of its time protecting the herd from predators. The protective forces are commonly centered on the food supply, more precisely, the dominant leader's personally determined portion of the food supply. Herd leaders will also use their dominance to move the group around, discipline members they consider vagabond or out of line, chase off intruders such as a dog or new member of the herd, or determine whether the group should accept and approach or avoid a visitor or new herd member.

The pecking order ranges from the most dominant to the most passive or submissive horse. The order is subject to some change but is tempered by the natural personality of each horse. For example, an extremely passive dam may become ferociously aggressive in protecting her new foal from other members of the herd, and may maintain her newly established dominant position well after the foal is weaned and grown. A young gelding may be on the passive end of the pecking order until he proves his strength in play battles and boosts his position in the hierarchy.

When horses within a herd look as if they are fighting, look closer. Most of the time you will find the horses are actually just playing together, although the play can be quite rough and injurious. I have witnessed horses tearing each other's flesh and tripping one another into falling by biting at the lower legs, all in the name of fun. Horseplay consists of shaking heads at each other, nipping, chasing, mounting as if to breed, rearing, striking, and kicking, and is most often enacted among the youngest members of a herd. Horseplay emulates real-life

A dominant leader using aggressive behavior to move the herd

fighting and breeding practices and helps teach proper interaction and establish dominance, especially among younger, unproven members, without a real show of force.

Rarely is the herd today made up of many mares and foals presided over by a breeding stallion. Most often a stallion never gets to enjoy the setting of a herd, as chance breeding is now frowned upon and the presence of a stallion often results in a higher injury rate among herd members. If you do see a stallion in a herd, it is most likely a young, unbred colt paired up with other colts of the same age, or a stallion placed with mares for the specific purpose of pasture breeding.

When a herd is made up of like-gender horses, hierarchy is based primarily upon the personalities and ages of the members. When mares and geldings are placed together, dominant positions usually go to the female members. Mares are almost always testier and more ready to defend themselves than geldings. The presence of a stallion among mares does not guarantee that the dominant position automatically belongs to the stallion, especially if the stallion is a newcomer presented during breeding season. In this case, the mare or mares might be severely dominant over the stallion in order to ensure that the decision to breed remains with the mare.

Foals are usually protected from any tests of dominance, not just by their dams but by other adult herd members. Although they are almost always considered the most submissive of the herd members, they are rarely picked on by more dominant members, unless there is another foal of like age with an aggressive personality. Foals have a unique way of communicating with other horses: they show both submission and a desire for acceptance by approaching an unfamiliar horse with jaws open and working up and down.

A passive horse can protect itself from more dominant members of the herd by always acting in a submissive manner. The submissive horse is by definition a follower and will avoid all confrontation by running away at the first sign of a threat, or removing itself from the hub of the herd. A very submissive horse may commonly be found standing alone while other herd members are gathered. Submissive horses are often the thinnest members of the herd due to their inability or refusal to compete for a fair share of the food supply.

Timid or weak horses on the low end of the herd hierarchy may need human intervention and protection if the herd's food supply is not plentiful or adequately spread out to ensure food for the most passive horses. On the same note, if a passive member is picked on to the point of receiving frequent wounds from bites or kicks, intervention is called for. Isolated, protected feeding areas may be needed, or a passive horse may need to be removed from the herd and paired with a less aggressive companion or herd.

Communication

Horses communicate by means of facial expressions, physical actions, and posture, as well as sweating, refusing to eat or perform, and vocalizing. Not only can a horse indicate what it wants (or doesn't want), it can give a clear indication of its moods and intents, if you know what to look for.

Greeting

When greeting someone familiar, a horse will most likely approach with interest, but not high excitement. The horse may nicker to draw attention to itself and will usually come forward until it can touch or nudge you with its nose. A friendly or curious horse's greeting is often so forward as to give a person the urge (perhaps common sense) to back away.

If the horse does not recognize the person or horse to be greeted, it may react with apathy, fear, or excitement. Some horses will blatantly ignore the visitor, while others put on quite a show. An unfamiliar greeting may consist of a hesitant approach with the intent to flee if necessary, trotting back and forth in order to get a quick look without losing its means to escape, or standing out of reach, puffing from the nose. When a horse does decide to actually greet a newcomer, the horse will most commonly arch its neck and point its nose at the visitor, puffing or blowing from the nostrils in order to pick up a scent. Horses that greet each other by this method will sometimes offer a flirtatious challenge by squealing and striking out. Such action can escalate to an out-and-out test of dominance if not stopped, especially among unfamiliar horses turned loose together.

Puffing or blowing does not always lead to a physical challenge. Friendly horses commonly greet each other in this manner, blowing directly into each other's nostrils. A person can also gain familiarity with a horse by blowing gently and directly into a horse's nostril to deliver his or her scent.

The attentive horse

Attention

A horse will show attentiveness by raising its head and focusing on whatever has its attention. Its ears will be held forward and its eyes bright and wide. The horse's tail will be held out slightly from its rump and might even be raised and held over its back. The more interested the horse is, the higher its head will be raised, the tenser its muscles, and the more upright its stance.

To beckon or seek attention to itself, a horse will whinny or nicker, toss its head, or approach with ears forward. It may also stomp or paw with its front feet. If you are within reach, the horse may nuzzle or bump you with its nose. When frustrated or unable to find the attention it seeks, a horse may react in an aggressive manner, possibly lunging out at passersby or attempting to bite.

Anger

An angry horse can be identified most easily by its facial expressions but also by its body language. When a horse is angered, it will lay its ears back flat and tense the muscles around its nose and mouth. Muscle tension will cause the lips to pull back a bit, forming wrinkles around the nostrils and sometimes exposing some threatening-looking teeth. If the intent of the horse is to threaten, it will point its nose out and shake its head at the object of its threat, often with its teeth bared, ready to bite. A bolder threat may include lunging or charging at the enemy, twitching or swishing the tail, and wheeling or turning away to put itself in a position to kick. If the horse has become angry enough to fight, it may also rear and strike out or bellow, a sound I can only describe as a horse's shout of rage. An enraged or aggressive horse may not be so courteous as to provide any warning, but may kick or bite with a mere flattening of the ears to let you know you're under attack.

There is an assumption that an angry horse under saddle will attempt to buck the rider off. This is not usually the case. Most horses buck because they are playful, frightened, surprised by an unexpected cue from the rider, or physically uncomfortable. Although bucking out of anger is certainly not unheard of, it is not a common reaction for a horse. More likely, a horse that is angered by the rider's demands or abusive signaling techniques will react by refusing to perform, moving in an opposite direction of that which was commanded, swishing its tail, rearing, or kicking out, which may be perceived as bucking.

Anxiety

A nervous or anxious horse will display a lot of quick ear movement and body tension. Characteristics of nervousness and anxiety are sweating, trembling, pacing, weaving, prancing, pawing the ground, or twitching the tail. An extremely anxious horse may even be seen to buck or rear. The horse is usually quiet, but may nicker or whinny. An anxious horse is generally flighty, prone to overreact to sounds and touch, and is easily distracted, unable to focus on anything or anyone for long.

Fear

Fear and anxiety often go hand in hand. The characteristics of a frightened horse are similar in many ways to those of a nervous or anxious horse, but a horse experiencing fear as a primary emotion tends not to fidget or dance around much. The frightened horse will be highly attentive; it will have its ears far forward to better identify what has frightened it, and may snort or blow loudly at the object. If a horse is frightened of its surroundings (a new stall, a ride in a van, etc.), it will act much like a nervous horse by sweating, frequently flicking its ears, and overreacting to sights, sounds, and touch. The horse is as nervous as it is frightened in such a situation. The frightened horse commonly reacts defensively by wheeling and running, backing up, cowering, or standing rigid, sometimes with its legs splayed. If it feels genuinely threatened, the horse may take aggressive measures.

Excitement

An excited horse differs from a nervous, anxious, or frightened one in that the reaction is usually a happy, playful one. The excited horse will be in a state of high attentiveness and will display this by carrying its head high and its ears forward. Its eyes will be widened, sometimes bugged out, and its nostrils flared. Often the veins stand out on the body as extra adrenaline encourages

These excited yearlings canter with high, springy steps; raised heads; and flagged tails.

blood flow and muscle tension. An excited horse will sometimes whinny, snort, or trumpet loudly from the nose. Sheer exhilaration often causes a horse to prance, buck, rear, or run wildly. The horse may carry its tail over its back and display gaits that are springier or loftier than normal, even at the walk. Extremely excited horses are usually not very responsive or attentive to their handlers and may even be quite unruly.

Relaxation

A relaxed horse is not normally a very energetic one. A horse in repose can usually be found standing in a resting position, with its weight on three legs and the fourth leg, usually a hind leg, resting on the toe. The horse's head will be lowered, its ears will be out to the sides and not flicking much, and its lips will look droopy and fleshy due to the relaxed muscles.

A horse can also be relaxed while performing, not just at rest. A relaxed horse will move with smooth, easy gaits. It will be mildly attentive but will not appear tense or hold its head or tail raised unnaturally. The relaxed performer generally sweats less, displays superior performance, and enjoys enhanced endurance due to the efficient use of its energy. Relaxed does not mean dull or numb; most commonly a relaxed performer is quite responsive and easy to get along with.

Need for Space

Horses learned early to stay in clear, open spaces, not only for better foraging but also to enable them to spot predators and run away without the hindrance of trees or other landscape barriers. Today, as in the past, horses usually opt to stay out in the open. Horses do not as a rule like to be kept in a wooded area or under cover and may stand in the rain or sun rather than stand under a grove of trees, a loafing shed, or open stall. This is not to say you cannot keep a horse in the woods or another confining area; horses are adaptable and will usually learn to accept whatever home is provided.

Horses consistently fed or kept within the shelter of a shed or stall are often more content and willing to use these facilities, but many remain just long enough to finish a meal before seeking more open ground, regardless of the weather. Horses in herds or pairs are much more willing to stand under a shed

Ample space is needed for herds to run and forage.

or trees than a lone horse because of the heightened sense of security company provides.

It's rather surprising that most horses are as cooperative as they've proven to be about being kept in a stall, since a stall is about the least likely environment a horse might choose for itself. The level of cooperation we see reflects the upbringing many domesticated horses receive.

Horses that have been raised to live daily in a locked stall seem generally accepting. Those that eat their evening meals and spend the night in their stalls may actually look forward to confinement, as this area is recognized as the source of food. In addition, a horse kept in a muddy paddock or exposed to severe weather may welcome the comforts of a clean, dry, protected stall. However, many horses show their discontent about being locked in through mild demonstrations such as hanging their heads over the door, staring out a window, or peering through knotholes or cracks looking for the horse next door or a possible escape route.

A number of horses suffer a higher level of frustration over being kept indoors and having their freedom of movement inhibited. Frustration and anxiety may also stem from the isolated situation a stall affords, especially if a horse is separated from mates. Horses such as these frequently develop a variety of bad habits such as chewing or kicking the walls, rattling their buckets, cribbing (sucking air into their bellies), pawing the ground, head tossing, pacing, weaving, or spinning in small circles. The horse's natural eating patterns may also be altered by its state of confinement. It occasionally will refuse to eat, overeat, or eat its bedding. Although these habits may stem from simple boredom, they are also signs of anxiety and frustration and can lead to more intense emotions. A horse may become claustrophobic, surly, or vicious as a result of stall confinement.

Horses kept in open areas also need a certain amount of space to allow for romping and grazing. This is especially true for horses kept in herds or pairs. Observation of herds kept in close quarters will usually reveal restlessness and surliness among the members and more nicks and bumps on the hides of the animals. Inadequate space can lead to constant bickering among herd members and vicious fights at feed time. A passive member will have less chance of escape if it is persistently picked on by a dominant horse, and a greater chance of missing out on meals it must compete for.

Self-Protection

In the case of attack by a predator, horses in the wild protected themselves by flight first, then fight. To this day, a horse's first reaction to any perceived danger or surprise is to get away from it . . . *fast*. Confidence and reassurance are found in numbers, so a horse will usually run to other horses. For the same reason, a horse will often run panic-stricken without cause if another member of the herd is startled into running.

Things a horse may consider dangerous or startling could seem ludicrous to you. A piece of litter rolling in the breeze, a sudden noise, another horse spooking, or a person walking unexpectedly around a blind corner may be all it takes to frighten a horse into flight. It takes study and practice to learn to predict what may spook a horse, but it's something you should be mindful of at all times. If you can anticipate what will likely spook your horse, you can often prevent the reaction by avoiding it or by reassuring the horse before panic sets in.

When a horse feels threatened and flight is not an option, it may fight. A horse's common fighting techniques are kicking and biting. Other methods of fighting include striking out with a forefoot, flipping over backward, or throwing itself to the ground, and leaning or pushing against the threat. This is frightening because the harder the enemy pushes to get free, the harder the horse will lean, possibly crushing whatever—or whomever—it is pushing against. A horse that feels threatened by a rider or handler may react by refusing to obey or freezing up, running off, running backward, rearing, flipping, or bucking.

If a horse feels fighting is useless, or the horse has been conditioned never to fight, it will either submit or freeze up, meaning it braces itself into a rigid, unmoving position. Beware the horse that freezes up because it will often come out of this state violently and without warning.

Cooperation

Cooperation is essential for horses to get along amicably in a herd setting. This also carries over to human interaction, providing the horse learns to view the human handler as dominant.

The most naturally cooperative horses are handled early and fairly. They cannot imagine life without the interaction of human beings. Cooperation is consistent with trust and can be lost if trust is forsaken. The older a horse gets before it is handled, the harder it is to gain its trust and cooperation, but a patient and conscientious handler can build a lifetime foundation of trust and cooperation in any horse at any age.

Oftentimes a horse actually enjoys cooperating with the reasonable demands of the handler because cooperation is known to result in pleasant and interesting experiences. At other times a horse will simply see cooperation as beneficial in avoiding negative consequences. When the choice is to cooperate or be severely punished, it is really not a choice at all. I believe many domestically raised horses see no alternative to cooperation and are unaware of their true physical power. It never occurs to them to challenge the dominance of their human counterparts or to resist handling and training. I don't say this in a derogatory way; this fact is simply further evidence of the horse's naturally easy temperament and follower instinct.

Temperament

Each horse is an individual with a unique personality and temperament, regardless of stereotypical breed or gender characteristics. As important as it is to understand the basic behavior and motives common to the horse species, it is also essential to see each horse in its own light—to understand that this is not a machine, but a living creature with thoughts, emotions, and personality traits of its own. They are born with some of these characteristics, which can be traced to their parents; some of their traits are learned and developed over a lifetime of experiences. Other personality characteristics or temperamental traits just seem to be part of a particular horse's makeup, with no obvious cause or beginning.

Breeds of horses are often stereotyped by temperament and personality. I've heard Arabians called flighty and silly, Appaloosas dumb and faithful, Thoroughbreds high-strung and unpredictable, and Quarter Horses steady and lazy. Someone else will tell me how absolutely steady an Arabian is, how strong and trainable an Appaloosa is, how intelligent a Thoroughbred is, and how high-strung a Quarter Horse can be. The fact is that you will discover different levels and types of temperament among all breed members. I believe it's dangerous and foolish to stereotype any horse's character by its breed. More important, look at the horse you are dealing with and learn as much about its background as you possibly can, then take time to get to know and evaluate the horse as an individual.

Understand that some horses are "bomb proof"—totally reliable and seemingly unafraid of anything—while others are untrusting, untrustworthy, or hopeless scaredy-cats. Know that there are people-lovers, people-haters, and horses that are indifferent. Some are willing, eager, and energetic, while others are chronically lazy, lethargic, and resentful of any demand. Some are calm and laid-back, while others are nervous and fretful. Some are quite tolerant of pain, while others fall apart at the teensiest discomfort.

As the handler, you can influence the way a horse behaves, sometimes imperceptibly and sometimes greatly, but the underlying personality and temperament of each horse will persist.

3

"Horsekeeping"

Creating a Good Environment for Your Horse

Before you bring a horse into your life you must plan and prepare a suitable environment. Not only is it vital to prepare a decent home for the horse, but you must also find a reliable food and bedding source and provide adequate storage for these items. You must collect a variety of tack, grooming, and first-aid materials so you can properly handle and take care of the horse. And you will need to gather some barn and stable equipment for cleaning and maintenance.

This chapter will enable you to figure some of the costs of keeping a horse. Specific dollar figures are not mentioned since they vary so much between regions and facilities, but it's important to understand what becoming involved with horses entails financially. The following information will provide a guide with which you can do your own research.

The Horse's Home

Once you've chosen a horse, you must meet the horse's primary need of a place to live. You should have your facility fully prepared by the time the horse steps off the van or trailer so it can be turned loose in its new home and left to itself for a while to adjust.

Fences

If the horse will be kept in a pasture or paddock, it is important to ensure all the fences are adequate. A poor choice of fencing material or a poorly maintained fence can lead to escape or injury if your horse breaks through, gets hung up in wire, or runs loose in unsafe areas.

Your horse's fence should be at least four feet high with a clearly visible top line consisting of a board, rail, or bright- or light-colored electrically charged tape. If your fence is higher than five feet, your visible line should still be four or five feet high. This will prevent a horse from accidentally running into or through an unseen barrier.

Electrically charged fencing can be used as a main fencing source or an addition to a weak or wooden fence that a horse might push against or chew on. Electrically charged fencing is connected to a battery, which sends an intermittent charge that will deliver a moderate electrical shock if touched. The shock will not cause injury unless contact is sustained but is severe enough to cause a reaction and teach the horse to avoid further contact. Brightly colored electrically charged tape has become quite popular but has in no way replaced the more affordable electrically charged (hot) wire. The downside of hot wire is its invisibility at all but the nearest range; a horse can run into it before realizing its mistake. When using hot wire as fencing material, tie lengths of bright- or light-colored surveyor's ribbon at intervals of no more than four feet, or wrap the ribbon loosely around the top wire in a continuous garland.

There are a variety of other types of wire fencing used to enclose horses. If you use wire-mesh fencing, make sure the wire is woven small enough to prevent a horse from putting a foot or leg through it, and strong enough not to be torn (this eliminates chicken wire). The safest fencing is chain link, two-by-four-inch mesh or V mesh.

Every time I turn around I seem to find a horse standing behind a barbed-wire fence. I have only one thing to say about barbed wire . . . *don't use it*! As often as I've seen horses standing behind this stuff, I've seen them injured and permanently scarred from it. Barbed wire is unforgiving. It does not usually hurt a horse at the touch, so it does not encourage a horse to stay away. It starts hurting when it cuts into a horse's flesh. This causes a fighting reaction, which too often results in entanglement and severe injury.

Wood makes fairly good fencing material, but be warned of its high maintenance needs. If you plan to keep your horse behind a wooden fence, first check the fence over carefully, even if it is brand new. Make sure there are no exposed nails or nailheads and that all posts are sound and firmly

A post and board fence, stout and easily visible

sunk. Boards should be attached to the *inside* of the posts to make it more difficult for your horse to push them off.

Most horses find wooden fences quite delectable and will chew your expensive lumber down to the nubbins if given a chance. You can protect your wood with a nasty-tasting wood treatment found at tack shops; creosote works well for most horses. Many people also use a line of hot wire just inside the top board.

You can use vinyl fencing material that looks just like a white-painted wooden fence. Vinyl fencing is expensive and may seem unaffordable, but you must take into account its long life and minimal maintenance requirements when figuring the actual fencing costs. Vinyl is also a relatively safe material, as it is inedible, difficult to break, smooth, splinter free, and is not put together with nails that can loosen or become exposed.

Your gates should be strong and swing freely. The latches should work easily so you can enter or escape in a hurry if necessary, but they should not be accessible to your horse. All gates should be latched or chained at both top and bottom and gate hinges should be secured if they are the lift-off type.

Open Shelters

If your horse is kept outdoors in a pasture or paddock, it should be provided with a shelter such as a loafing shed or access to an open stall. Your horse may choose not to use this, but it should at least have the option of getting out of the weather. Regular feeding in the sheltered area will encourage your horse to use the facility more and will result in a healthier coat and hooves.

Your shelter should have at least two walls, one being to the weather side. If the shelter is intended for use by more than one horse, there should be separate feeding areas and an escape route to prevent one horse from being trapped inside by another.

Your horse's shelter should be kept fairly clean and dry. No horse likes to stand in muck or mud, and it's unhealthy for their legs and hooves. During inclement weather the shelter may be your horse's only relief from the conditions. A choice bedding for an outdoor shelter is hog fuel made up of large wood chips and bark strips. Hog fuel is cushiony, can soak up and eliminate a good deal of moisture, and will last a fair amount of time before it needs to be replaced.

If your horse is fed outdoors, keep its hay and grain off the ground so the horse will not ingest parasites, sand, and other contaminants that may lead to colic. Always feed your horse under shelter and from a clean container raised off the ground. If the container

A simple loafing shed

is set on the ground, it should be made of a soft, flexible material that won't injure a horse if it steps in it, falls, or rolls against it. A hard container set inside an old tire works well to protect the horse from injury and is difficult for the horse to overturn.

A hanging bucket works well for grain as its depth will keep most of the grain from being pushed out. For hay, a rack with vertical slats will allow the horse to pull hay out by the bite without dumping it on the ground all at one time. A rimmed base under the hayrack is handy for catching fallen hay and for feeding grain. A hay net can be used in place of a rack, although some horses find this a good toy once it is emptied and will chew holes through the mesh. If you do use a net, hang it so it is tied above your horse's chest level to prevent the horse from entangling a leg. Keep the hay net filled or remove it once it is emptied.

Enclosed Stalls

Some horses spend a great deal of their time cooped up in a stall. If this is your stabling intention, it's essential that you ensure a maximum level of comfort and safety for your horse in such a confining space.

The stall should be a minimum of ten feet by ten feet, twelve by twelve being standard. The walls should be built of two-inch-thick lumber at least five feet in height. Concrete walls are not uncommon but must be used with care, as they will cause injury if the horse kicks or rolls up against them. If your stall walls are concrete or brick, you should line them with securely bolted plywood or rubber mats. Plywood is occasionally used as the primary wall material in stalls, but I do not recommend this. A horse can easily kick through plywood, causing injury and providing a means of escape. The money initially saved by using plywood will be lost as you continually repair or replace it. In addition, some wafer boards or impregnated plywood materials are chemically treated, which can be harmful to a horse that chews or licks the walls.

Your stall should have a level, hard-packed dirt floor. If the floor is concrete, it should be covered with rubber mats that are heavy and dense enough to resist pawing. Don't expect extra bedding to make up for the hard surface of concrete, as a horse will commonly push the bedding aside when rolling or lying and will end up lying or standing on the unhealthy hard surface. This is a common cause of capped or abraded elbows and hocks.

The stall door should be at least four feet high with a latch the horse cannot fiddle open. An iron gate, stall ties, or webbings are commonly used in place of, or along with, the stall door. The most common iron gate is hung about two feet off the ground and allows for easy crawling access to the horse and stall. The iron gate also allows for more ventilation than a closed door. Stall ties are heavy chains encased in plastic that are secured across the front of the stall. Webbings are made of wide nylon strips woven in a mesh pattern; they also stretch across the opening of the stall. Both webbings and ties work on the same principle as the iron gate but do not offer the same level of security.

Some of the nicest horses become aggressive or overexcitable at feed time and are best left alone. Unless you have a loft feeding system in which you can drop the horse's feed from overhead without entering the stall, buckets and feeders should be placed at the front of the stall, preferably in the corner where they are least likely to be bumped. They should allow access for dumping feed without entering the stall. If you have an especially aggressive horse, or trouble with a horse that rubs against or poops in its buckets or feeders, you can sometimes hang the buckets outside the stall where the horse can reach them easily by hanging its head out.

Stick to water and grain buckets and containers designed for horses, not just in the stall but anywhere you keep your horse. Those five-gallon, paint-type buckets I often see are too deep and narrow for a horse to reach bottom, and the edges are sharp enough to cause injury.

The stall can be bedded with a number of materials, the two most common being straw and wood shavings. Do not use sawdust or fine peat, which are too fine and can be inhaled; large wood chips, which are rough and not very absorbent; or hay, which will be eaten. Occasionally, shredded tires and newspaper are used to bed a stall, but without much success. Newspaper tends to saturate and pack down; rubber is cushiony but not at all absorbent, so puddles of standing urine are left underneath. It is also much harder to dispose of newspaper and rubber after use, as they can't be used as fertilizer.

Some people will use a layer of sawdust underneath a bed of straw as bedding. This system allows for maximum moisture absorption, but it is tedious to clean a stall bedded this way. I find that one material when adequately applied and mucked out daily is sufficient for absorbing the average horse's urine output.

Stall Preparation

Before your horse first enters its new stall, the stall should be cleaned out completely and all buckets and feeders sanitized to get rid of mold and infectious germs from previous inhabitants.

Check the walls carefully for exposed nails or nailheads, and make a habit of checking for nails on a weekly basis. They are often hard to detect if the walls are dark, but if you don't find them, your horse surely will.

A dirt floor should be level, hard packed, and dust free before adding bedding. You can keep the dust down by sweeping the floor first, then sprinkling it lightly with a hose. If your floor is wooden, check for and replace any cracked or rotten boards. Both wood and concrete floors should be covered with rubber mats.

If you choose straw for bedding, expect to use a full bale to bed a stripped stall. After the stall is bedded, however, you need add only about a third of a bale daily after mucking out. Shake the straw into a level bed with a minimum of a four-inch depth, twelve inches being ideal. Bed a little deeper in areas where the horse will spend the most time standing, such as the gate and feeding area. If the straw is a little dusty, sprinkle it lightly on the surface with water after you shake it out. If it is dusty enough to make you cough when shaking it, you probably shouldn't use it, as it can cause respiratory problems for your horse.

If you bed with shavings, shredded newspapers, or tires, spread them evenly at a depth of two to six inches. Again, it's wise to add a little extra where the horse stands most often and where it urinates.

Stall Maintenance

Stalls should be cleaned every day if a horse spends half its time or more there. A daily cleaning provides your horse with a comfortable home, reduces the need to completely strip the stall of material, and eliminates the growth of mold or build up of dust.

To clean the stall, remove all the wet material and manure. Push the dry bedding off to a clean corner or side, then rake the floor of muck and dust before respreading the used material and adding some new. Once a week or so you should strip the stall completely, fill any holes or dips, and rebed with all fresh materials. If there are areas of the floor that are especially wet, rake dry bedding through these to soak up excess moisture, then sprinkle the areas generously with dolomite lime before rebedding.

What you do with the material you take out of a dirty stall depends on your circumstances. Large stables often find a source, such as a mushroom farm, that will either pick up the used bedding or accept it upon delivery for fertilizer. Others use the dirty bedding for field fertilizer. Used shavings are occasionally added to arena or trail surfaces. Some haul it off to landfills. It can also be sold or given to gardeners for mulch and fertilizer. Whatever you decide, be warned that if you simply let it pile up around the barn you will create a health hazard, attract an extraordinary fly population, and stink up your property.

Grain and water buckets should be scrubbed at least once a week. Water should be changed at least every other day, every day if the weather is warm or icy. Uneaten hay or grain should be removed if it stands more than a day since it could contain mold, dust, or rodent droppings that can make your horse sick.

Always look inside your horse's containers before feeding and watering to make sure they are clean. You might find bedding or food in the water bucket and moldy grain in the feed tub, and horses will sometimes poop in their buckets and contaminate their water and food supplies. I've found some funny things in feed tubs and water buckets over the years—like dead mice and fresh-laid chicken eggs that a horse might not care to eat or drink around (although I knew of a horse that actually ate chicken eggs, shell and all). An automatic watering system does not excuse you from daily checking. A malfunctioning waterer can quickly lead to your horse's dehydration and illness, and can be avoided simply by pressing the lever each day to see if water flow is normal. Checking containers is also a good habit to develop to keep track of how much your horse is eating and drinking.

Food and Water

Water

Horses drink only water, simple enough. They can drink as little as two or three gallons a day or as much as twenty-five. If your horse is kept in a stall and you find the bucket empty more than once when checked twice a day, hang an extra bucket. If you use a large outdoor water container, check it daily and change it at the first sign of algae growth.

Excessive drinking may occur because of a hot or humid climate, hard exercise, nervousness, or excessive salt intake. Whatever the reason, your horse should not be deprived of water while resting. In fact, the only time your horse's water intake should be controlled is during and after strenuous exercise when a horse is likely to gulp enormous amounts into an already stressed system and wind up colicky or foundered. Control does not mean deprivation, however; this would be cruel and could delay your horse's recovery time. Simply offer the water in small amounts (about ten swallows) at short intervals (about every five minutes) until the horse is cool, rested, and no longer interested in drinking.

If your horse does not seem to be drinking much water—less than five gallons a day—don't panic. There may be several reasons, including cold weather, a sedentary life-style, a deficiency of salt in its diet, or the consumption of wet grass, which will satisfy its thirst.

Make sure the water supply is clean and uncontaminated, cool—not ice cold or warm—and easy to get to. Then check to see if your horse is getting enough salt. You can provide a salt block or add a small amount (one or two tablespoons) of mineral salt, available at a feed store, to your horse's grain.

Grass

Your horse needs a good supply of roughage every day to meet its nutritional needs and to prevent boredom and munching on inappropriate material such as bedding and wooden fences. If your horse eats pasture grass, keep an eye on the supply to make sure it doesn't run out. Short-cropped grass that shows no new growth is obvious, but also watch for patches of deceptively long, lush-looking grass that your horse ignores. Your horse is not being finicky; this grass is most likely contaminated by manure and urine or contains weeds that are poisonous or stalks that are unappealing and difficult to digest.

To maximize your grazing crop and promote healthy, even pasture growth, fertilize your fields regularly with an organic product. Rotate any grazing animals to give each pasture area time to recoup. If you have only one pasture area, run a fence down the middle so half the pasture can rest while the other half is grazed. In addition to fertilizing and rotating, your fields should be mowed occasionally. Mowing will reduce weeds and tough stalks and promote the new, tender growth considered ideal by your horse. Mowing is also helpful in reducing manure to mulch, but don't consider mowing as a means of eliminating manure; it will still be there, along with any parasites it might contain.

Good pasture such as this will help this pregnant mare maintain her health and nourish her unborn foal.

You must make a habit of removing the manure at regular intervals in order to control parasites and allow for more grazable area.

Beware of lush, extra-rich spring grass. Turning your horse out on this is like turning a child loose in a candy shop, with similar results. Gorging on lush grass can cause obesity, colic, or foundering (laminitis), a painful swelling or disfigurement of the neck and hooves which too often results in irreversible crippling.

To prevent problems linked to overeating, limit your horse's grazing time on lush grass to about two hours a day and supplement with timothy or dry grass hay. You can increase the grazing time gradually until grass growth slows down a little and your horse's digestive system adapts to it. To gauge how your horse is doing, look at its manure droppings. If its system has adjusted to the grass, the manure should be firm and chunky, not loose or soupy.

Hay

Hay is a common substitute or supplement to grass. It is purchased by the bale or ton from feed stores, truckers, or directly from growers. Depending upon the region you live in, you might not be able to rely solely on locally cut, generally more affordable grass hay, as it is often deficient in nutrients. But you can use this hay as a pasture grass supplement or combined with a higher quality hay as a filler to give your horse more munching time and replace the urge to graze.

Timothy and alfalfa are two of the most common quality hays, although clover or bluegrass may be more readily available in your area. Ideally you should mix hays, such as clover and grass or timothy and alfalfa. Check with local feed suppliers and stables to see what's available.

Alfalfa is a rich, high-protein hay, and probably the most fattening. By feeding only alfalfa or mixing it with local grass hay you might save some money, but it could be too rich if your horse is not accustomed to it. Keep an eye on your horse's manure and reduce or replace the alfalfa with a dryer, less green hay if diarrhea occurs.

There is no standard as to how much hay a horse should eat, although an estimate for a medium-size horse not supplemented by pasture is about two ninety-pound bales a week. To gauge your horse's needs, ask the previous owner how much hay the horse is accustomed to eating and confirm the portions with your veterinarian. Watch to see if and how much hay your horse wastes, but be careful not to assume you are feeding too much if hay is left uneaten. This may be a sign of poor teeth, illness, or bad hay. A horse will also leave hay uneaten if it is difficult to pick out of dirt, mud, or feces. Look at the condition of your horse now and watch it closely in the future; if weight loss or gain occurs, consult your veterinarian and make *gradual* adjustments to your feeding program.

If your horse is clearly fat, cut its hay supply down slightly and slowly. If it is thin, especially if it vacuums up its hay in a short amount of time or you find it eating sticks, leaves, and wood, increase the amount you're feeding.

When determining the thinness of your horse, look beyond the size of its belly, which may only indicate bloating. A healthy horse should have a uniformly well-padded frame. A thin horse generally displays a narrow neck, hollow flank, and jutting bones at the points of the shoulders and hips, as well as a knobby spine and outlined ribs.

If you can't judge the fatness of your horse at first glance, try grabbing the flesh at the crest of the neck and wiggling it. If your horse is fit, the flesh should seem firm and hard to move. If it jiggles loosely, this is a good indication your horse is overweight. You can also push in on the flesh around the horse's shoulder, girth area, and rump to see how pillowy it feels.

Never confuse straw bedding with hay; your horse should be discouraged from eating straw, as it is devoid of nutrients and difficult to digest. Eating straw can cause bloating and colon impactions. If you're losing bedding overnight and your horse is not fat, this is an indication you need to increase the amount of hay you're feeding. If you think your horse is getting enough hay, you can add some local grass hay to give it more to munch on, or switch to shavings for your bedding material.

Grains and Supplements

Many horses have their diet supplemented by grains. Certainly any horse will benefit by the added nutrition and energy grains supply, but there are particular horses that depend on grains for optimal health: those that are regularly exercised, foals and horses not fully matured, pregnant or lactating mares, aged horses, and horses that are ill or rehabilitating from illness.

The safest bet in selecting grains is to buy premixed feed designed to suit your horse's age and activity level. Unmixed grains such as straight oats or corn won't offer your horse as high a level of nutrients. Be especially careful about a diet of straight oats or a high ratio of oats, as this seems to be a rather hot food for horses, that is, it provides a high amount of energy, which may cause an inadequately exercised horse to become nervous or unruly.

As with hay, the amount of grain you feed varies with the individual horse. A sedentary, average-size, healthy horse should need no more than a gallon a day if it has a good hay or grass supply. A high-performance horse such as a racehorse or jumper in training will eat as much as eight gallons a day. I recommend you consult with the horse's previous owner and your veterinarian when determining your horse's grain mixture and rations. Seek further advice when changing the horse's level of exercise, its hay or grass source, or when the horse is ill or has stopped eating.

Vitamins and food supplements can also be added to your horse's diet to make up for any deficiencies. As mentioned earlier, make salt available by setting out a block to be licked at will. If your horse eats the salt block, as I have seen a few horses do, you should remove the block and instead supplement the grain with a granular mineral salt.

Pellets

A less common type of food is processed alfalfa pellets. Alfalfa pellets may or may not contain other grains or nutritional supplements. Pellets can replace the need for hay in some circumstances such as trail riding in areas where grazing is poor and you need to limit what you pack, or when your horse has bad teeth and can't chew hay well. For this, the pellets can be softened by soaking them in water to make a mash. Pellets are also useful to encourage a horse with a small appetite, such as one that is recovering from an illness, to ingest more nutrients.

Under normal circumstances, I would avoid using pellets because they don't seem to satisfy the urge to graze. Furthermore, the average horse's system is not accustomed to the high-concentrate nutrients of the pellets and will have difficulty keeping up with digestion. This can lead to diarrhea, painful gas retention, or a more dangerous colon impaction. If you choose to feed your horse pellets, you must be careful to add them gradually to the horse's diet while slowly cutting down on its normal hay or grass supply in order for the horse's digestive system to adjust.

Professional Services

The need for professional help is an inevitable part of horse ownership. It's been my experience that cutting costs by putting off calling for help or trying to deal with circumstances on your own invariably costs more in the long run.

Horseshoer

One professional person you will need to employ is a farrier, or horseshoer. Horses that are not ridden or exposed to rocks or paved surfaces may be able to get by just fine without shoes. Whether or not your horse is shod, it will

Corrective shoeing will help to repair this neglected hoof.

The horseshoer trims and shapes the hoof.

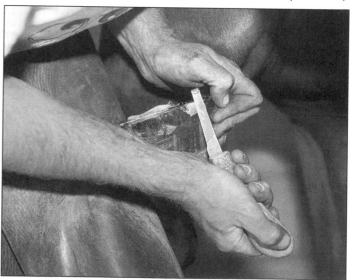

still need regular hoof maintenance in order to stay sound. The wall of a hoof grows continually, similar to our finger- and toenails. The longest portion of the wall will become brittle as it grows out and will crack or chip easily. In addition, the extra length of the hoof can alter the horse's natural stance and gaits, putting undo pressure on joints, tendons, and ligaments and causing frequent stumbling. A horse should not go more than three months without having its hooves trimmed and shoes replaced. If your horse has a lot of hoof growth or wears its shoes down rapidly on pavement or other hard surfaces, it will require more frequent farrier service.

A good horseshoer can help determine the source of a lameness problem if it involves the horse's hooves. Tests a horseshoer might perform include removing a shoe to see whether a high nail is causing pain and using an instrument called a hoof tester to apply pressure to points of the hoof to help discover a puncture wound, bruise, or abscess. A horseshoer can also detect fungal infections of the hoof, often before you are aware of the problem.

Veterinarian

Another professional you can't do without is your veterinarian. You should select and become acquainted with a veterinarian before ever taking possession of a horse. This person can be vital in helping you choose a horse by examining it thoroughly before you commit to the purchase. Information about choosing a veterinarian is provided in Chapter 4.

The sharp nail ends are clinched downward for better hold, then they are rasped smooth to prevent injury to anyone handling the hoof.

The shoe is shaped first, then nailed onto the hoof. The nails are placed in the nerve-free wall of the hoof and are not painful to the horse.

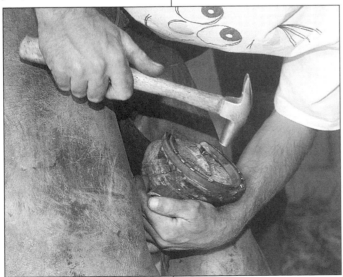

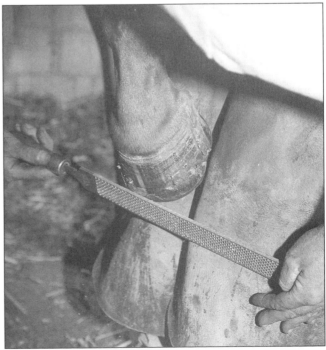

Once you've selected a horse and brought it under your care, consult with your veterinarian to determine a good immunization, dental, and deworming schedule. Your vet will also be able to help you figure out what and how much to feed your horse. Write down your veterinary care schedule and follow it faithfully. This is where the adage "an ounce of prevention is worth a pound of cure" almost always rings true.

Keep a record of all veterinary and farrier services. Not only will this help you keep track of the care your horse receives and your budget, but you will find farrier and veterinary services often complement each other when dealing with a lameness problem. Each professional will appreciate being able to look up the record of the other.

Trainers and Instructors

Although I believe it's advisable for all beginners to enlist the help of a trainer and riding instructor, at least on an as-needed basis, these professional services are certainly optional.

If you plan to take riding lessons, it's wise to start well before you bring home a horse of your own. Ride as many school horses as you can to get the feel of different mounts. These horses are generally safe and fairly docile and work well to build confidence in beginners. Ideally, once you have your own horse to ride you will continue lessons on this horse until you feel comfortable enough to ride without assistance.

If you obtain the services of a trainer to work with your horse, decide whether you prefer the horse trained at your facility or the trainer's. Many trainers will only work out of their own stables. This is often best because the trainer will have established adequate riding and training areas and have on hand the equipment he or she needs. This also gives the trainer the freedom to work with your horse on his or her own schedule, which often means the trainer spends more time with your horse than if it were trained at your stable.

When shopping for trainers and instructors, word-of-mouth recommendations are often best. Many trainers and instructors never advertise their services but rely solely on the power of a good reputation. However, recommendations do not excuse you from checking into the trainer or instructor yourself, as you might have different expectations than the person giving the referral.

Spend some time watching a prospective trainer or instructor work before committing yourself. He or she should be willing to give you a tour of the facilities, but you may want to pop in unannounced as well. Pay special attention to the condition of the barn, the equipment, and the horses stabled there. The quality of care and level of maintenance you observe are a likely reflection of the services you and your horse will receive.

When making a final decision, know and state your goals. Ask the trainer or instructor to clearly explain his or her methods and give you a time estimate for reaching the desired goals, but be aware that it is difficult to accurately estimate how much time each horse or rider will need to show improvement.

Once you have chosen a trainer, make a point of visiting regularly to check the conditions under which your horse is living, and watch the trainer work with the horse. Suspect any trainer that demands an appointment for a visit or dis-

Your grooming supplies should include a bucket or box for carrying and a variety of brushes, combs, sponges, and hoof-care items

courages frequent visits, unless you are one of those pesky types that expects a trainer to stop work to entertain you. You may not always get to watch your horse's training session if you show up unannounced, but you should still catch the trainer at work with other horses if you're there during training hours, and this should prove to be worth your while. Good trainers are proud of the work they do and have nothing to hide.

Supplies and Equipment

A substantial amount of your investment in horse ownership will be in what lies in the tack room and stable. Bear in mind when you go shopping that quality equipment will pay for itself in durability, effectiveness, comfort for you and your horse, and increased safety. Be aware, though, that the highest quality is not always the prettiest nor the fanciest. Don't compromise quality for decorations unless your only goal is to shine in the show ring.

Grooming Supplies

Before you buy your first brush, pick out a container that will make carrying your grooming supplies convenient when working around a horse. Loose brushes get misplaced and stepped on and pick up a lot of dirt. A plastic bucket with a handle works well, but I prefer a shallow plastic box with a handle and several compartments. You can buy one of these at most hardware or variety stores in the cleaning supplies department. I like the box because you never have to dig deep for your supplies and it doesn't tip over easily.

For hoof care, the minimum you will need is a hoof pick. Since these are relatively inexpensive and tend to disappear easily I recommend buying several. Keep one or two in your brush container, one hanging in the tack room, and one tied to your saddle.

Since a hoof pick can cause injury if lost and left in a stall, it's advisable to tie a bright-colored (not yellow if you bed with straw) ribbon or a bell, such as you'd find on a cat's collar, to the handle of your pick.

I recommend buying a hoof brush if there isn't a brush attached to the hoof pick. Almost any small, stiff utility brush with a handle will do. The hoof brush is used to clean the outside wall of the hoof. I also recommend buying hoof dressing to ensure healthy, pliable hooves.

To brush your horse you will need at least two types of brushes: a stiff curry for removing caked dirt and loose hair and a soft-bristled brush for smoothing the coat and brushing the sensitive areas on your horse. My favorite curry is the round rubber curry with shallow teeth since it's not too harsh on a horse's skin, is easy to clean, and will not become clogged with hair or dirt during use.

For a soft brush, the best is a long-bristled natural horsehair brush, but any soft-to-the-touch bristled brush will do. You will also need a hard- or medium-bristled brush for a horse with a thick or long coat.

To finish the coat and really make it glow you can use a simple rub rag, towel, or cloth diaper, or you can buy a rubber mitt from your local tack shop.

The mane and tail will need regular maintenance to keep mats and impossible tangles from developing, but too much combing can thin and shorten a beautiful tail. A hard plastic mane and tail brush or a stiff human hair brush is the easiest and quickest to use for brushing out a mane and tail, but a metal tail comb will do the most meticulous job.

The supplies listed above are the basics for grooming, but if used regularly and properly are really all you'll need. There are many more products and tools available for grooming that you may wish to purchase for specific circumstances. For example, the shedding blade will help get rid of loose winter hair during shedding season, but a rubber curry can do this job as well. A bot blade can help remove stubborn bot eggs deposited on your horse's legs, but a razor blade with one edge taped over is equally effective. Use your judgment and your pocketbook when deciding how extensive your grooming supplies will be.

Medical Supplies

There are some basic first-aid supplies you should always keep available. First and foremost you will need an adequate container to store your first-aid supplies. A permanently fixed cabinet with a latching door is ideal and will enable you to find what you need without searching when an emergency arises. Inside your medicine cabinet you should have scissors, electrician's tape, horse-bandage safety pins, one-edged razor blades, and a hoof pick. Bandaging supplies should include gauze patches, sheet cotton or paper towels, quilted or padded bandages, stretchy rolled bandages, and Vetwrap or another self-sticking, gauze-type bandage roll. Clean, lint-free towels, rags, or cloth diapers are essential, and cotton balls are handy for cleaning small wounds. You will need antiseptics to clean wounds, wound ointments, iodine-based liquids or wound powders for treatment, and a soothing ointment such as aloe vera, zinc oxide, or bag balm to relieve chafing or galls. Liniments are handy, as are poultices and fly repellents. Don't forget your own needs; keep a supply of surgical rubber gloves to wear while treating a horse and a box of adhesive bandages for mishaps around the barn.

A more detailed discussion of medical supplies is offered in Chapter 9.

Barn Equipment

For cleaning and maintaining stalls and loafing sheds you will need at least one pitchfork. There are different types of pitchforks for different jobs. If you bed with straw, get the longest, widest-spaced tines you can find. For shavings use a pitchfork with tightly spaced tines. When gathering clean shavings to fill a stall, skip the pitchfork and try a snow shovel for easiest pickup.

You should have a spade shovel on hand for filling holes in stalls and other miscellaneous chores. You will need a lawn rake and broom for sweeping stall floors, shedrows, and feed and bedding storage areas. Make a habit of keeping these areas clean and you will have a better looking stable and reduce dust buildup, mold growth, and risk of fire.

A wheelbarrow or garden cart is essential for moving around manure, bedding, bales, grain sacks, and other heavy or bulky items. Some people forsake the wheelbarrow for a small tractor with a bucket and trailer.

You will need at least one hose for watering, cleaning equipment, and bathing your horse. You should have a scrub brush for cleaning buckets, and wire cutters and a pocketknife for opening bales and grain sacks. A hammer and a few other hand tools, such as screwdrivers and chisels, are handy. I also keep a couple of pairs of heavy work gloves for chore duty, but don't wear bulky, awkward gloves when handling horses. For riding and handling horses, get a pair of formfitting riding gloves, baseball gloves, or (my favorite) water-skiing gloves.

Feed Storage

Grain and vitamins should always be kept in secure, watertight storage containers to avoid rodent invasion, moisture, mold and dust contamination, and an unplanned gorge-fest if a horse gets access to it. Plastic or metal garbage cans with tight lids work well. You can double-secure the container by stretching a bungee cord from handle to handle over the lid. I have also seen retired chest freezers used to store grain, but these must be kept secured to prevent the possibility of trapping and smothering a child.

Hay and straw must never be laid flat on the ground, tarps, or a concrete surface, as they will soak up trapped moisture and spoil quickly. If you don't have a wooden floor or loft to store your bales, lay them on boards or board pallets, with the stem ends down, so air can circulate underneath them. Once the bottom bales are laid properly, the rest can be stacked tightly on top and beside each other. Make sure your storage area is weatherproof, with a good roof and walls to keep rain or snow from blowing in and wetting the sides of your bales.

Watch out for hot hay. If you open a bale of hay and find it feels warm to the touch, it is contaminated with moisture trapped during baling and should be thrown out. These bales have been known to get hot enough to catch fire. In addition, if hot hay is stacked among other bales, it may cause spontaneous combustion and destroy the stack, the barn, and everything in it. Knowing your hay source and whether the hay was baled during or too soon after a rainy spell may be your only way of preventing a hot bale from entering your barn.

∩ ∩

The information in this chapter should go far in enabling you to prepare a proper home for your horse. Tack needs also play a large role in handling and keeping a horse and will take up a good chunk of your budget. This information will be covered in Chapter 5.

Checklist for Basic Supplies

Grooming

- ☐ hoof pick
- ☐ hoof brush
- ☐ mane and tail comb
- ☐ plastic curry
- ☐ rubber curry
- ☐ soft-bristled brush
- ☐ stiff-bristled brush
- ☐ rags

Medicine Cabinet

- ☐ scissors
- ☐ electrician's tape
- ☐ razor blades
- ☐ thermometer
- ☐ cotton balls
- ☐ gauze patches
- ☐ sheet cotton or paper towels
- ☐ padded leg bandages
- ☐ stretchy rolled bandages
- ☐ self-sticking rolled bandages
- ☐ lint-free rags
- ☐ nonstinging antiseptic
- ☐ wound ointment
- ☐ wound powder
- ☐ gall or rash ointment
- ☐ rubbing alcohol
- ☐ fly repellent
- ☐ rubber gloves
- ☐ adhesive bandages (for your injuries)

Barn Equipment

- ☐ hose
- ☐ shovel
- ☐ rakes (metal and lawn)
- ☐ pitchfork
- ☐ wheelbarrow or garden cart
- ☐ knife
- ☐ wire cutters
- ☐ scrub brush
- ☐ hammer
- ☐ chisel
- ☐ buckets
- ☐ extra chain, ropes, snaps, and eye screws

Feed Storage

- ☐ pallets or boards
- ☐ tarps for exposed hay
- ☐ watertight, sealable containers
- ☐ measuring scoops or cans

Depending upon your situation you may find other items necessary or convenient for keeping a horse. Many stables now have automatic fly-control systems, watering systems, and hotwalking machines. Some are equipped with hot- and cold-water washracks and laundry facilities. You may think a stable office, kitchenette, or heated viewing room mandatory for your needs.

If none exists, you will probably want to plan for a riding area you can use regularly without transporting your horse. This may mean building an arena or leveling out a pasture area and adding surface material. This could also entail bulldozing or cutting a trail through available property, or just investigating the trails or open areas in your neighborhood that are within safe riding distance. I will cover this subject more extensively in Chapter 10.

If you plan to transport your horse on more than the rare occasion, you might think of buying a van or trailer; this decision might further require the purchase of a vehicle capable of pulling the load. This is a personal decision, but I will cover the safety requirements of a horse-hauling vehicle in Chapter 4. It is worth your while to keep in mind that a horse is a large and powerful creature that will not travel well or willingly in a rickety, bouncy, open container or one that is too small for the horse to stand comfortably and well balanced. I can tell you from experience that breaking down while hauling a horse is a very unpleasant experience, so the working condition of your vehicle should be attended to before you start even a crosstown trip.

4

The Smart Shopper

A Buyer's Guide to Finding the Right Horse

Choosing a horse for personal use carries the same weight and variables as choosing a personal vehicle. The difference lies in the fact that the horse is a living creature. Once the decision is made to purchase a particular horse, you become completely responsible for the well-being of that horse. If your decision is regrettable, you cannot simply push the horse aside; it requires daily care and attention, and if you decide to give it up, will need a decent replacement home. A good choice in the first place will prevent many future headaches and make the difference between enjoying the time you spend with your horse, or dreading it.

Where to Look

There are three basic ways you can have a horse of your own. You may be given a horse, you may lease a horse, and you may buy a horse. Purchasing a horse is by far the most prevalent method, and the one that carries the most risk.

Finding a Free Horse

It may surprise you to find there are many free horses available. The presence of these horses is not widely known or advertised since a person willing to give up a horse at no cost generally does not want it to end up sold as meat.

Many free horses are elderly and considered retired. Although the horse may not be able to meet the needs of a more experienced rider, it may be perfect for a first-time horse owner and may very well thrive with good care and attention.

Some free horses are chronically lame and will only do as pets or companions; the present owner may not be willing to keep the horse around indefinitely but may care enough for the horse not to send it to auction or to be killed. Some have fallen into poor health due to neglect. The owner may realize the financial sense of giving up the horse rather than spending excessive amounts of money in an attempt to rehabilitate the animal.

There are racehorses available that are ready for retirement or have proved failures in competition. Most are geldings since these cannot be used for breeding, but some mares and stallions unsuited for breeding will also be made available.

Racehorses are retired for several reasons. A horse may earn retirement upon reaching the age of eight or ten without mishap. The horse may be crippled from injuries and not suitable for racing or riding. A horse may suffer from leg problems that are not crippling but bad enough to risk permanent injury with further racing stress. The horse may be a "bleeder," one that suffers from ruptured vessels of the lungs that can result in nosebleeds when the horse is raced or stressed past its limits. Bleeders are generally not affected by normal exercise and riding.

Any of these horses may need retraining, but some are quite gentle and all have had extensive handling and a decent amount of care. Think hard about the free horse you choose, especially if it is one that needs retraining or rehabilitation. The gift horse may turn out to be quite expensive in the long run. If you are set on finding a free horse, contact 4-H and pony clubs. Haunt local stables and the racetrack if there is one in your area. Probably the best method is to advertise; horse show arenas, stables, racetracks, and auction yards almost always have a bulletin board or area where you can tack up a flyer.

Leasing a Horse

An alternative to buying a horse is to lease one or share ownership. Lease deals can best be found through referrals, from stables or riding clubs, but you will occasionally see a horse for lease advertised in newspapers or other publications. Often this can be a free lease with the stipulation that you pay for care and boarding.

Leasing can be a good way to get started because you can be more assured of the honesty of an owner that retains interest in the horse. In addition, the owner will remain available for consultation if there are any problems, and you can return the horse if necessary.

The downside of a lease is that you don't really own the horse and may have to return it after you have become attached to it. A good contract is essential in any lease deal, and a lease with option to buy is ideal if you think you want to keep the horse.

If you enter into an ownership-share agreement, you should have the terms written into a contract. Determine who is going to be responsible for care, both financial and physical, when the horse will be available for use by either party, and what the horse will be used for at any time. Be mindful of the rights of either party to loan out or let others ride the horse.

Purchasing a Horse

You will find horses advertised for sale in the newspaper, on flyers posted at stables, in horse publications, and by word of mouth. There are also auction yards that hold regular horse sales; this is a great place to find a bargain—and a greater place to get stung.

At an auction you will find a variety of horses available. Unless they are registered and their papers and possibly performance videotapes are available, these horses must be considered as having no history. Without documentation, anything you are told about a horse is suspect. The opportunity to ride a horse at an auction is limited, if allowed at all, and you can't realistically judge a horse's behavior or performance by watching it being maneuvered inside a tiny ring. Veterinary examinations are often not allowed, and the horses are not tested for the presence of drugs that may hide lameness or ill temperament. The auction yard is a quick way to get rid of an unwanted horse and is used frequently as a dumping ground for the most undesirable animals. My recommendation is to avoid the auction yard altogether.

There are people that make their livings buying and selling horses. Many horse traders are trainers that are willing to put some time into a horse to make it look good and perform well, then take their wages in the profits of a sale. Other horse traders hit auctions looking for big, attractive horses or family-type ponies. They then advertise these animals in the newspaper, often making up histories on the horses, and gain a quick turnaround on their money.

Whether or not a horse trader is honest, he or she often hasn't spent enough time with the horse to be a fair judge of its temperament, performance, or soundness. You may find, however, that the selection through a horse trader is better and more accessible than what you will find by chasing around the countryside answering individual advertisements. If this is so, stick with a trader (often operating under a stable name) you can check through referrals, even if this means actually going out to see a horse that the trader has already sold. If patience allows, take time to watch the activity in a trader's stable. Suspect any horse trader that brings in horses by the truckload or has different horses in the stable every time you visit.

Newspaper or other advertising publications are decent places to find horses for sale. You are often dealing directly with a long-term owner or even the original owner or breeder of the horse. But be aware that horse traders also use this medium to sell their horses.

When answering an ad be sure to ask how long the present owner has had the horse, whether the horse is registered, how it has been used and who has been using it, and why the horse is for sale. Determine whether the owner is willing to show the horse multiple times, submit to a veterinary exam (at your expense), and ride or pay for a professional to ride the horse in your presence (assuming this is a trained riding horse). If the horse is not registered, ask for any other evidence of the horse's bloodlines, such as pictures of its sire and dam. Speaking of pictures, ask that any photographs or video recordings of the horse be made available. This may give you a good indication of the horse's history since many owners photograph and record events such as horse shows, mountain rides, or a horse's willingness to carry five children on its bare back.

Perhaps the best way to find a horse is by word-of-mouth referral. Some of the best horses are never officially advertised through a publication because there is no need. It is common to first tell those within a circle—club members, boarding stable clients, instructors, and trainers—and let those people spread the word for free. If you are taking riding lessons, ask your instructor and the stable trainer to help you locate a suitable horse. Joining a riding club, even before you own a horse, will put you in touch with many connections. Contact 4-H and pony clubs even if you are not looking for a child's horse. These clubs turn out many wonderfully trained animals of all sizes and breeds. Most people that know you and plan to be around you after you have purchased a horse will do their best to help you find one that will not hurt you or soak you financially.

Shopping Guidelines

Budget

Before you look at your first horse there are several things you need to do. First and foremost, if you are planning to purchase, determine your budget and the absolute maximum amount of money you are willing to pay. Some horses can be bought on credit, but most are cash-up-front deals. If you buy a horse on installments, bear in mind that the horse is your responsibility the minute you take possession. If it dies or becomes lame or injured, you must still continue your payments. If you fail to make your payments for any reason, the horse can be seized and you will lose the horse and the money you've invested in training, board, feed, veterinary, and shoeing expenses.

When setting your dollar limit keep in mind that the purchase price is only a token payment on the long-term investment you are about to make. Horses are constant and substantial consumers; they need regular care, a decent home, services from professionals, and tack and equipment. I can't realistically predict your expenditures since they vary by area and market, but it would pay for you to do some research in this area. Talk to an instructor, a trainer, a stable owner, and other horse owners. Find out what it takes to care for a horse by minimal and ideal standards, and see where you fit in.

Preparation

Before you start on your shopping expedition you should ready yourself with knowledge and skills. My first recommendation, of course, would be that you read this book (the whole thing). There is more you must do, however, since certain skills can be learned only from hands-on experience. For this reason I suggest strongly that you take some riding lessons. Find an instructor that has several schooling horses available for you to ride, as each horse will feel different and respond differently to your commands. Whatever your ultimate preference, ask your instructor to allow you to ride both English and Western styles, and possibly bareback.

My favorite type of instructor is one that asks the student to participate in some of the chores. You will limit your learning experience if the horse is tacked and ready when you begin and led away saddled after you are finished with your lesson. You should (enthusiastically) help catch, groom, tack, bathe, and cool your schooling mount. If time is limited, do at least one of these chores at each lesson. If the instructor doesn't offer, don't be shy about asking to help out.

There are other ways of getting involved and learning about horses before you go shopping. Spend some time at horse shows, not just watching the events but visiting the stabling and warm-up areas. Observe, and when possible, ask questions; a lot of knowledge and skill float around these areas.

Volunteer at a local stable to do barn chores. You may or may not be abused in this situation, but as a volunteer you can always walk away. The willingness to clean some stalls, though, may buy you some riding time or the opportunity to tag along with a trainer or instructor.

If you can, get a job at a stable or racetrack. There are many top-class trainers and riders that started out as stall muckers at minimum wage or less. The opportunity to learn and advance from this position depends on how much you want it.

You may want to join a riding club to meet others of similar interests. Most club meetings are also gab sessions where knowledge and tricks of the trade are swapped, and you may even get the opportunity to participate in a ride or event, regardless of whether you own a horse.

Assistance   Even with the accumulation of some knowledge and skills you should not shop for your first horse without some help. Take someone with experience on your shopping expeditions. This may be a knowledgeable friend, a trainer, or a riding instructor, although you may need to pay for the services of the latter two. If this is the case, you may want to do the preliminary looking first, then bring the professional along for confirmation on a second or third look.

Never, never, never buy a horse without the approval of a veterinarian. Many people scoff at this as an unnecessary expense, but it can save you many times the money in the long run, as well as a bit of emotional stress. Your veterinarian doesn't need to tag along as you shop; wait until you have narrowed your choices to one or two before you call in his or her services.

When choosing a veterinarian, think of this as the start of a long-term relationship. Bouncing from vet to vet is not ideal as each new veterinarian must get to know both you and the horse in order to offer the best service. At the same time, it is unreasonable to expect one veterinarian to take care of all services at all times. For this reason, you may want to interview several veterinarians to choose a backup, or select a practice of two or more veterinarians that work closely together.

The veterinarian you choose should be an equine or large-animal specialist. After-hours services or referrals should be offered for emergencies; you don't want to be caught flipping through the yellow pages while your horse is colicking at three A.M.

Your veterinarian should be willing to give advice and answer questions over the phone without making you feel ignorant or intrusive. This can save you a lot of time and money by avoiding some unnecessary veterinary visits. Your veterinarian should never sound curt or exasperated over even the most basic questions, as long as you do not hound or pester to excess.

Word-of-mouth referrals are very common in choosing a veterinarian, but don't take for granted that you will like a veterinarian as much as the next person. Take time to interview the veterinarian and possibly watch him or her work. Most veterinarians would not be offended and might enjoy having you come along for a few farm visits. Contact and interview at least three veterinarians before making a decision, assuming there is a selection of that size in your area.

The Right Horse

There are many types of horses available for the beginner, all of which have merits and downsides. Research into the type of horse that might suit you best is fundamental and should precede any shopping excursion.

Age

With good care and regular exercise, the elderly horse can be as robust as the juvenile.

Age is a primary factor in choosing a horse. If you are eager to step into the saddle, an unbroke or greenbroke horse is likely unsuitable. You may, however, wish to start with a young horse or foal for several reasons. Obviously, youth promises longevity and a long-term relationship is, for most, the ideal. Some also choose the unbroke horse in order to experience the breaking and training process and to participate in the horse's development as a mount—to place a personal stamp on the animal. This is a wonderful concept, but I caution beginners of the danger of ruining a horse or getting injured trying to break and train it without the necessary skills and knowledge. If a young, unbroke horse is your choice, you should be prepared to send it to, or work closely with, a reputable trainer.

Many people are unwilling to take on an older horse. The aged horse is thought more likely to have health

problems, and be set in its ways, therefore being less trainable. And it is feared the older horse will die too soon, causing grief and possible financial loss.

The negative factors concerning the elderly horse certainly hold some merit but are usually somewhat exaggerated. A well-cared-for aged horse can be as robust in health as a two-year-old and has probably passed through most of the viral illnesses young horses are subject to. Fitness is a major—though mostly ignored—factor in keeping the older horse healthy. If you are willing to put in the time to ride an aged horse on a regular, moderate schedule or otherwise provide it regular exercise, you will minimize many health problems.

Concerning training, an older horse may have picked up some tricks and undesirable habits and be less pliable to your demands. I've seen this just as commonly, though, in the three-year-old as in the twenty-three-year-old. Bad habits don't take years to develop—they take days, sometimes only hours or minutes. More likely, if you choose a well-trained, well-treated older horse it will be more docile and cooperative than a young one still testing its limits.

"You can't teach an old dog new tricks" does not apply to the older horse (nor to the old dog, in my experience). I believe horses enjoy learning at any age if the learning experience is not painful or frightening. I know of many horses that have had multiple careers, changing with age.

The old horse may indeed die before you're ready. Humans outlive most animals; this is unavoidable. There are degrees of agedness, however, and if you choose carefully, the older horse can provide years of use and enjoyment. If you decide on an older horse, you will likely be rewarded with the company of a gentler, more predictable animal that will give you confidence during the time you need to build skills.

Gender

Gender is not even thought to be a factor by some, but should be considered by the novice. If your horse is to live with others in an open area, it must be able to get along. This pretty much excludes stallions or the ungelded colt. Mares and geldings usually get along quite well in a herd or pair setting, with mares being the less predictable of the two.

If raising a foal is on your mind for future plans, you will likely choose a filly or mare. Stick to the female end of the breeding business; raising and keeping stallions to breed is strictly for professionals.

As general advice, you are better off avoiding a stallion or ungelded colt for any purpose. There are some exceptionally well-mannered, well-trained stallions out there; they *are* the exception. Stallions as a rule are more headstrong and aggressive. They are more likely than a mare or gelding to physically challenge you and less likely to back down to your authority. A stallion, even in play, is more likely to bite or strike at a person, and if you enter the enclosure of a stallion that is loose, it is more apt to attack you. Usually this attack is a form of play, but the results are hazardous regardless. I have worked with and trained many stallions and ungelded colts. They can be completely compliant for extended periods, then become completely unmanageable in the presence of a mare or other distraction.

The gelding is the most reliable animal for temperament. The gelding's behavior is not influenced by hormonal changes and is, therefore, more predictable. The mare often seems to suffer from similar emotional upheavals during her heat cycles as a woman does during menstrual cycles. In many you may hardly notice the mare is in season; in others it creates a Jekyll-and-Hyde personality.

Size

Size cannot be ignored when choosing a horse. Horses and ponies are powerful creatures—most can carry a sizable person for an adequate distance. But this does not mean anyone should ride any size horse or pony.

If you choose a horse that is too small, your horse will tire more easily and suffer more back strain. Ideally for the horse, your weight should be less than 25 percent of the horse's estimated weight. You will also be affected by the inadequate size of your mount. If your legs dangle and your hands can easily reach over the horse's ears, you will feel awkward and look odd. Your hands will tend to be a bit heavier on the reins than is ideal, and you will not be as effective with your leg signals.

If your horse is too large, you will have problems mounting and dismounting, as well as properly placing the tack on the horse. A large horse may also be less responsive if the rider is frail or if the rider's legs are set so high that the horse doesn't receive proper leg signals. Big does not mean uncontrollable, though; a very small horse can be more unmanageable than a large animal. Training and proper equipment are much greater factors in control than is the size of the horse.

So how, you may ask, is the perfect size determined? This is very simple. While standing at the horse's shoulder you should be able to peer just over the horse's withers. If the horse forms a wall you cannot see over, even when stretching on tiptoe, it is too large for you. If you can rest your chin on the horse's withers, it is too small. These size specifications are for mature mounts; a young horse or foal, or a carriage or cart horse, will not fit within these guidelines. Also keep in mind that size specs are not written in stone. Rarely will you see a rider *perfectly* matched to a mount.

The ideal horse for a beginner is one that is gentle by nature, not cooperative by force.

Temperament

Temperament should probably be your most important consideration when choosing a first horse. Just about any horse can be beaten into a submissive attitude, but this does not create a genuinely loyal, trustworthy temperament.

The ideal horse for a beginner (for anyone, actually) is one that is gentle by nature, not cooperative by force. The horse should be relaxed and friendly in the presence of people and should show interest and willingness when approached. The horse should accept your touch without flinching or dancing away and should be tolerant of your awkward movements. A truly gentle horse by nature will display these characteristics even before it has been trained or handled extensively.

Breeds and Performance

Choosing a horse by breed, color, or performance is wholly arbitrary according to your personal needs and desires; I cannot guide you any more than I could tell you what make and model car to buy. I do have some comments, though.

When choosing a horse by its performance abilities, the novice will do best to find one that is finished at its training level. Leave the greenbroke or potential performer for the more experienced buyer. If you do choose an unfinished horse, I strongly suggest you do not try to complete the training without help. Either hire a trainer or work directly under the supervision of a trainer.

Preferring a breed is quite common, often the major factor in choosing a horse. You would be wise to ignore any stereotyping about the breed you've chosen and look at each horse as an individual. Every breed has its rogues and its sweethearts. In addition to temperament, members of any breed will vary in size, endurance, soundness, beauty, conformation, and performance ability.

The Physical Exam

A non-horsey friend of mine accompanied me to a horse auction recently. Though not interested in horses, and not at all in the market for one, he was dazzled by a shiny black mare circling the ring and was highly dismayed when I refused to let him bid on her. My friend saw a fine, coal-black steed—a worthy mount for a proud rider. What I saw was a thin, aged mare, narrow chested and cow hocked, with osselets formed on both front ankles and signs of foundering in the hooves.

It is frighteningly easy to miss the physical flaws in a horse if you don't know what to look for, especially if the horse is a dazzler—of a brilliant color or with a flowing mane and tail. Understanding the ideal, and not so ideal, physical attributes of the horse, as well as learning the signs of aging, health, and soundness problems, will simplify your final decision and help prevent you from setting your heart on an unsuitable horse.

Aging the Horse

Clearly the simplest method of aging a horse is to shop only for registered stock. Providing the registration papers are authentic and the horse matches the physical description on the papers, you can rely on the date of birth listed as an indication of the true age of the horse.

Physical appearance will give you a clue about a horse's age, but with mature horses this can be very inaccurate. I once owned a twenty-one-year-old Appaloosa that could have passed unquestioned as a six- or seven-year-old, and there is a five-year-old Thoroughbred in our barn that looks to be in his late teens.

A horse with clear signs of aging will have a sunken or hollow eye. The skin will be looser when pinched or pulled and the coat may be shaggier or shed later in the season. Muzzle hairs are often whitened. The muscles are less defined and the back may be swayed. The teeth are longer, yellower, and protrude farther to the front.

The teeth are a practically foolproof determinant of a horse's age, but examination of the teeth is difficult for two reasons. One, to get a good look you must open the horse's mouth and keep it open while you stick your face close enough to see the surfaces of the teeth. Most horses are highly uncooperative about this. Two, you must be knowledgeable enough to determine the differences without constantly referring to a chart or graph, again because the horse isn't going to stand there all day with its mouth forced open. My suggestion is to have your veterinarian examine the horse's teeth. He or she will have the instruments necessary to hold the horse's mouth open and will have the knowledge to make a quick determination.

Your veterinarian will look for the number of permanent teeth (all are in place at age five); the number of teeth with blackened surfaces, actually hollow spaces crammed with food gunk, which indicate a horse between three and seven years; the stage in which the blackened surfaces are worn clean (around age eight); and the length of the Galvayne's Groove, a vertical groove that begins growth at the gum base of the incisors.

The Galvayne's Groove begins forming about age nine and extends to half the length of the incisor by age fifteen. A twenty-year-old horse will have a full groove, from gum base to the bottom of the tooth. As the horse ages, the groove begins to smooth with wear and disappear, starting again at the base. A horse of about twenty-five will show the remaining groove from about the center of the incisor to the bottom tip. If the groove is completely worn away, you can assume the horse to be well over twenty-five and probably not suitable for purchase.

Judging by Conformation

Conformation is a measure of how a horse is put together and balanced. Ideal conformation will help a horse retain its soundness and will make for a more balanced, comfortable mover. Conformation attributes vary in some ways breed by breed, but there are ideals and flaws common to all breeds.

Keep an open mind when judging a horse by conformation. Many flaws that are frowned upon in the show ring will have no effect on the horse or the pleasure you receive from the horse. I used a severely pigeon-toed Quarter Horse for years as a pony horse, one of the most physically demanding jobs a horse can perform. The horse was quite comfortable to ride and never lame until a well-meaning farrier took it upon himself to correct the horse's stance by chang-

This foal's excellent conformation will help it to develop into a sound, strong, and balanced adult and thus a more valuable horse.

ing the shape of the hooves. If the conformation defect is not grotesque, the horse moves well and comfortably, and the legs show no sign of unsoundness, you may get a decent horse at a discount price by overlooking the flaw.

The first thing to look for in conformation is the horse's overall balance. All parts of the horse should be in proportion, but you need not carry a measuring stick to determine this. Stand well back and observe the horse standing still. The horse's legs should be lined up and squared, the head raised and faced forward, and the horse should not be leaning or resting a foot. If the horse looks proportional, then it is. That simple.

Legs

Balance and smoothness in a moving horse are determined largely by the conformation of its legs. Again, while the horse is standing squared observe it from all sides. (This time a measuring stick or other straightedge could be helpful.)

First, observe the horse from the front. The legs should appear to come straight down from the center of each side of the chest. If the legs are splayed or widely set, they will put undo pressure on the knees. If the legs are narrow from the chest or narrowly set at the ground, this indicates weakness in front and commonly creates a choppy stride. The knees and ankles should be aligned with the center of the foreleg and the center of the hoof. Knees that point in (knocked) or bow out will not withstand a lot of stress. If the hooves point to the center, the horse is pigeon-toed, and this can lead to stress on the ankle joint. If the hooves point out, they are splayed and can, again, put stress on the ankles.

Move to the rear of the horse. The legs should fall straight from the center of each side of the horse's rump to the ground, all joints in alignment. The most common defect you will find are cow hocks, or hock joints that point in. This flaw may reduce the strength of the hindquarters and create a rather loose-jointed action behind, but is generally not very consequential for moderate riding. Hocks that point out are more troublesome, as the hock and hip joints will be unduly stressed. Also, beware the horse that stands narrow at the ground. Its balance will be reduced, it will be more likely to hit a hind ankle with the opposing hind hoof during exercise, and more stress will be added to the hock joints.

When you observe the horse from the side, you must be sure to look at both sides, as you can't assume they will match. The front legs should line up from the center of the shoulder to the center of the knee through the center of the cannon bone to the back of the heel. Don't even consider buying a horse that doesn't align in front from a side view, and if you need to use a straightedge to determine this, don't be shy. If the knee is over (slightly bent) or back of the line, the horse is almost certain to suffer from knee problems. Look also at the angle of the pastern and hoof. A long, vertically straight pastern or a pastern with extensive horizontal slope will put undue pressure on the ankles. An ideal

Correct Conformation of the Legs

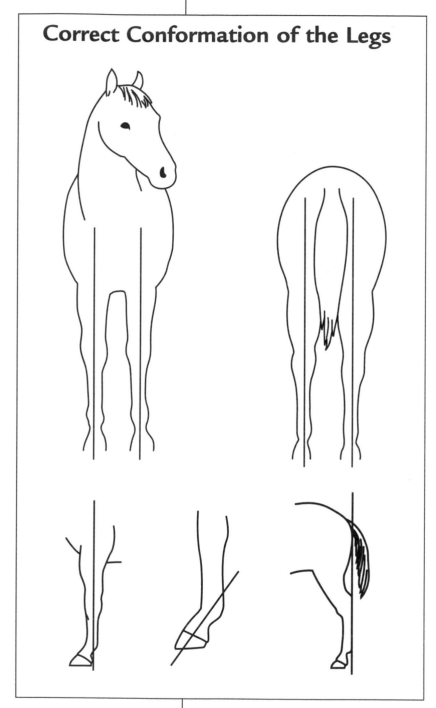

pastern is short and moderately sloped. The hoof should have a nice forty-five-degree slope in front. The heel bulbs should not touch the ground, but should have a bit of hoof below them; this will protect them from easy bruising.

A side view of the hind legs should show straight alignment from the base of the tail to the back of the hock, lower leg, and fetlock. The heel should be slightly inward from the line. A horse that stands under or is angled in from the hock down will be poorly balanced and choppy to ride. This horse may have a tendency to clip its front heels with the hind toes. A horse that stands out behind will also be poorly balanced and tend to have less strength in the hindquarters.

Body

Conformation attributes of the body are harder to determine than those of the legs because of the variables by breed. Still, there are flaws and ideals to look for that are appropriate for all horses.

An attractive head is just that—one you look at and say, "Gee, that's pretty (handsome, nice, etc.)!" Some attributes are based on more than aesthetic judgment, however.

The mouth can have deformities that make eating difficult. This can be a detriment to the horse's health and your feed bill. Lift the lips while examining the horse's head and make sure the horse has front teeth that line up well enough to graze or pull hay. A horse with a severe parrot mouth or overbite almost always needs extra grain or alfalfa pellets it can suck in and chew with its back teeth; it will not do well on pasture. An underbite is fairly rare, but a severe underbite will result in the same problems as a parrot mouth.

Don't neglect to examine the eyes. They should be well placed on the head, not too high or too close together. Look for large, clear, bright eyes and avoid horses with spots or clouds over or near the lens area, as they will likely have sight problems. Look under the eye for raw spots, scarring, or hair loss, which may indicate chronic eye infections. This may not be a reason to turn the horse away; it could be caused by sensitivity to flies or dust and could improve with better care.

Ideal conformation requires a strong proportional neck in all breeds. The crest should be straight or convex and firm to the touch. If it is concave, or slopes in and down, the horse is considered ewe-necked. This will not greatly affect the performance of most pleasure horses but does tend to weaken the front end of hard performers such as jumpers. You may need to sit on or stand above the horse to examine the alignment of the neck, but it is worth the trouble. If the horse has injured any vertebrae in its neck, the neck might show a crook along the mane line. This type injury is chronic and the horse should probably be avoided. If the crest has a curve to it, this is a good indication the horse has foundered, another chronic ailment you do not want.

The withers should be examined closely for scars, which indicate past injury. This may not affect the horse further, having possibly been caused by ill-fitted tack, but it could be a chronic problem if the horse is especially high at the withers. Besides problems with tack, extremely high-withered horses are miserable to ride bareback, so consider this if you plan on bareback riding.

Flat- or mutton-withered horses can also be a problem. Most saddles will not sit well on a mutton-withered horse; compensation to stop saddle rolling usually means an extra-tight girth or breast collar, both of which may cause galls, swelling, or a nasty attitude on the part of the horse.

The first line of the shoulder, where it meets the neck, should show slope. A vertically straight shoulder is usually weak and may cause a choppy, pounding effect on the front end. The shoulders should be evenly developed on both sides and should not appear dropped on one side when viewed from the front.

The spine should appear straight and well padded, without knobs protruding. A straight spine, though, does not guarantee a healthy back. If the horse has a weak back or an injury, you can check for this by placing a thumb and finger on each side of the spine at the withers, then running your fingers the length of the spine, applying a fair amount of pressure. If the horse sinks down, it likely suffers from some sort of back problem, either spinal or muscular. Brush or rub the back vigorously to double-check that you haven't just tickled the horse into crouching, then run your fingers down its spine again.

The hindquarters should be well padded and equally proportioned. Hip problems can best be detected by examination. Stand at the rear of the horse while the horse is made to stand square. If one hip is dropped lower than the other or one hindquarter looks significantly less muscled than the other, this indicates hip weakness or injury.

I've stated that the spine and hindquarters should be padded, the neck sloped, and the withers not too high. In a thin horse this will not be the case and cannot, at least at the moment, be considered a true conformational defect. You must take into consideration the overall condition of the horse while judging by conformation.

Determining Soundness

Your veterinarian will be your judge and jury on the soundness of a prospective horse. However, your veterinarian will likely not follow you around on all your shopping expeditions but only examine the horse or horses you are most seriously considering. You may be able to eliminate some horses by detecting a few soundness problems yourself.

When I speak of soundness I am mainly referring to the condition of the bones, tendons, and ligaments of a horse. Soundness also includes the condition of the horse's respiratory system as well as its overall health. I've previously covered some of the soundness problems you should look for when examining the spine and hips. Obviously conformation and soundness blend together in some respects, but a soundness examination goes beyond judgment of a horse by conformation.

Hooves

The hooves are truly the foundation of the horse and a good place to start your check. First, I must comment on the color. It is widely believed that a white hoof is softer than a black hoof. The worth of this statement is largely determined by the hoof care your horse receives, but color could be a real consideration if you plan to keep your horse barefoot in a wet or muddy environment or ride your horse barefoot on rocky or rough ground. If these are your intentions, you will do best to find the hardest-hoofed horse available, and this would probably mean a black-hoofed animal.

If the horse you are examining has had poor hoof care, you are likely to find small cracks or chips at the bottom of the hoof wall; this is easily correctable. Long cracks, though, that extend past the nails or nailing area may not heal or may heal improperly, causing chronic lameness. The heel bulbs and coronet band should show no signs of inflammation and should not be tender when pressed. The floor of the hoof should be smooth, dry, and reasonably odorless. You should be able to press on the sole, avoiding the frog, with the blunt end of a hoof pick without causing the horse to flinch or pull away from you. All areas of the hoof should be cold to the touch, unless of course the horse has been standing in direct sunlight or intense heat.

Look closely at the hoof for any sign of curving at the toe, which is an indication of advanced laminitis. A person can sometimes successfully hide this condition by cutting the hoof extremely short, but if left untrimmed the hoof will actually grow off the ground at the toe until it forms a curl. Laminitis is an almost always incurable and extremely painful condition and you absolutely want to avoid this animal. Other signs of laminitis are heat in the coronet bands or hooves, a cresty or deformed neck, and a leaning stance in which the horse attempts to place most of its weight on its heels.

Hooves can tell a bit of the history of a horse. When a horse suffers severe stress or a serious illness, the coronet band will become inflamed. After the horse has recovered and the hoof continues to grow, a raised ring will show up on the wall of the hoof, indicating the time at which the horse was stressed. The wider the ring, the longer the illness or stress. Multiple rings could be the sign of a not-so-happy life for the horse. Poor nutrition will also cause formation of these rings.

Legs

The legs of a horse have no muscle or fat from the knees and hocks down. These areas have low blood flow and are cold to the touch. When an injury occurs, blood rushes to the area to aid healing, thus creating heat. So unless a horse's legs are exposed to direct, hot sunlight, any heat you find indicates a problem.

An injured area will also usually show some swelling. Since there is no fat or muscle tissue from the knees or hocks down, including the hooves, any squishy, puffy, or unusually thick, hard areas must be considered signs of injury. Since the areas of the legs are so crucial and complicated I will explain them individually.

You will not have the real skills to test a horse for soundness by watching it move; nevertheless it is a good idea to try to detect problems this way. Always observe the horse at a trot, either with a rider on its back or being led by someone skilled. Watch it move from the front, behind, and side. Many leg injuries will not be indicated by a limp, so look beyond the exaggerated gimp and head nod for other indications, such as a short or wide-based stride, stiffness in the joints, overflexion, stumbling, and refusal to perform. If the horse shows an obvious limp, have the hooves tested first, as this is the area most blatant in indicating lameness.

Ankles

A working horse's ankles receive a great amount of stress and are often the first trouble spots. Many ankle problems will be difficult for you to detect and may not be detected by your veterinarian without an X ray, but some are readily apparent even to the amateur.

Windpuffs are perhaps the most common ankle ailment and are generally not a serious problem. They are swelled areas on the sides of the ankles, just above the joint between the center and the back of the ankle, and are most commonly seen on the hind legs. They indicate hard use of the animal and can be relieved by rest, cold-water bathing, and bandaging. A horse with windpuffs often never shows signs of lameness or discomfort and may be perfectly usable long-term, even if you can't rid the horse of the windpuffs. Other common causes of windpuffs are poor conformation, stall confinement (especially after hard use), pregnancy, and hot weather.

In the same area, but lower than the windpuff, you may find a hard, bony growth that makes the ankle, just forward of the fetlock, jut out unnaturally. This is probably sesamoiditis, or inflammation of the sesamoid bone, and it is serious enough to inhibit your purchase of the horse.

Swelling on the side of the ankle forward of the center is not considered a windpuff but indicates a more serious injury, such as to the extensor tendon or ankle joint. Swelling accompanied by heat in this area is reason to reject the horse, or at least to insist on a careful examination by your veterinarian.

The front of the ankles should be fairly flat and hard. If the forefronts of the ankles appear to protrude and look rounded, they have probably formed osselets. Osselets are bony growths that indicate injury caused by excessive pounding, either because the horse has been ridden on hard surfaces or the horse has poor, upright conformation of the pasterns. Osselets don't go away but should not cause lameness after formation is complete and the area shows no further heat.

Similar to osselets are ringbones and sidebones. These bony growths form on the pastern, either just below the ankle or at or below the coronet band. They may or may not be detectable unless they are fresh and heat and swelling are apparent. As with osselets, ringbones and sidebones usually do not cause lameness after they are set, but this can take a very long time, even years.

Examine the fetlock for raw spots or scarring. This is a sign that the horse hits the ground with its fetlocks when galloping and indicates weak pasterns, which can lead to ankle and pastern (suspensory) ligament injuries. Occasionally hitting or burning the fetlocks is caused by poor shoeing, so you may want to consult a farrier or veterinarian before you give up on such a horse.

If the entire ankle joint looks enlarged, you should avoid this horse. This indicates serious past injuries such as bone chips or a chronic present malady such as arthritis.

Horses with ankle injuries often limp at the trot, but not always. Watch out for a shortened pogo-stick stride (most apparent at the canter) or a wide-based stride.

Cannon Bone and Flexor Tendon

The cannon bone is the main support between the ankle and the knee or hock joint, and can be thought of as the horse's shin. There is a major supporting tendon that runs from knee to ankle along the back of the cannon bone, actually two tendons sheathed together—the deep and the superficial flexor tendons.

The flexor tendon should be absolutely straight and of the same thickness from top to bottom. A bowed tendon, one that curves or bulges outward, is very undesirable. Although the tendon can be set and healed, given much time and attention, it will always be vulnerable to rebowing. A horse cannot function soundly with a bowed tendon. When examining the tendon, use your hand and fingers to measure its straightness and thickness. Don't be fooled by thick hair around the fetlock, which might cause the tendon to appear bowed, but at the same time don't let thick hair hide a bow. The bow might run the length of the tendon, part of the length, or appear as a slight "wow" just above the fetlock. Don't discount a bow by its size; they are all serious. Don't bother giving the horse a trot test if you suspect a bow. Just walk away.

The cannon bone should be thick, hard, straight, and cold. The most common injury involving the cannon bone is a splint injury. These are bony growths that form on the splint bones to the side of the cannon bone. They are commonly the result of riding on hard surfaces. Generally splints do not cause pain after healing, but will not disappear. A green splint is one that hasn't healed. It will have heat and be tender if pressed, and may cause lameness. A horse shouldn't be used until the splint is completely healed, but this is a fairly rapid process.

The cannon bone may also show swelling or a hard lump on the front surface. This is called a shin buck and is a hairline fracture caused by fast galloping on hard surfaces; it is especially prevalent in young horses. The bucked shin will heal with time—anywhere from one to six months—and tends not to recur easily. It may or may not leave a lump on the shin, depending on the severity of the injury. The bucked shin is very painful and a horse should not be used until healing has occurred.

A horse with a cannon bone injury may not limp, especially if both cannon bones are affected. Commonly you will see the horse take shorter, stilted strides at the trot.

Knee

The knees have been trouble spots for many athletes, including horses. Knee injuries are much harder to detect unless they are severe enough to cause excessive swelling or protruding lumps. The best way to examine the knee is by feel. Feel for heat and squishy spots. With the knee fully flexed, press your fingers into the front of the knee joint to test for pain; the horse will flinch or pull away if there is an injury.

When watching the horse move at the trot, look for a distinct limp with a head nod. The horse will probably not shorten its stride or change its knee flexion.

Avoid any horse that stands back at the knee or stands bent at the knee. If the horse is not unsound now, it will undoubtedly become so in the future.

Hock

An unsound hock can often be detected by swelling in or on the joint. Look for swelling in the depressed areas on the sides of the hock, both inside and outside the joint. If there is swelling on the outside of the joint in the (normally) depressed area, the horse is termed to have a thoroughpin. These, like windpuffs, are usually caused by exercise and might not go away. They rarely cause lameness or any decrease in performance, though, so are considered more an aesthetic flaw than unsoundness.

Swelling or bony growth inside or on the front of the hock joint is called a spavin and is far more serious than the thoroughpin. A spavin is a form of osteoarthritis and is incurable. Spavins are not always detectable but can be tested for by raising the hind leg and flexing it high, holding it one or two minutes, then dropping it and immediately trotting the horse. If the horse is spavined, it should be visibly lame on the affected hind leg.

If the cap or hind tip of the hock is swollen or fluid filled, it is termed a capped hock. In this area swelling is commonly caused by lying on hard surfaces or kicking stall walls or fences, and can be cured by eliminating these problems. A capped hock does not often cause lameness but may remain fluid filled long-term if not drained.

Stifle

You cannot realistically detect swelling or heat in the stifle joint, as it is layered in fat and muscle. The best way to detect unsoundness is to physically test the horse. Horses with stifle problems often cannot back up, so this is a good first test. Watching the horse move at the trot might reveal a limp behind or a hind leg raised unusually high. Flexing and squeezing the stifle will also indicate unsoundness but cannot be done well or reliably by anyone other than a veterinarian.

Respiratory System

Horses with chronic respiratory ailments will rarely demonstrate them at rest or during easy exercise. A horse should be lunged at the canter or ridden at a brisk canter in order to detect any breathing problem.

The two most common respiratory problems are obstructive pulmonary disease, commonly called heaves or broken wind, and laryngeal paralysis, also known as roaring.

Certain horses are, or become, sensitive to dust spores found in dried hay. These spores build up in their air passages and cause obstruction to breathing, or obstructive pulmonary disease. The horse develops a chronic cough and exhibits labored breathing characterized by a hitch during exhalation, during or after brisk exercise. Horses with OPD can have their symptoms reduced by keeping them in a dust-free environment (now think about that) and avoiding hay as feed, but the horse's symptoms are always subject to recurrence, and I cannot recommend a horse with this ailment.

Horses with laryngeal paralysis suffer from a paralyzed nerve that prevents the muscles that open and close the horse's airway from functioning properly. The horse will make a roaring sound during heavy exercise. Laryngeal paralysis often has no effect on a horse's performance, especially during moderate or light exercise.

Horses may breathe loudly during exercise for several other reasons. Some horses simply have a flappier nose passage that makes their breathing sound like trumpeting. Others will have their air cut off by a throatlatch fastened too tight or by tucking their head so far as to tighten the throatlatch, which results in labored breathing. Occasionally a horse, especially one that is tense, will press its tongue against the back of its throat while being ridden; this will cause a gurgling sound and will make breathing difficult for the horse, especially if the horse does not breathe well from the nose. A horse that does this is sometimes said to have swallowed its tongue, but this is not the case and is not really possible. This condition is not a physical defect and can be corrected by tying the tongue down or placing a snug nose band or cavesson.

Overall Health

You're always a step ahead if you choose a healthy horse rather than one that needs some work. You can forgive short-term viruses or minor wounds, but you may want to hold off on the purchase to see that they are truly short-term problems and that the horse at least appears on the road to recovery.

You're always a step ahead if you choose a horse with overall good health.

The coat of a horse often reflects its health and the care it has received. The horse's coat should be shiny, full, and free of mats or weepy sores, no matter what the season. During warm seasons or in warm climates the coat should be short and smooth. Some consider dappling a sign of robust health, but not all horses will dapple out, so be careful not to prejudice yourself against an undappled coat. Lift the mane and forelock to check for excessive dandruff or lice, and check the ears, between the front legs, the underbelly, and the genital area for any strange growths, especially on gray and Appaloosa horses.

The skeleton should be well padded, firm to the touch, and have muscle definition. Don't be fooled by the pot-bellied, spindly framed horse, which is probably not fat but full of parasites.

The horse should be alert and interested in its surroundings. It should not be hesitant or refuse to perform as asked, given reasonable demands. The horse should not sweat without cause and should not sweat buckets if exercised moderately in fair weather. It should be able to turn its head back to its belly on both sides and be able to walk in small circles without stumbling.

The eyes of the horse should be clear and bright; its nostrils should be clean or exhibit no more than a trickle of clear fluid. The horse should hold its head straight without tilting to one side and should not shake its head excessively. Feel under the jaw and throat for any swelling, scabs, or weepy sores, which may indicate highly contagious strangles or lymph node inflammation.

The Test-Drive

The ability and willingness to perform on command is a reflection not just on the horse's good health and temperament, but on its training and the amount of handling it has received. You are likely to focus on the riding aspect of the horse's training, but you cannot bypass testing the horse's manners when handled on the ground.

The number one rule when testing the horse's abilities, manners, and performance is that you not be the first person testing them. You are the observer; you do not help or interfere in any way except to request the handler do certain things with the horse. The owner should demonstrate all the horse's skills for you before you lay a hand on it; if the owner is not capable, that person should have a competent assistant or hired professional to show the horse. The reason for this, and I do not mean to take the fun out of your shopping experience, is that you don't know what the horse will do until you've seen it in action. Don't take anybody's word on the safety and reliability of the animal until you have witnessed this as a fact.

After the horse has been demonstrated sufficiently, and you are confident it is safe to handle or ride, you must still be aware that the horse might react differently under the handling of another person, especially an amateur who might be rough handed, awkward, unbalanced, and unpracticed in the finer signaling skills. With this in mind, you must take precautions to prevent your-self from being injured. Handle and ride the horse within a safely enclosed area (a pasture fenced with barbed wire *is not* acceptable) and do not go far off on your own. Move easily and quietly around the horse, use the lightest hands and signals the horse will respond to, and don't get in a hurry. When riding, walk the horse before you trot, and trot the horse before you canter. Stop the horse several times at each successive gait to ensure you are main-taining control. Don't even think about testing the horse for speed. Wear pro-tective gear such as well-fitting, rubber-soled boots, long pants and sleeves, and a helmet.

Ground Handling

When you make an appointment to see a horse, ask that the horse, if kept in a pasture or paddock, be left there until you arrive. This will give you an oppor-tunity to see how easily the horse can be caught, or if it willingly approaches and surrenders itself. Observe the methods the owner uses to catch the horse, for instance by bribing it with food, chasing, or calling. From here you can watch the entire process, from haltering to leading to grooming and tacking the horse. If the horse has already been brought in and tacked, you must insist on a second visit in which this has not been done in advance.

Some horses are kept in a stall; it would be unreasonable to ask the owner to turn it out in an open area just so you can watch the capturing process. You can still get a measure of the horse's temperament by its willingness to be approached and captured in the stall.

The owner should not be pressed for time; determine this when you make the appointment and you will avoid any lame excuses over why the owner doesn't bother cleaning the horse's hooves before saddling it or other such nonsense. Insist on full grooming before the horse is tacked, including hoof picking, brush-ing the entire body, head, legs, and ear area, and combing the tail and mane. This will show you if the horse is nastily oversensitive to the brush, flighty or nervous about the movement of the handler, or uncooperative about having its hooves or ears handled. Don't hold the horse while the owner is grooming or allow the owner to groom the horse untied, as you can use this time to test the horse's willingness to stand tied without fidgeting or pulling back.

You've probably already observed the horse being led; if not, ask the owner to lead the horse with a halter and lead line at both the walk and the trot. The horse should follow willingly without trying to rush forward, pull away, dance, buck, or rear.

The horse should be saddled before it is bridled, but don't expect this as a hard-and-fast rule; many people bridle first. When the saddle is placed on the horse's back, there should be no crouching or shying away. As the girth is tight-ened, watch for tail swishing or attempts to bite or kick, which indicate the horse has learned to expect a painful experience and is uncomfortable and intemper-ate enough to threaten the saddler. The girthing process is not pleasant for many poorly handled horses, but with easy, gradual girthing there should be no pain or protest.

Test Performance Checklist

When shopping for a horse, a checklist can be a valuable tool. Not only will you have a reminder of each horse you see, the checklist will also ensure you don't skip some of the performance tests. The following is an example using a fictitious horse. If possible, attach a photo of the horse to your checklist for future reference.

Name of Horse: *Trygve*
Owner: *Mary Johnson*
Address & Phone: *111 Cherry Lane, 555-1111*

Ground Test

Capture: *Approached when bucket of grain shaken, easy to catch while eating grain.*
Leading: *Whinnied and tried to turn back to pasture mates, but followed easily when out of sight of them.*
Tying: *Stood quietly.*
Brushing: *Pinned ears when brushed on belly. Otherwise good.*
Picking hooves: *Cooperative.*
Saddling: *Pinned ears when cinch tightened.*
Bridling: *Cooperative.*
Bathing: *Pulled back from handler when sprayed with hose, but cooperative when sponged.*
Turning loose: *Strong on lead after spotting pasture mates.*

Under Saddle

Mounting: *Stepped away from rider first try; stood well after yelled at.*
Rider weight shifting: *Stood still, cooperative.*
Patting and boot rubbing: *Tucked tail and tried to move forward when patted behind the saddle.*
Moving forward: *Responded to leg squeeze and chirping, didn't rush.*
Turns: *Cooperative in circles. Tried to turn the wrong way on first figure eight.*
Control while cantering: *Had to be kicked into canter; kind of lazy, but nice.*
Speed and stopping control: *Very cooperative.*
Backing: *Tossed head, shuffled sideways.*

Reactions to Distractions
(Substitute other test scenarios if necessary.)

Traffic: *No reaction to slow-moving car and passing tractor.*
Crossing stream: *Refused, then jumped it.*
Hose on ground: *Stepped over it willingly.*
White blanket on ground: *Backed away, refused to approach it, even when whipped with reins.*
Running and barking dog: *No reaction.*
Pasture mates: *Whinnied, tried to turn back once after passing, but obeyed rider's kicks and chirping to move on.*

During bridling, the horse should not throw its head up out of reach, try to back away, or clench its teeth to prevent the bit from entering. Again, these are bad habits learned from poor handling, but they are hard to break.

After the horse has been ridden, ask that it be bathed, either with a sponge and bucket or with a light hosing; the horse should stand cooperatively and should not show excessive fear of the hose or water. When all is done, watch as the horse is turned loose that it does not drag the handler or wheel and kick at the handler after it is set free.

Riding

You already know you're not going to ride the horse first, right? As observer you can still be in some control of the situation. Decide what you want to see the horse do under saddle and specify this to the owner or rider. Don't allow him or her to just show off the most practiced steps, and don't let the rider take off and leave you observing from a distance.

The first demonstration you will observe is the mounting process. The horse should stand still without being held from the ground or tied up. Shuffling is no big deal, but spinning, running backward, or rushing forward are all no-no's. Watch the horse's spine to see if it raises and stiffens (humps up), a sign that the horse is thinking about bucking. Some horses won't bother with humping but will go right to the point and buck; avoid this sort.

Before the rider moves off, ask that he or she shift his or her weight around on the horse's back. The rider should be able to raise his or her arms, pat the horse on the neck, rump, and near the ears, and gently rake the horse's sides from shoulder to flank with his or her boots without a negative reaction from the horse.

The most basic mount should be able to walk, trot, canter, and stop on command, the first command being ideal. The horse should also be able to back on command, do circles at all gaits, and do a halfway decent figure eight at any gait. Watch out for horses that need to be kicked repeatedly or slapped with the reins to get them going or keep them going; a lazy horse is desirable to some extent for the beginner, but a determinedly lazy horse can be quite impossible for an amateur. In addition, beware the horse that snaps or swishes its tail when signaled to move forward, or that shakes its head or bucks or kicks up a little. These are signs of protest and can also be considered threats of further action if the rider insists on forcing the horse to perform.

You can usually forgive the horse that tosses its head when asked to back; it probably has had little experience or training. Head tossing during normal riding is not so acceptable. Watch especially for horses that toss their heads while being asked to do turns or figure eights; these horses are demonstrating a lack of compliance that often will not show up while being ridden in a straight line.

Pay special attention to the horse's stops. The horse, again, should not throw its head up when signaled to stop but should ideally tuck its chin and give to the bit. The horse should slow itself by dropping its rear end slightly, rather than jamming the front legs and pitching the rider forward. Unless the rider has asked the horse for a quick slide-stop, the stop should be a gradual, but not enduring, process and the horse should stay in a reasonably straight line. If the rider needs to point the horse at a wall or fence to get it stopped, you may do best to avoid this horse.

If the rider has been demonstrating the horse's skills inside an arena, ask that the horse be ridden outside the enclosure, provided there is a safe area. It is wise to test the horse for its spookability, but don't hurt the rider unnecessarily by jumping out from behind a tree or waving a jacket; any horse would justifiably react to such treatment.

If possible, ask the rider to walk the horse through a puddle or stream—you can make one with a hose if necessary. The horse should be able to walk up to and past a vehicle; a slow-moving one should be used to test the horse. The horse should not overreact to the presence of people walking around, sitting, or crouching, to other horses, or to animals such as dogs, goats, and cattle. If any people or animals are moving erratically or suddenly, though, I would forgive the horse for any reaction.

Other good spook tests include strollers, umbrellas, loose clothing, bicycles, and objects on the ground such as crumpled paper, a rag or blanket, barrels, or a pile of lumber. You can expect most horses to show some reaction, but it is the depth to which they react that counts. If a horse throws an absolute fit, perhaps wheeling back or rearing, when asked to pass a Styrofoam cup on the ground, this horse is probably not ideal. If a horse is frightened but shows some willingness to explore or some trust in the rider's judgment, or at the very least shows it has enough training to hang in there and obey rather than run for cover, this horse is probably not a lost cause.

Some horses are "barn-sour" or mate-spoiled. They will perform brilliantly with another horse but can think only of getting back to the gang when ridden alone. Make sure the horse proves it can be ridden without a fight away from the barn or pasture, and don't allow the owner or rider to show the horse in the company of another horse until it has proven it will perform well on its own.

No matter how unshakable the horse has proved itself, when it is your time to ride you must take precautions to ensure your safety. There is always the possibility that the horse will react differently to an unfamiliar rider and the probability that your skills won't equal those of the horse's owner or first rider.

Before mounting, check your girth or cinch to see if it has loosened, a not too uncommon event, as many horses tense and push out when first cinched, then relax, loosening the girth, during riding. Have someone hold the horse while you mount, even if it stood stock-still for the first rider. Stay in an enclosed area and ride easy. Don't jerk the reins, whip, or pound the horse with your heels, and don't use spurs, even if the owner insists you must. I'm not sure I'd choose a horse that needed spurs for everyday riding anyway.

Outside an enclosure, don't go faster than a trot. Stay off roads and away from steep hills or bluffs. Stay within reach of help and don't ask the horse to do anything it hasn't already demonstrated it could or would do successfully. Finally, be considerate of the animal. It has already been ridden by one person and could be tiring by now. You can, and should, come for another ride, so don't overdo it the first time.

After dismounting, observe the horse between unsaddling and bathing. Look for any raw marks or welts around the girth, the withers, and at the chin-strap line. Chafing from the tack is not normal but might not be a reason to turn away from a horse. The horse might chafe because it is obese and has extra folds of flesh to rub against the girth. The horse might have poor conformation, such as jutting withers, that cause it to sit tack poorly. The chin-strap line might be raw because the horse is harder on the bit than it should be (you could be unaware while riding because the chin strap is doing the work for you). Consider the horse and the circumstances and try to decide whether this is a long- or short-term problem.

Taking Precautions

There is a wide variety of tranquilizers and pain relievers available to horse owners, many of which can enhance a horse's performance without giving any clue the horse is drugged. A horse can be tested for the presence of drugs, but this is not a simple process and not all that realistic for the normal shopper.

A person might also make a horse appear more docile than its nature by exercising it heavily before you arrive. Don't expect to find signs of hard work on the horse; the owner could have worn it out hours earlier, then bathed and groomed it. There are a few signs to look for, though, that the owner might have missed cleaning up. Check the hooves to see if they are filled with sand or arena material. Look high between the horse's hind legs for signs of dried sweat, which often forms a foam. Other areas to check for sweat marks are behind the ears and at the girth. Horses also kick up mud, dirt, and sand onto their bellies, which might be missed in the cleanup. Check the tack the horse normally wears to see if it is still damp from sweat.

The best way to prevent being duped is to buy from or through someone you trust, but quite often you must shop for horses from people you don't know or can't trust. The second best protection you can give yourself is to visit the horse several times, at least twice unannounced. You can warn the owner in advance that you plan on visiting without an appointment and gauge the reaction you receive. Even an honest person might not welcome unannounced lookers, but it must be understood that you can't buy the horse just by watching rehearsed performances.

When dropping in unannounced, don't expect the owner to spend a great deal of time showing the horse, but plead to at least be allowed to handle the horse, or watch it being handled, around the barn or stable area. If the owner or another responsible person is not present, be careful not to trespass and don't handle the horse at all.

You might also try to get a written guarantee that the horse has been shown and performed without the aid of drugs; an honest person should not hesitate to sign this, even though it's not really worth much. A previous owner could get away with blaming you or the horse's new environment for changed behavior or lameness.

Of course you will have your veterinarian examine the horse as final confirmation of its soundness and temperament. Your veterinarian may not detect the presence of drugs without a test but may be able to see beyond the drugs and find the unsoundness or note a behavioral problem. If the horse carries a costly price tag, a blood test would be in order, as well as X rays of the legs and hooves.

Patience is sometimes hard to come by when you are eager to bring a horse home; this will make you vulnerable to the hard sell—a seller that tells you the horse is sure to sell *that very weekend* or how three people are lined up to see the horse the next day, etc. Horses don't often sell that fast, and you will not be doing yourself a service if you rush into a purchase without making multiple visits and taking time to have your vet or other professional look the horse over. There's always another horse to be had even if you miss out on your original dream horse.

Further precautions must be taken to determine the legality of your purchase. You must make sure the person selling the horse actually has the right to do so. Even a horse that is not stolen might be offered for sale by an unqualified person. There are legal tangles between stable owners or trainers and clients delinquent in paying bills. There could be a horse involved in an unsettled estate or divorce. Make certain before you accept a bill of sale that it and any registration papers are made out in the name of the person signing them, and ask that person for identification.

If the owner listed on the registration papers is different than the person selling the horse, the seller should still be able to show you a legitimate bill of sale signed by the person listed on the papers. This would validate any excuse the present owner might give, such as never having gotten around to transferring the horse's registration papers.

The New Addition

Whether you've purchased, leased, or been given a horse, you now have on your hands a substantial addition that will affect your life and life-style. Ideally you will have prepared an adequate home for the horse so that you are not stringing wire while the horse nervously explores its new territory, or rushing to the feed store an hour past the horse's regular feeding time.

Transport

Occasionally a person will choose a horse from a facility that will remain the horse's home. For instance, if you bought a horse from or through your trainer or instructor, you may choose to keep the horse at that stable for convenience. You may buy a horse and admire its present stabling situation so much that you continue to board the horse there. For whatever reason, this certainly simplifies the horse's adjustment period, not to mention reducing your work load in preparing a new home.

If, as most people, you need to transfer the horse to a new home, your first concern is transportation. Hauling horses has its hazards and should not be attempted without some knowledgeable help.

The horse owner might volunteer to deliver the horse. This is not a bad idea, but there is a gray area between when the horse is purchased and when it arrives at its new home. If there is a mishap during transport, who is responsible? The best protection you can give yourself is to wait until the horse arrives to complete the transaction. Many sellers won't agree to this, understandably, and in this case I would find an alternate method of moving the horse.

You can hire a professional horse hauler. This person will send a certified vehicle with a trained driver or handler; you will not have to lift a finger. The professional horse mover must also carry insurance and is liable if anything happens during the trip.

If you choose to move the horse yourself, you can rent, borrow, or use your own van or trailer. Whatever you use, be careful to measure the height and length. Many vans are too small for a large horse; trying to force a horse into cramped quarters often raises a protest on the part of the horse. Even if the horse walks in it will have more trouble balancing and might get claustrophobic over its lack of head space and start fighting midway through the journey.

Examine your trailer or van beforehand. Check under floor mats for rot. I once heard of a horse dropping through a rotted trailer floor on a freeway (just its front legs, but that was enough). Make sure there is some sort of bedding or no-slip surface as well. There should be a short, high tie with a breakaway snap to secure the horse's head, and the anchor for this tie should be bolted or welded. There should be a partition strong enough to help the horse stay in one place and balance itself, and it is best to have a butt chain in addition to the back door or ramp door. Check and double-check your ball and hitch to see that they are secured, and use safety chains as a backup.

Don't plan to load the horse without help. If the horse proves it will walk in on its own, great; you can load it yourself next time. The first time have someone help that has done this many times before. Have someone lead the horse in while another shuts the back door immediately. Don't secure the horse's head or the butt chain until the door is shut; the horse can break either one if it tries to rush out backward.

Some horses load easily but are afraid to back out of a trailer, especially if there is no ramp. Again, you should have help at your unloading spot. Have someone at the horse's head while another person stands at the rear of the trailer. The horse should be untied and the butt chain removed before the back door or ramp is opened, as some horses will rush out the moment they sense freedom. If the horse is hesitant to back, the tail person should speak reassuringly and pat the horse on the rump (standing to the side) while the head person pushes the horse back from the chest.

Patience and temper control are vital in loading and unloading a horse. If the horse is causing real trouble or absolutely refusing to cooperate, there are several methods you can use, which will be covered in Chapter 7.

Adjustment

You've just removed a horse from its familiar environment and plunked it into a new one. Depending on the personality of the horse and the severity of the change, there will be some adjustments to be made before the horse is comfortable enough to act as you'd normally expect.

Stabling

If your horse has been kept in a stall and you plan to provide it with a large, open pasture, this will be a major adjustment. The horse may not be used to the freedom and may run itself through a fence. A transitional area large enough to allow the horse to gallop but small enough that the horse can clearly see the boundary lines will help the horse to adjust while learning its limits. An arena or stall turn-out paddock would be ideal. This area will also give the horse a chance to let off some steam and be less willing to run mad in a larger enclosure.

Likewise, if you plan to convert a pasture horse to a stall-bound one, be prepared for some anxiety on the horse's part. The horse will do best with a daily turn out in an arena, paddock, or pasture. Lacking that, you should provide the horse with daily or twice-daily exercise.

When introducing a horse to a new pasture or paddock, even if you feel the boundaries are clearly marked, walk the horse along the fence lines. Some people force a new horse to touch an electrically charged fence so it won't try to run through it later. I must discourage this, as the horse may react as if *it* were electrically charged. Besides, it's cruel and unnecessary. Far better is to clearly mark the hot wire with surveyor's ribbon or strips of white cloth. Walk the horse near enough for it to see the lines and let it discover the zap on its own if necessary. Before you are through with th tour, lead the horse to its feeding station and water source and show it where the gates are. This is not to encourage the horse to escape—your gates should be more secure than that—but to let the horse know where to find you when you visit or where to come when called (some actually do that).

Companionship

Horses are social creatures and bond quickly and strongly to their turn-out mates. If you've removed a horse from a herd or a mate, the horse might spend days running the fence looking for its mates, or it could become depressed and stop eating. Your best solution is to avoid isolating the horse; provide a new mate or add the horse to a herd. It will act the loner for a short time but will most likely seek companionship at the first opportunity.

If you cannot provide another horse, think about getting a low-cost animal as companion, maybe an elderly pony or a goat. A companion will keep your horse more content and less likely to try to escape or pick up bad habits such as walking the fence.

If isolation is your only option for your new horse, *you* will need to provide the horse with companionship. This entails daily visits at the least, and ideally, daily grooming, riding, and exercise sessions. Don't expect an occasional visit from a neighboring horse to fulfill your horse's need for companionship;

this will often upset the horse rather than give it comfort, as the visitor will be unfamiliar and untrusted.

Diet

A horse's diet is generally regulated; it will eat the same thing day in and day out, perhaps shifting from pasture grass in the summer to hay in the winter. Changing the diet, even beneficially, can upset the horse's digestive system or throw the horse off its feed.

If the horse you buy shows signs of thriving, you might want to stay with the regimen of the former owner, including following the feeding schedule. If you choose to change the horse's diet and feeding schedule, you must do it gradually. Consult with your veterinarian to ensure you provide the horse with the proper nutrients and amounts, then take your time. Increase or decrease grain rations by no more than a half gallon a day. If the horse is to be introduced to pasture grass from dry hay, turn it out for only an hour the first few days, then increase it by an hour every other day or every two days until the horse is free to graze. If you are changing hays or grains, mix them, gradually increasing the ratio of the new to the old. If the horse stops eating at any time or develops diarrhea or constipation, reverse your procedures until the horse straightens out and resumes eating well.

Handling and Riding

Unfamiliarity often breeds fear. The horse that performed complacently at its old stomping ground might appear flighty, nervous, and uncooperative in its new territory. Time and patience should prove the horse to be as reliable as you originally believed.

Take time to lead your new horse at a walk through the stabling, grooming, and riding areas you plan to use. Stand it in the area where it will be saddled and bathed, without doing either of these things. Don't tie the horse in any unenclosed area until the horse proves itself calm and cooperative. If the horse is snorty, arch-necked, or tense, stop and give it a breather until it finds there are no boogers out to get it. Patting the horse and talking reassuringly and calmly will often work wonders in restoring a horse's confidence.

When grooming and saddling for the first time, it is best to tie the horse inside an enclosure such as a stall. Work slowly and quietly until the horse becomes familiar with the way you do things. Don't rush into riding the horse; you are best off giving it a couple of days to relax and familiarize itself with the whole scene. This time may seem like an eternity to a new and eager owner but will usually pay off by beginning a smoother and more successful riding relationship.

Even after waiting to ride and walking your horse around the riding areas, your horse might be nervous on its first outing. Stay at a walk until you've covered all unfamiliar territory by horseback, even the inside of an arena. Sometimes riding with another can make a world of difference in building confidence in a new horse. Follow and let the more experienced horse show the way until your horse proves it wants to move forward boldly. Once you've familiarized your horse with a particular riding area, stick with it for a few days or weeks before moving on again. This will give you more time to adjust to your new mount as well.

∩ ∩

Remember always that horses are creatures of habit; they thrive on routine. Whatever changes you make in your horse's life, try to stick with them and create a routine that is workable for you and acceptable for the horse. At the same time, watch that your routine does not promote the development of bad habits in the horse. If you show up at four o'clock every day, catch the horse and immediately saddle and go for a strenuous ride, your horse might start hiding at about ten minutes to four. Try showing up at your normal riding time just to visit and feed the horse some carrots to break this habit. If you habitually feed your horse immediately after riding (not a good idea, healthwise) your horse might start trying to cut short your ride. Change your feeding routine so the horse doesn't associate riding with eating.

When things aren't working out the way you hoped, try something else. Maybe stall life just isn't going to work for your range-raised horse. Find a place to board the horse that has pasture turn outs. Perhaps your evening ride coincides with your horse's internal dinner gong. This horse will undoubtedly perform poorly, so you will have to change your riding time or add a midday feeding. You can't fail if you are open to suggestions and experimentation.

5

Gearing Up

An Introduction to Tack and Equipment

ack is a term for the tools people use to handle, control, and ride horses. Tack is generally worn by or attached to the horse. Other items used for control and to increase the horse's comfort are simply described as equipment. The term *equipment* might cover such items as saddlebags, twitches, bell boots, polo bandages, and whips.

Walk through a good tack store or leaf through a tack catalog and you will be overwhelmed by the various types of tack and equipment available. You might think, "Oh my gosh! I could *never* learn to use all this stuff!" Relax, you will never need to use much of this stuff; if you do, it will be on the recommendation of a trainer or instructor who will advise you as to its purpose and function. There are, however, a good number of tack items common to everyday use, and it's essential that you have a basic understanding of them so you will know which to buy and how and when to use them.

Halters

The first item you cannot function without around horses is the halter. This is the head harness your horse will most likely wear anytime you handle it from the ground; it is used primarily to lead the horse and tie it.

Halters are made of three basic materials: rope, nylon, and leather. Rope halters are inexpensive and fairly ineffective. They stretch and are sloppily fitted, so they are easy for a horse to slip out of or catch on something such as a branch, post, or hoof. A horse should never be tied or turned loose in a rope halter.

Nylon halters are the strongest and most durable. They come in many sizes and can be fitted to your horse. The nylon halter is ideal for tying a horse or leading it because the material won't break or stretch. For the same reason, this is not a good halter to turn out your horse in, even in a stall. The nylon halter has virtually no give; it can kill your horse if the halter gets hooked on something unbreakable or your horse catches a foot in it while scratching its head with a hind toe or pawing at the ground with its head down. The most common reaction for a horse that gets caught and can't feel any give is to fight to free itself. With its immense strength and capacity for blind panic, a horse can strangle itself, break its neck, or bash its body and legs in the scramble.

There are breakaway nylon halters designed with hardware that releases when extreme pressure is applied, thus supposedly freeing the horse of the halter. They probably work, but I wouldn't care to test them on my horse. Your safest bet is to leave all halters off your horse when it's turned loose. If you feel you absolutely must leave your horse turned out with a halter, use a leather halter, which will almost surely break if your horse gets caught in it—although not necessarily before your horse has sustained injury.

Leather halters also have appeal in their classic good looks and soft touch on the tender skin of your horse's face and ear area, but leather takes more care and maintenance than nylon, is more expensive, and since it *can* break is not ideal for tying a horse or attaching one to a hotwalking machine.

Use a halter that won't break when tying your horse, although it is extremely important that your horse not get caught in a situation in which the halter won't give. You should always be around to help or free the horse if it starts fighting. You tie a horse because you want the horse to stay put. Getting loose by breaking a halter would most likely cause a chaotic situation and possibly teach your horse a bad habit of yanking back to free itself when tied.

The halter should not be fitted snug against your horse's head; a tight fit will cause discomfort and chafing and reduce sensitivity of the horse to your handling cues. On the other hand, a halter fitted too slack will be pulled off easily and is more likely to get caught on something. When properly fitted, the nosepiece should lay well above the nostrils but below the point of the cheekbones on the side of the face so the side rings of the halter don't bump or rub them. You should have ample space to lay your hand flat between your horse's jaw and the underside of the nosepiece and between your horse's throat and the underside of the throatpiece.

Lead Lines

The lead is the line you use to lead and tie your horse. Like the halter, the lead comes in several materials, most commonly leather, nylon, and cotton rope. The leather lead looks good and is nice to hold due to its soft, sticky texture. It won't

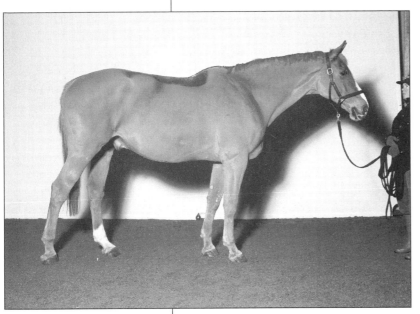

The halter and lead line

The chain shank, used for enhanced control

slip easily through your hand when jerked, so it is great for leading, but it breaks when stressed and should not be used to tie a horse. Many horses find leather an irresistible chew toy, so make sure your leather lead is out of reach when not in use.

Nylon leads come in rounded, braided lengths or flat lines. These leads, if fitted with strong snaps and hardware, are virtually unbreakable, but the smooth surface of the nylon makes for poor gripping and "bites" when the lead is jerked through your hands.

Most rope leads are very strong and durable. They come in different thicknesses and are made of a variety of fibers. Avoid thin ropes and those made of rough or too-smooth fibers that will burn and slide through your hands. A good rope (*hint-hint:* a thick cotton rope) will feel good in your hands.

There are snap leads and shank leads. Snap leads are fitted with a snap commonly attached to the bottom nosepiece ring of the halter under the horse's jaw. The horse is moved around or kept stationary by the pressure of the halter.

Shank leads have a length of chain attached with a snap on the end of the chain, although some shanks are separate from the lead and attach to the snap on a normal snap lead. A shank can be used like a normal lead line by running the chain through the bottom halter ring and snapping it back to itself, but its real purpose is for extra control. The chain is meant to be looped through the rings of the halter nosepiece so the horse is moved around by the pressure of the chain against its jaw and nose, or for extreme control, under its upper lip.

There are many ways to use the shank, which will be discussed in detail in Chapter 6. The important thing to remember now about shank leads is that they are meant only to lead horses, never to tie them. The chain is fairly thin and vulnerable to breaking if a horse is tied with it. If the chain doesn't give and break during a struggle, it can cause serious injury to the horse's face and jaw.

When you buy (or make) your lead line, be sure it is at least eight feet but no more than fifteen feet long. It is hard to tie a horse and easy to turn one loose with a short line. An extra long line is awkward to use and can get tangled or tripped over.

Pay special attention to the snaps and hardware. Look for firmly secured hardware and high-quality steel or brass snaps that open and shut easily, preferably with one hand. It doesn't matter how strong your lead line is if the snap breaks or the hardware pulls free.

Make a habit of tying a knot in the end of all your lead lines. This will help you stop the line if it is pulled through your hands and can prevent a horse from getting loose.

Related to the lead line is the lunge or jip line. This is an extra long lead line, usually made of nylon or rope, used to exercise a horse in a circle around you while you hold the line. This is a wonderful method of exercising a horse in hand but is not mandatory for every horse. You may never need to buy a lunge line, so it is best to hold off purchasing one until you see the need and receive training from a professional in how to lunge your horse; it is far too easy to lose control of a horse or be kicked if you don't know what you're doing.

There is one other item related to lead lines that is not really meant for leading or moving horses at all. The bungee tie is a thick (approximately three-quarters or one inch in diameter), stretchy, rubber tie less than three feet in length with heavy snaps on each end. It is used only for securing by snapping to an eyebolt or ring.

The idea behind bungee tying is that a horse can pull back and stretch the tie without injuring itself. Supposedly the stretchiness eliminates that no-give feeling of a hard tie and discourages a horse from fighting the tie. The problem with the bungee, though, is that if a horse *does* fight, it will stretch a long way, then break, snapping like a very large rubber band. The force-driven rebound of a snapping bungee can cause severe injury; horses have been known to lose eyes when broken bungees snapped back in their faces. For this reason, the bungee tie should only be used in enclosed spaces such as a stall or a horse trailer, where the horse's space for pulling back is limited. In addition, it must be hung at or above the level of the horse's head to prevent a horse from putting its leg over the tie.

Stable Blankets

A stable blanket is sort of like a jacket for a horse. It covers the horse's body from neck to tail. Some also come with hood attachments that cover the horse's head and neck. Stable blankets are made in varying degrees of thickness to accommodate different weather conditions.

Light blankets, called sheets or coolers, are usually made of a single layer of cotton or denim but can also be made of cotton mesh or wool. Sheets are used to cool a horse after exercise, to keep it warm until it dries after a bath, rainstorm, or excessive sweating, or to keep the horse clean during mild or warm weather.

Medium-weight blankets are usually two layers thick, made of an inner absorbent layer and an outer cotton or canvas material. They are meant to keep a horse clean and warm in cold, but not severe, weather.

Heavy blankets are quilted and are meant to keep a horse clean and warm in frigid weather and to prevent a horse from growing its natural winter coat so it can look slick throughout the year, usually for show.

Waterproof blankets can be an outer layer of waxed or oiled canvas and an inner absorbent layer or a plastic sheet, like a cheap raincoat. They are meant to be used outdoors in inclement weather but are minimally effective in heavy rains because of seepage at the openings and seams.

In my opinion, if you don't show your horse, you shouldn't blanket it. A horse's coat grows in direct relation to the climate to provide adequate, natural, twenty-four-hour-a-day protection from the elements. The more you blanket your horse, the less its natural winter coat will grow, and the more dependent upon the blanket your horse will become. There is nothing ugly about a well-groomed, thick winter coat, so put away the blanket and get out the brushes.

Even if you choose to blanket while your horse is kept indoors, avoid blanketing a horse that is turned out. Your horse should have adequate shelter in its paddock or pasture to keep dry during inclement weather. A blanket, even a waterproof one, won't substitute for shelter. Blankets become sodden and mucky after being worn outside for a while and can actually chill your horse by not allowing it to dry underneath the soggy covering. In addition, a blanket can twist uncomfortably when the horse rolls and a horse can catch a foot in one of the blanket straps while romping around.

There are certainly times when a blanket will benefit your horse's health. If you haul your horse in cold weather in an overly ventilated trailer or van, a blanket will help keep your horse from becoming chilled. If your horse is ill and chilled from fever, a blanket could help stabilize its temperature. A horse suffering from muscle cramps (azoturia) will often recover faster if the muscles are warmed with the help of a blanket. If left outdoors, a horse with a sunburned or rainscalded back must be protected from the elements with a blanket. If an aged or very thin horse is unable to stay warm even though it has grown a thick winter coat, a blanket would be in order. Any horse moved suddenly from a warm to a cold climate, or from a sheltered stable to an unprotected outdoor environment during a cold spell, should be allowed to wear a blanket while adjusting, and anytime an unusual cold snap hits your area you may want to supplement your horse's winter coat with a blanket.

Most blankets are measured in inches. Measure your horse from the point of its shoulder to the end of its rump below the tail to determine the appropriate size blanket. The fit is important if the horse will be left alone wearing the blanket, say overnight. A sloppy blanket will become twisted when the horse rolls or frolics, and feet and legs can get tangled in loose straps.

If the blanket is used only when handling the horse, such as cooling it after exercise, a strap across the chest and a strap around the girth and barrel are adequate to secure the blanket. If the horse is to wear the blanket for long, unattended periods, you should use one with additional straps that encircle the upper hind legs to hold the blanket more securely in place.

Bridles

The bridle is the head harness your horse will wear for riding. It is used to control your horse's movements by applying pressure to certain points of the horse's head and mouth. The bridle works as the rider's primary braking and steering control mechanism.

Every bridle has a bit or a hackamore nosepiece, a headstall that holds the bit or hackamore in place, and reins that act as the rider's steering wheel, brake pedal, and occasional accelerator. From those basic pieces come a large variety of bridle types. I will hit on the basics. You will choose your bridle based on your individual horse, your riding style and skill, and I hope, the advice of a trainer or instructor and the horse's previous owner.

The majority of bridles are made of leather or nylon. You can also find headstalls made of braided horsehair and reins made of cotton rope. As with halters and leads, each material has its pros and cons. Leather has a classic look that makes it ideal for the show ring and is easy on the hands and the horse's skin, but it requires more maintenance (cleaning and oiling by hand) and can break under pressure or if allowed to rot or stretch.

Nylon is strong and can be thrown in the wash but looks a little tacky in the show ring and is slippery to grip and a bit abrasive on some tender-skinned horses. You can buy reins made of a wide nylon strap with a strip of ribbed rubber sewn over the area on which your hands might rest. The rubber greatly enhances your grip while riding with nylon *or* oily leather reins.

Thick, cotton rope reins are my favorite for casual riding but would be considered unacceptable in a horse show. They're my choice because they are soft and easy to hold on to and are not adversely affected by wet weather. In addition, they're great on the trail because you can use them to tie, provided they have a good snap or you bypass the snap.

It is not uncommon to see materials mixed and matched on a bridle, and this is sometimes the best solution for the comfort versus durability versus maintenance versus grip dilemma. You might use nylon for the assurance of a nonbreakable headstall with leather reins that you find more comfortable to grip. A leather headstall might be worn by a sensitive-skinned horse, while the rider uses cotton rope reins for comfort and tying. You also might find you pre-

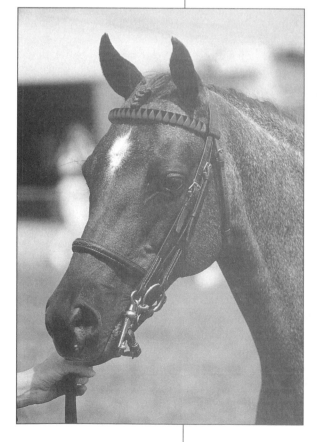

The bridle is the head harness your horse will wear when you ride it.

fer an all-leather bridle for fair-weather riding or show purposes but switch to a low-maintenance nylon rig for rainy days or schooling sessions.

Bits

The bit is probably the most significant piece of the bridle in determining control. There are numerous bit styles, the most common being the snaffle and the curb, with countless variations of each of these.

Snaffle

A snaffle bit has a jointed bar for a mouthpiece. The joint lies on the horse's tongue. A ring or "D" snaffle has rings (round or D shaped) attached to each end of the mouthpiece. The headstall and reins both buckle onto these rings. The pressure exerted on the snaffle when the reins are pulled is directly against the horse's mouth. As you pull on the reins, the snaffle is pulled back in a V position, pressing against the tongue, the bars (spaces on the horse's gum line where there are no teeth), and the corners of the mouth.

If you use a ring or D snaffle, I recommend using a chin strap. Although it will have no effect on stopping or turning your horse, it will prevent the bit from being pulled through the horse's mouth when you pull on one rein to turn. This is less likely with larger rings on your snaffle and can also be prevented by using a snaffle with prongs. A pronged snaffle is one that has straight prongs attached to the rings so they extend above and below the rings against the horse's cheeks. These will help keep the rings outside the horse's mouth and greatly enhance your turning cues.

Snaffles also come with shanks in place of rings. A shank in this case is a bar (bent or straight) attached at each end of the mouthpiece so it extends a short length above the mouthpiece and a longer length below it. The headstall is attached to a ring or slot at the top of the shank and the reins are attached at the bottom.

A chin strap must be used with the shank snaffle, attached to the same rings as the headstall or separate slots at the top of the shank. The chin strap lays under the jaw of the horse in the crevice just above the horse's chin.

When shanks are used with a snaffle, the pressure points for stopping are tripled. Pressure is applied not only by the bit, but by the chin strap and crownpiece of the headstall. You are still tweaking the horse's mouth, but when you pull on the reins the bottom of the shank is pulled toward you and the top of the shank is pushed forward; this pulls the chin strap in against the jaw and presses the headstall down against the poll, a sensitive area at the

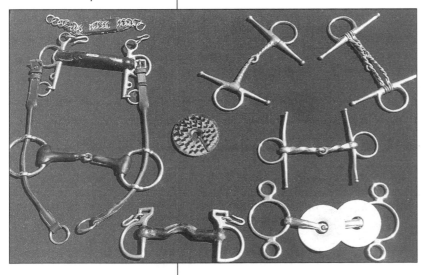

There are countless varieties of bit styles, the most common having a jointed snaffle or curbed-bar mouthpiece.

top of the horse's head behind the ears. The longer the shanks, the more lever-age is applied, given the same degree of pull from the rider.

Curb

The curb bit almost always has shanks and works in much the same way as a snaffle with shanks, except instead of squeezing the corners of the mouth the curb puts pressure on the roof of the horse's mouth.

The curb is a bar mouthpiece with a rounded or V-shaped hump in the center raised to varying heights, commonly one-half to one-and-a-half inches. The raised bar or curb lays against the back of the tongue when the reins are slack but is pushed forward and bumps the roof of the horse's mouth, which is quite sensitive, when the reins are pulled. Obviously, the higher the curb the more severe the pressure.

Some curb bits are made with a small metal roller, sometimes called a *cricket*, placed inside the area of the raised curb. Some believe a roller curb entertains a horse by giving it something to play with; that is, a horse can work the roller with its tongue to amuse itself. Other riders do not consider the roller a toy at all; it is meant to be used as additional control. When the reins are pulled and the curb is raised toward the roof of the mouth, the roller rakes along the horse's tongue, emphasizing the signal.

Spade

A spade bit is an extreme version of the curb bit, replacing the curb with a spade-shaped metal piece extending high above the bar of the mouthpiece. Spade bits are used with and without a chin strap, as the spade is believed to be severe enough on its own to disallow the need of a chin strap. If used improperly the spade bit can cause injury—both to the horse and to the rider when the horse reacts to the pain. I only mention spade bits because I dread the thought of a beginner getting his or her hands on one accidentally. *Spade bits should never be used by a novice or anyone with heavy hands or a hot temper.*

∩ ∩

Although each type bit varies in its method of stopping, all help turn a horse when you pull on a rein by putting pressure on the off side of the mouth and jaw and pulling down on the inside corner of the horse's mouth. The horse's head will be pulled in the direction you want it to go, with the body following. Rely-ing on the pressure of the bit to turn a horse without the aid of rein or leg pres-sure is termed plow-reining.

Deciding on the perfect bit for both you and your horse is not easy and may take some trial and error. Once you've made a decision, though, there is not much to fitting a bit. Bits commonly come in horse or pony sizes. There are cer-tainly some size differences, however, so you should take a measurement of the width of your horse's mouth at the corners before you purchase a bit.

Always buy a bit slightly larger than the width of your horse's mouth to pre-vent chafing or pinching. Your horse should wear the bit high in its mouth, rest-ing along the space on the gums where there are no teeth (the bars). Adjust the headstall so the bit is snug enough that there are two or three wrinkles formed in the skin at the corners of the mouth and loose enough so you can lay two fingers' width or a flat hand between the horse's cheek and its headstall. You are not being kind by letting the bit hang loose and low, as it will bump painfully against your horse's teeth and possibly allow your horse to put its tongue over the bit, which is incredibly painful for the horse when you pull against the bit.

Hackamores

The hackamore is a bitless bridle. This is a shank hackamore.

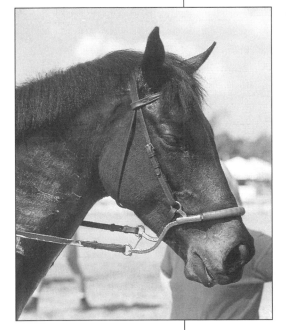

The hackamore is a nosepiece that works in place of a bit so your horse wears nothing in its mouth while being ridden. There are two basic types of hackamores: the shank and the bosal.

The shank hackamore works on the same principles as the shank bit except pressure in the mouth is replaced by pressure against the bridge of a horse's nose. Shank hackamores work well on most horses. Some people use them because they believe they are kinder than a bit, but this is not necessarily true. The chin strap is just as severe or kind on either a bit or hackamore, and the bridge of the nose is at least as sensitive as a horse's mouth.

The bosal is a stiff, upside-down-teardrop-shaped nosepiece with a knob on the lower end with which you fasten both reins. The headstall attaches directly to the sides of the bosal. This hackamore uses pressure only against the bridge of the nose and the sides of the jaw. It is popular for breaking and training horses but doesn't offer a lot of control for the novice rider.

Hackamores work to push a horse into a turn by pressing against the outside cheek and lower jaw. Unlike the bit, the hackamore places no pulling pressure against the mouth. Because of this, most hackamore-ridden horses are trained to neck-rein as well as to plow-rein; that is, to turn away from the outside rein as it is placed against the horse's neck.

A problem I have found with hackamores of all kinds is that a rider has difficulty pulling a horse's head up if it gets too low, as the horse can continue to push through the noseband. This can make it difficult for the rider to stop a horse from snatching grass, trying to run off, or bucking.

The hackamore should be fitted so the noseband lays against the center of the bridge of the nose and the chin strap lays just below the midpoint of the jaw between the horse's chin and cheekbone. A hackamore placed too low can press on the horse's nostrils and cut off the horse's air when the reins are pulled. One placed too high can rub or bump painfully against the points of the horse's cheeks. Furthermore, a too-high hackamore will reduce your horse's sensitivity to signals and cause your horse to carry its head higher than normal or point its nose forward to escape the higher, tighter pressure of the chin strap.

Chin Straps

Since a chin strap is essentially your main brake on many horses, it's important it fits properly. You should be able to lay your fingers flat between the strap and the horse's jaw. If the strap is too loose, it won't tighten against the jaw when necessary and you'll lose much of your stopping power. If it's too tight, it will be a constant irritant on your horse, causing it to overreact to any pressure on the reins or to become numb and unresponsive to any signal to stop or slow down.

Chin straps are most commonly made of flat leather or nylon straps, or chains. The chain bites harder with less pressure than a flat strap, which is good for lighter control but bad for the horse of a rider with heavy or clumsy hands.

It is important to understand that the chin and jaw area in which the chin strap lays is very sensitive, which is why the chin strap works so well for stopping control. To prevent injury to your horse in this area, steps must be taken. First, always check your chin strap to make sure it is smooth and clean, whether it is a chain or flat strap. A twisted or dirt-encrusted chain can easily cut into your horse's tender flesh, as can a frayed or twisted strap. In addition, make sure there are no buckle ends or strap keepers on the surface that will poke against your horse's jaw. Second, use your chin strap gingerly. Yanking on the reins or using constant, hard pressure will not necessarily increase your stopping power. The pain you cause with heavy-handedness can cause your horse to fight and react in opposition to your demands.

Headstalls

A headstall is a single strap attached at both ends to the bit or hackamore. Its anchoring point is behind the ears of the horse and its main purpose is to hold the bit or hackamore in place. Almost all headstalls come with a throatlatch—

A Western-style split-ear headstall with a shank (curbed-mouthpiece) bit

An English-style bridle with browband and throatlatch and a separately placed flash noseband. The bit is a ring snaffle.

a strap that runs from the temples under the throat. This is a safety strap used to prevent the headstall from being accidentally pulled over the horse's head.

To be effective, the throatlatch shouldn't be loose enough to swing against the horse's jaw, but it is not meant to be worn tight, as it will press against the horse's windpipe and interfere with its breathing during exercise. Keep in mind that a horse at rest, such as when you are bridling it, will have its head extended and breathe shallowly. While you are riding, the head is usually tucked in more and the breathing heavier, both of which add to the expansion of the throat and windpipe. Adjust your throatlatch so you can slip a hand easily between the strap and the horse's throat.

Most headstalls also come with a browband, which further ensures the bridle won't be easily pulled off the horse's head. The browband rests from temple to temple over the horse's forehead and is usually not adjustable in width.

In place of a browband on some bridles is the split-ear headstall. This headstall has a slot, either literally split from the headstall strap or made from another sewn-on strap. The slot is fitted to go around one ear and hold the headstall in place. Split-ear headstalls must be carefully fitted to properly enclose the ear without pulling or rubbing against it.

Some headstalls come with nosebands (cavessons) attached, which are adjusted to fit snugly to prevent the horse from opening its mouth while being ridden. I personally find attached cavessons awkward to work with while bridling and prefer the separate cavesson attached to its own thin single-strap headstall. I can put this on the horse's head first, then bridle it, adjust it more accurately to fit each particular horse, or leave it in the tack room when I don't need it. The noseband fits ideally about an inch below the point of the cheekbone and is meant to be worn snug but not so tight as to pinch skin.

Reins

Reins are the lines you hold in your hands to keep in touch with your horse while riding. The simplest is a single line extending from one side of the bit to the other side. This is my favorite rein for the novice rider because the uninterrupted single line is easy to hold, hard to get tangled in, and impossible to drop on the ground while you are mounted.

There are split reins, which are two separate lines, and more complicated sets of reins such as double reins and draw reins. Double reins are made to be used with a double bit or a pelham bit, one set attached to a snaffle bit or top ring and the other attached to the bottom of a shank bit. Draw reins are attached at the girth of the saddle and run through the rings of the bit, coming up either along the shoulders of the horse or between its front legs, then running back to the rider. Double reins and draw reins are intended only for experienced riders trained in their use.

If you use split reins, I highly recommend tying them together at the point at which your hands will rest. I suggest this because it is deceptively easy to drop one while you're riding. Tie your knot while you are mounted so you can choose the right length at which you want them tied. To find the right length, lift the reins about a foot above the pommel of the saddle or the horse's withers, with most of the slack taken out. Wherever your hand is resting on the rein is where your knot should be. Reins tied too short will leave you riding with your arm extended uncomfortably over the horse's neck. Reins tied too long will leave you with a handful of slack when you pull on them. It's pretty amusing to see a rider holding a hand up behind his or her ear, pulling on reins that are too long.

Bridle Hardware

The hardware used to put your bridle together is of utmost importance and should be examined before choosing any bridle. Your bridle is useless if it falls off your horse's head or a rein becomes detached. I avoid headstalls that attach to the bit with Chicago screws, screws that are slotted on one end and flat and smooth on the other. Chicago screws are hard to tighten properly, and loosen at will. After having enough of these screws fall out and detach the bit at inconvenient times, I now automatically replace them with a buckle before using the bridle. I would rather use baling wire as a fastener than a Chicago screw. If you must use Chicago screws, tape over them with electrician's tape. If this is too unsightly, dab rubber cement on the screw before fastening it to help stop it from loosening.

It's hard to tell a good buckle from a bad one, and any buckle will break or bend, given enough stress. The best deterrent for broken or bent buckles is watchful maintenance and proper use. Check your buckles *before* bridling for bent or rusty spots or breaks. Sometimes the buckle is fine but the leather underneath the buckle has rotted due to trapped moisture and extra wear, so be sure to always check the condition of the leather when checking your buckles.

Some headstalls are attached to bits by thin leather thongs or cords. These work well to stay attached but will wear and stretch with time, so they should also be checked and replaced if necessary.

The reins can be attached to the bit by being looped through themselves if a strap is provided, or they can be attached by buckles or snaps. A popular snap for reins is the scissor snap because it's lightweight and easy to open and close with one hand. But these snaps are made of very thin, light metal where the two sides join and will break easily; they are absolutely not for tying.

Speaking of tying, bridles as a whole are not meant to tie horses. Even if you have heavy-duty hardware and thick nylon, the shanks of the bit can easily be bent or the ring snaffle can be pulled through the horse's mouth during a struggle. In addition, the headstall is more apt than a halter to be yanked over a horse's head if your horse pulls back, throatlatch and browband notwithstanding.

If you think you might tie your horse at some time during a ride, place a halter under its bridle or carry one tied to your saddle which can be pulled right over the bridle for a short tie up. You can carry a lead line suitable for tying, or you can use a nylon or rope rein to tie if you detach it from the bit and attach it to the halter, either by tying it or snapping it on with a strong (not a scissor) snap. If you are tying the horse for a long period, be nice and remove the bridle so the horse need not wear such heavy gear on its head. Another word of caution concerns letting your horse eat with the bit in its mouth. It is difficult for a horse to chew with a hunk of metal in the way, and the food, particularly hay or grass, can ball up and choke the horse.

Saddles

The two glaringly different saddle types are the English and Western saddles, with a wide variation in both types. There are also Australian stock saddles, plantation saddles, McClellan (army) saddles, sidesaddles, racing saddles, and bronc saddles for rodeo.

English

The English saddle is the type used in hunt scenes. It comes in different styles for different riding purposes such as jumping, saddle seat, and dressage. There is also an all-purpose type. The English saddle is almost always made of leather. It is fairly lightweight and compact, elegant in its simplicity. This saddle has no horn at the pommel (the front of the saddle seat) and has thin stirrup leathers that attach to bell-shaped metal stirrups. On each side of the saddle the girth is attached by buckles to two straps called billets, and it can be made of leather, padded nylon, neoprene, or string (actually lines of rope braided at intervals).

The English saddle is raised at the pommel to provide space for the horse's withers. It is padded underneath, with particularly dense padding under the seat so it can be used without a saddle pad, although it rarely is. The pad increases the horse's comfort level and protects the underside of the saddle from caking

A Western (stock) pleasure saddle

An English jumping saddle

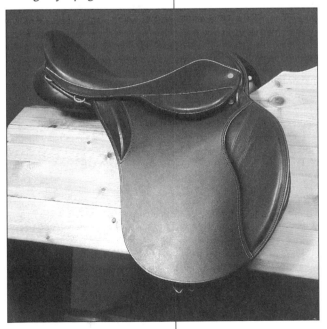

with sweat and hair. The raised pommel and cantle, or back part of the saddle seat, also serve to provide the rider with a comfortable, balanced seat.

Western

The Western (stock) saddle is the one you see all the cowboys using. Again, there are different styles for different purposes, such as barrel racing, roping, and equitation showing.

Almost all stock saddles have a horn at the pommel, although there are a few exceptions. The horn is meant to anchor a lasso while the rider is roping cattle. Contrary to popular belief, it is not meant to be used as a safety hold or a handle to pull yourself up when mounting, and could be eliminated from most saddles.

Other features of the stock saddle include a wide stirrup leather (fender) that protects the lower leg from rubbing on the cinch and cinch straps (latigos), and a wooden or metal stirrup, often encased in leather. The cinch is made of string, neoprene, or padded nylon and has large rings that are either buckled or tied to a wide latigo strap on each end.

Like the English saddle, the stock saddle is raised at the pommel but lays fairly flat along the rest of the horse's back. It has a cantle—a raised piece that makes up the back of the seat to hold the rider forward. There is a thin layer of padding—commonly sheepskin—underneath, but this saddle is not meant to be used without a pad, or at least a saddle blanket.

The Australian stock saddle, characterized by the polies at the pommel

The side saddle. The rider's right leg rests on the top appendage, the left leg over the bottom appendage.

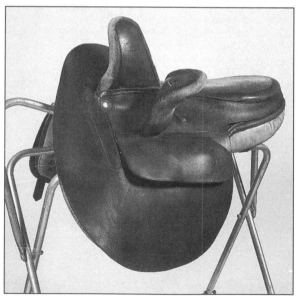

**Australian
Stock**

The Australian stock saddle looks like a cross between an English and a Western saddle. Many come with the pommel and horn of a Western saddle. Others come with an English-style pommel. The Australian saddle may come with the thin stirrup leathers of an English saddle or the wide fenders of a Western saddle.

Among the unique features of the Australian saddles are the polies—stiff appendages designed to rest against the front and back of the rider's thighs to help hold the rider more securely in place.

The Australian saddle is usually girthed like an English saddle but is also made to be used with a surcingle or overgirth—a second safety girth that goes over the top of the saddle and the first girth.

Plantation

The plantation saddle is a flat version of an English saddle. It was originally used by Southern gentry to oversee vast plantations and was designed for comfort, with heavy padding in the seat and long, wide, smooth flaps under the stirrup leathers to protect the rider's leg from the girth buckles and the horse's sweaty sides. Plantation saddles are hard to find but a pleasure to own if you are planning long-distance riding.

**McClellan
and Sidesaddle**

The McClellan saddle was designed and issued for the U.S. Army cavalry units. This saddle is basically a wooden frame held together with leather straps. It is meant to be ridden in the Western style and is shaped with the high cantle and Western-type stirrups. The McClellan saddle is also cinched Western style with latigo straps and a ringed cinch. McClellan saddles are surprisingly comfortable in light of their economical construction. Riders I know who use them swear by the comfortable seat and free leg movement the design allows. The light weight and good shape seem to suit horses well; this saddle has become popular as an endurance-trail saddle.

The sidesaddle also comes from days past when it was considered obscene for a woman to ride straddled. The sidesaddle is built quite similar to the plantation saddle, except it has only one stirrup. The sidesaddle is equipped with a bent horn at the pommel area; the rider hooks one leg over this horn so both legs are on one side of the saddle.

Riding sidesaddle takes some practice and skill, but the saddle itself makes this a comfortable and not-so-difficult endeavor. Very few of these saddles are used now for everyday riding; they are usually reserved for use in show-ring events and parades.

**Fitting and
Selecting a
Saddle**

To ensure a minimum of saddle sores, your saddle should be fitted for both horse and rider. The most important fit for the horse is over the withers.

Some saddles are made for high-withered horses and others for mutton- or flat-withered horses. The flatter saddles are often categorized as Arabian saddles or as having a Quarter Horse tree, due to the characteristic flat, rounded withers of those breeds. If you put a too-flat saddle on a high-withered horse, the saddle will likely press down and chafe against the withers, thus causing a wound or abscess that is extremely hard to heal. If you use a high-withered saddle on a flat-withered horse, the saddle won't sit well and will easily roll side to side. It will also put undo pressure on the shoulder muscles just below the withers and may cause soreness or lameness.

For the rider, the seat should be ample to prevent pinching and chafing but not so large that the rider appears to swim in it. The saddle should also have long enough stirrup leathers to accommodate a tall rider and should be easily adjustable to a short length for shorter riders. This is especially important for Western saddles, which have wide, rather stiff fenders and limited room for adjustment. Another problem with the wide, stiff fenders of a stock saddle is the unwillingness of some to swing forward and back, especially when the stirrups are shortened. This swingability is vital in allowing you to place your feet and legs where they are most comfortable and to shove your legs forward when a horse props or bucks.

The easiest way to choose a saddle that fits you is to sit in a few, or even better, ride in several. Can you sit erect in the saddle without effort? That is, does the saddle push you unnaturally forward, arching your back at the lumbar region, or slump you back, giving you the feeling you might slide on to the horse's hips? Do the stirrup leathers and fenders swing and adjust easily? Does the fender of a stock saddle bulge out when the stirrups are shortened? Can you feel the buckles, straps, or latigo knots with your knees or thighs? Do the lower edges of the cantle press into your thighs? If you leaned or fell forward suddenly would a saddle horn punch you in the stomach?

When you find a saddle that feels good, take a measurement in inches from the pommel to the cantle, as this is how saddles are sized. Take note of the manufacturer's name and perhaps take pictures of the saddle from several angles so you can remember what suited you so well when you shop elsewhere.

Finding the right fit is not the only factor in choosing a saddle. The quality of saddles varies greatly and matters a lot since the saddle gives and takes a tremendous amount of stress.

Beware the new saddle with the bargain-basement price. In this case you almost always get what you pay for: a cheaply constructed, poorly fitting, uncomfortable saddle. If you are on a budget, skip the frills—the silver and fancy leather tooling—and stick with quality. Take a knowledgeable person along to shop with you if you aren't sure you can recognize quality yourself.

Some things to look for are good fasteners and the quality of attachments (stitching or rivets) for the latigo or billets and the underpadding. Automatically eliminate any saddle that is stapled together. Feel the leather, especially the leather underneath that isn't easily visible. This is where many manufacturers cut costs by using low-grade leather. I don't know exactly how to describe good, grain leather except to tell you that when you look at enough saddles you will eventually be able to tell the difference. In a used saddle it is especially apparent—higher quality leather will develop a supple sheen as it molds to use, rather than stretch marks and cracks as it gives in to use.

If you are shopping for a used saddle, again consider that quality is often reflected in the price. Used saddles, like used cars, are subject to wear and tear and the quality of care they've received. Examine any used saddle carefully, inside and out.

Saddles are built around frames called trees. Trees are commonly made of wood, although many recently built Western saddles have fiberglass trees, which are virtually unbreakable. Some saddles, such as my old Aussie saddle, are built around a metal tree.

A wooden saddle tree is not hard to break. It can be cracked or broken by being dropped, thrown, or by having a horse fall or roll on it. A broken tree will not only cause excessive wear on the saddle, it will also sit wrong on a horse's back or move in a rubbing motion at the joint of the break, which will cause sores or back injuries to the horse.

Since saddle leather is tightly attached to the tree, you often cannot detect a broken tree by looking. A good test is to lay the saddle on the ground, press your knee into the center of the seat, and pull up and side to side on the pommel and cantle. If there is movement or give when you apply pressure to the tree, it is probably broken. If you're not sure, have someone familiar with broken saddle trees look at the saddle with you.

Saddle Accessories

There are several accessories to the saddle, including the pad or saddle blanket, the breast collar, and the backcinch.

Pads

The pad is a thick layered or quilted piece that fits under the saddle to protect the saddle and the horse's back. It can be made from sheepskin, neoprene, foam rubber, or any dense but flexible material. English pads are often closely fitted to the saddle so there is not much overlap past the saddle. Western pads are usually rectangular.

Some pads are cut back at the withers. A cut-back pad is used for high-withered horses to prevent the pad from pressing down on the withers and causing a sore. There is also the split pad, which is actually two pads joined at the spine by fabric. The density of the pad allows the saddle to sit up off the spine without placing any pressure on the spine of the horse from either the pad or the saddle.

Blankets

A saddle blanket is a dense, tightly woven, single-layer blanket. It is commonly made long enough to be folded into two layers but doesn't offer a lot of cushion either way. Some people prefer saddle blankets over pads because they allow the saddle to sit truer on a horse's back, which reduces saddle slippage and rolling. Saddle blankets are often used underneath a pad to protect the thicker pad, which is hard to clean, from sweat, hair, and dirt from the horse.

Towels

Another way to protect the pad from the horse and the horse from the pad is to use a saddle towel—a linen, denim, terry, or cotton sheet laid between the horse and the pad.

Saddle towels can be thrown in the wash after each use and are cheap to make or buy, so you can keep several around and toss them out when they become worn. I especially recommend the use of saddle towels when one pad is used by more than one horse. This will help prevent the spread of contagious skin diseases.

Some saddle towels slip easily and can actually fall out from under your pad and saddle while you're riding. To prevent this you can attach the towel to the pad, either by folding it over the front of the pad or by pinning it on. If you're ambitious, you can also sew Velcro or snaps on both the towel and the pad so they can be fitted together easily.

Breast Collars

A commonly used accessory to the saddle is the breast collar. A breast collar can be worn with all types of saddles. Although different breast collars are intended for different saddles, they all serve to stabilize the saddle by keeping it from rolling to the side or slipping back, thus allowing for a somewhat looser cinch or girth.

The ideal breast collar is Y shaped, with the center of the Y resting on the horse's chest, the top legs of the Y attached to rings below the pommel on each side of the saddle, and the bottom of the Y run through the horse's front legs, snapping to or encircling the girth or cinch.

There is also a breast collar that embraces the horse's chest and shoulders horizontally. This breast collar attaches at each end to the girth or latigos and is held up and in place by a strap that lays over the horse's neck near the withers. This breast collar works well to keep a saddle forward but does not do much to stop saddle rolling.

The breast collar needs to be fitted firmly to be effective but with enough flexibility to allow the horse free shoulder movement and prevent chafing. In addition, if a strap is attached to the girth or cinch from between the horse's front legs, it is essential the strap be centered. An unevenly placed strap can cause a severe girth gall from rubbing under the elbow areas. I have seen this happen before and it is wicked to heal this area, not to mention painful enough to the horse to prohibit riding until the area has healed.

A Western-style Y breast collar

Backcinch

A backcinch is added to some Western saddles. The backcinch—a flat leather strap—acts as a second cinch attached near the back of the saddle. The backcinch is not meant to be worn tight. It is used to keep the back of the saddle from lifting, specifically for roping when the saddle is jerked forward by an animal tied to the horn. For casual riding, the backcinch has no real function and many people remove it.

Bareback Pad

The bareback pad is not really an accessory, nor should it be considered a type of saddle. This piece of tack is a cushioned pad with a strap attached to fasten it around the horse's girth. This strap is *not* a cinch or girth and *cannot* be tightened properly to ensure that the pad, which has no tree or set shape, won't slip. Bareback pads should be used only to protect your bottom from dirt, sweat, and a bony spine while you are riding bareback—not as a substitute for a saddle.

A few bareback pads can be found with attached stirrups. These stirrups should be discarded immediately and the straps that hold them cut off. They pose a serious hazard. If a rider uses the stirrups, any unbalanced pressure in the stirrups will cause the pad to roll to the side or all the way under the horse's belly. The rider will, in this case, almost certainly fall off or wind up with a foot caught in the stirrup and be dragged.

Common Equipment

There are many items you will find around the barn that are helpful in handling and riding, or maintaining safety and soundness while handling and riding, your horse. These items are not tack items but are directly related to tack.

Restraining Devices

I consider the halter and lead line or tying line restraining devices. A shank attached to a lead line will also serve to restrain a horse if wrapped around its nose or placed under its lip or jaw. The horse's size, strength, and will have brought about the invention of many other types of restraint, the most common of which I will discuss.

Twitch

The twitch is a loop of rope or cord attached to the end of a medium-length handle such as an ax or sledgehammer handle. The cord loop is placed around the horse's top lip and twisted until it is very tight. This is painful and allows the handler not only to keep the head of the horse immobile, but usually to control a horse's unwanted movements.

I have never owned or used a twitch, but it is a common sight around many stables. Most veterinarians and farriers carry twitches to be used during treatment or when shoeing an unruly horse; their need for control is understandable and I have never stood in the way of the use of one in such circumstances. I will not recommend the use of a twitch by a novice, however, because of the damage that can be sustained by mishandling such a severe device.

Hobbles

Hobbles are a very different form of restraint. There are many, many types of hobbles and it seems that inventing new hobbling techniques is quite a popular pastime. The basic purpose of the hobble is to restrict a horse's movement by tying the horse's legs together or to another part of its body in some manner. Probably the most common hobble is one that "handcuffs" a horse at the front pasterns with leather straps. This is popular on long trail rides where it is not possible (or humane) to keep a horse tied overnight or while resting. To prevent a serious escape attempt, these hobbles restrict the horse's movements to a short-strided shuffle.

Other hobbles are meant to restrain a horse's movement during breaking or while treating or bandaging a leg. A common breaking hobble is made of thick cotton rope. The rope is looped around the horse's neck, run back and tied around a hind pastern, pulled back up to the neck loop, and tightened until the hind leg is forced off the ground. This puts the horse in a three-legged position in the hope of preventing the horse from bucking or lunging while it is becoming familiar with the feel of a new rider. My experience with this type of breaking method has shown that most green horses don't understand the concept of hobbling until *after* they've bucked or lunged and fallen down. I won't use such hobbles and I cannot recommend their use by an amateur.

Cross-Ties

A cross-tie is a method of tying a horse for safety and restriction of movement. Cross-ties are two lines or chains three to five feet in length. Each line is attached to a post or eyebolt on opposite sides of where a horse is expected to stand. The horse will be secured to the cross-ties by the side rings of its halter.

Cross-ties are better than a single tie for keeping a horse from moving sideways or turning, and make grooming, bathing, or otherwise working around a horse safer and easier. There is also restriction from two opposing sides rather than one forward restraint, which discourages a horse from trying to pull free.

Leg and Hoof Protectors

When riding, transporting, or turning a horse loose to play, you may at times need to use protection to prevent injury to the legs or hooves. Standing bandages and wound treatments will be discussed in detail in Chapter 9.

Horseshoes

Horseshoes are perhaps the most obvious and common protection for hooves. Horseshoes are most commonly made of iron, steel, or aluminum. Iron is the most popular material for riding horses because of its longer life and hardier protection. Steel and aluminum are generally lighter and are used more often on high performance horses. Dense rubber shoes are worn by some horses that are used primarily on paved surfaces, such as carriage horses and police mounts.

Shoes are generally attached by nails to the wall of the hoof. Occasionally a horse's hoof is too weak to hold a nail. In this case the shoe will be attached by glue or clamped on with lipped shoes to the wall of the hoof.

Felt, rubber, or neoprene pads can be added between the hoof and the shoe for extra cushioning effect. The pad can cover only the area of the shoe or the entire sole of the hoof.

Farriery is an advanced science; not only can a well-placed shoe protect the hoof, but it can change the horse's stance and gaits to improve soundness or conformation. A skilled farrier can change the shape of a hoof by cutting and rasping. He or she can raise a heel or toe by the thickness of the shoe and can add to the shoes such items as bars, toe grabs, and stickers, which increase traction or help change posture and movement.

A rubber boot which clamps or glues over the horse's hoof can be a temporary hoof protector. Some people swear by these boots and find they save money on horseshoeing by using them. As far as hoof protection, they do seem ideal, but a consistent problem is that the boots allow dirt and sand to enter at the top opening in the pastern area. This dirt can be quite abrasive against the edges of the boot and often results in bloody chafing. Keep this fact in mind when you use hoof boots; use a thick ointment around the pastern and coronet band to protect from chafing and remove the boot often to clean underneath.

Bell Boots

Bell boots are bell-shaped rubber pieces that fit over the hooves at the pastern area. The bell boot's purpose is to protect the tender heels and coronet bands from being nicked or bruised by a hind or off toe. High performance horses often are seen in bell boots, as overreaching (the term for a hind toe touching a front heel during a stride) most commonly occurs at high speeds or during athletic action such as jumping or quick turns.

Shipping Bandages

Shipping bandages are used to protect a horse's legs from bumps and bruises during transport. Shipping bandages are generally very thick, as their purpose is to protect from blunt trauma and the horse is not likely to move fast or far in them. You can purchase a bandage made especially for shipping; you might find it called a boot in your tack shop. This is usually one dense piece—foam rubber glued to stiff vinyl or canvas. It generally wraps around the leg once and zippers shut or is attached by Velcro.

You can also use a standing-type bandage for shipping. This consists of a quilted bandage underneath secured by a stretchy, longer bandage layered over the top. Methods for applying this bandage are discussed in Chapter 9.

Riding and Exercise Bandages

Horses that are strenuously or athletically exercised or have some problems with soundness may do best to wear bandages during exercise sessions. An exercise bandage is used to maintain pressure against the joints and tendons, but must also allow free movement of the joints and not apply such pressure as to strain tendons or ligaments.

A fairly safe and effective support bandage for exercise is the polo bandage. These are long leg wraps made of a soft, fuzzy, stretchy material. They are meant to be wrapped directly against the leg from just below the knee to below the ankle and are commonly fitted with Velcro for easy attachment. A bandage offering more support than the polo bandage is the trace bandage. This long leg wrap is made of thin, very stretchy, elastic material most commonly secured by Velcro. Vetwrap is a type of fabric gauze leg wrap that sticks to itself as you wrap. Although the bandage is fairly stretchy, it is much stiffer than the polo or trace bandages. This is a plus for extra support but can be a hazard for an amateur bandager.

There are also neoprene or foam rubber boots made for exercise. These boots do not cover the hoof—they reach from below the knee to below the ankle and are meant to keep constant pressure on the ankle joint and tendons to provide extra support. Exercise boots are molded and fitted to wrap once around the leg and attach by vertical or horizontal strips of Velcro, buckles, or zippers.

Bandage-type leather boots are also worn by many horses during exercise to prevent a horse from injury if it overreaches or "speedy cuts"—hits one leg with another toe. These boots are commonly seen on performers such as roping and gaming horses and jumpers. A boot such as this may be padded at the fetlock area or the inside of the cannon bone–shin area. They are usually strapped on with buckles and are not really meant to be used as support bandages.

I hesitate to give instructions on how to bandage a horse for exercise because of the possibility of serious injury if bandaging is done improperly. I strongly recommend you stick with polo bandages if you do choose to self-bandage. The pressure of a trace bandage or Vetwrap can be severe enough to bow a tendon. In addition, if improperly applied, a trace bandage can fall and trip a horse. Because of this, these bandages should only be used under the guidance of your veterinarian or a professional with experience in bandaging. I also find many people improperly place exercise boots, even with much practice, so I really can't recommend this leg wrap.

Stick with the polo bandage if you feel your horse needs protection during exercise, as it is the easiest to apply. The polo is thick enough to protect a horse from overreaching and speedy cuts and is adequate as a support bandage. Prewrap your polo so the Velcro is rolled into itself first; this is the opposite of the way a new polo is packaged. Hold the end of the bandage against the depression between the cannon bone and the flexor tendon on the inside of the leg, about midway between knee and ankle. Wrap down, pulling the polo *slightly* snug with each wrap. Your layers should overlap so a half inch of the previous layer shows. Wrap securely around the ankle and fetlock *twice*, until it is entirely covered save an upside-down V at the front of the pastern. Wrap back up the leg until you reach the top of the cannon bone. Do not cover the knee in any way and always end your bandage at the top. Until you get the hang of bandaging, have someone with experience check your job; also check your bandages often during use to determine if they are slipping or loosening. Never leave the exercise bandage on longer than necessary.

Whips

There are a number of whips available; most are designed for a specific purpose. The real purpose of any whip is to cue a horse to move faster or in a forward or backward direction, to turn sharper, extend its gaits, or to pay more attention to other cues such as hand, leg, and voice signals. Whips are also used to force a horse to keep its distance from the handler or to prevent a horse from kicking when lunging or during ground handling. If your intention is to punish a horse by beating it with a whip, you may find your actions counterproductive and hazardous to your health.

Riding Whips

A riding whip goes by many names, depending on your region and style of riding. At the racetrack a whip is called either a whip (fancy that) or a stick. English riders often use a riding crop, while Western riders use a quirt. There is a difference in each type. A racing whip is heavy, made like a golf club handle. It has a stiff leather popper and is often feathered with short leather pieces to add a little sting. A riding crop is light, thin handled, and longer than a quirt or racing whip. The crop usually has a frayed cord end. A quirt is a short, light whip, similar to the racing whip. The handle is thinner and there is often a leather wrist strap. The popper is a folded-over piece of soft, floppy leather, usually about two inches in length.

Ground-Handling Whips

I can't say I know anyone that uses the Indiana Jones–style coiled bullwhip to work with horses. The ground whip you most often see is a flexible whip of varying lengths with a frayed cord end. The ground whip is most often used for lunging horses and loading them in trailers or vans but is also used for leading and ground driving. The length of the whip varies, depending on its use. A lunging whip must be quite long with an extended popper cord to keep the horse moving in a wide circle away from the handler. A whip used to encourage a horse to load for transport should be medium length—short enough to direct the horse without allowing a lot of swing to the side and long enough to protect the whip handler from being kicked. A whip used to guide a horse while leading should be about the same length as the body of the horse so the handler doesn't need to turn or reach back to pop the horse on the hind legs.

Tack Care

You've probably found by now that a collection of tack, even for one horse, is pricey. If you are even slightly frugal you will want to protect your investment with good care and maintenance.

All tack should be stored in a locked, weatherproof, well-ventilated area. To prevent mildew and rot, it should be hung on racks or hooks so air can move around it. Leather should not be hung on nails; the ungalvanized metal will damage the leather. In very moist climates, leather tends to mildew despite hanging and ventilating. If this is the case in your area, you may need to store your leather items in a heated room or use a dehumidifier.

Avoid storing tack in crates, trunks, or barrels long-term. Not only will your leather tack quickly rot (and stink), but most tack can't take the stacking and mashing of cramped storage and will be permanently creased, bent, or damaged by the treatment. I also find people quickly lose track of tack stored in closed containers. You can spend a great deal of money replacing tack you forgot you owned.

Your tack, especially leather goods, will last much longer and look better if kept clean. I'm lazy and will use tack that can be tossed in the wash whenever possible, but the use of some leather is inevitable, and cleaning such material is not so simple.

Leather should be cleaned with saddle or oil soap on a regular basis—at least once a week if it's used frequently. If it is filthy or muddy you may have to scrub it first with soapy water, then towel dry, otherwise you will just be sealing in the dirt with your saddle soap. You should also oil leather occasionally with an oil soap or leather oil to keep it supple, but be conservative with your oil as it will eventually stretch and weaken the leather.

Keep your bit clean by dipping it in a bucket of water or rinsing it as soon as you take it out of your horse's mouth. This is much easier than scrubbing off caked gunk after it has dried, especially if it is left long enough to build into several cementlike layers. If a bit is used by more than one horse, add a capful of disinfectant or bleach to your dipping bucket to help prevent the spread of disease or virus carried in saliva.

In addition to making bit cleaning more difficult, if you wait to clean your bit and allow crusty gunk to dry and build up, the crud will act as an irritant on the corners of your horse's mouth and possibly cause a hard-to-heal sore. Pain caused by the bit is one of the most common reasons horses develop head tossing and rearing habits under saddle.

Use your cleaning time to inspect all your tack. Look under buckles, fasteners, flaps, etc., because this is where rot and wear are most prevalent. Clean and dry these areas thoroughly and replace any piece that looks worn. It is far less costly (and risky) than having a piece of tack break while you are using it.

6

By Hand and Foot

*Effective Methods for
Handling Horses on the Ground*

The importance of learning and practicing good habits during ground handling cannot be overstated. More injuries happen on the ground than during riding—injuries as a result of being bitten or kicked, stepped on or knocked down, whacked by a horse's head or knee, crushed, jerked, dragged, and tangled up in lines.

Surely there are more ways for a person to get hurt on the ground than those I have listed. There are also countless ways a horse can be injured, abused, spoiled, or traumatized as a direct result of human mishandling and ignorance.

Catching and Haltering

**Catching a
Horse in
the Stall**

We'll begin with a bare horse, loose in the stall. To do anything safely with this horse you must first catch it and place the halter and lead line.

When you enter the stall, stand at the unlatched gate and wait for the horse to approach you. Most horses do this willingly, as stalls are boring places and visitors are usually appreciated. If the horse does not approach you, but is facing you, walk quietly toward its head, leaving the gate closed but unlatched as an escape route.

Keep an eye on your horse's facial expressions. If it is interested in or accepting of your approach, its ears will be forward and it will be quiet and complacent. If the horse feels in any way threatened or invaded, it will lay its ears back and shake its head in your direction or move evasively. If the horse is frightened by your presence, it will display a lot of ear flicking and body tension. It will probably retreat to the farthest corner and may blow or snort at you.

If your horse is aware of your presence but continues to face *away* from you, paces the stall, or takes action to avoid your approach, heed this as a warning that you are not welcome. Exit the stall, but stand right at the gate. Signal your horse to come to you by calling to it. If you get no response, try tempting it with a food treat. Stay out of the stall until the horse approaches quietly with its ears forward, or at least stands quietly facing you. It's too easy to get trapped in a stall; if the horse doesn't want you there it may act against you with aggressive or defensive behavior, leading you to panic—thus leading the horse to panic.

If your horse has shown no intent to approach after you've called, cajoled, or tried a bribe, or if it approached at a lunge with its ears pinned flat and its teeth bared, should you give up and leave? If you lack experience and help, *yes*. Wait for an experienced horseperson to help you. It's not normal for a horse to refuse to let you catch it in the stall. It is a sign that something is wrong.

Catching a Horse on Open Ground

Catching horses that are turned out in a pasture or paddock is another story. Horses have a lot more fun outside than they do in a cubicle and are more resistant to human interference.

In a large enclosure you almost always have to enter to catch the horse, although some horses will trot eagerly to the gate when they see you or hear you calling.

If your horse is turned out alone, signal it at the gate to come to you. Try calling or shaking a noisy grain bucket. If the horse doesn't come straight away, go in after it. Walk up to the horse, approaching from the front. If it moves away from you, follow it, always at a walk. Never run. Running will start a panic flight or a game of chase you won't win.

If the horse continues to avoid you, just keep following it, always walking, even if your horse breaks and runs. The horse will eventually give up and stop if you are persistent. When it stops, approach from the front. If the horse turns away, back off and reapproach from the front. Start following again if your horse takes off before you've caught it, and remember to stay at a walk. This slow-motion chase may seem futile, but your persistence will pay off and the horse will almost always be compliant when it gives up on running away. You very well may have to sacrifice an afternoon of riding in your attempt to wear down your horse, but once a horse realizes it cannot elude capture by running away, your next attempt at catching will most likely be much easier and faster. As a bonus, if it takes so long to catch your horse that you don't have time to ride, you can use the shortened period to feed and groom your horse and turn it out again; this will reinforce the idea that being captured is a positive thing.

If you absolutely can't catch your horse by following it, try beckoning with a bucket of grain. This won't work more than a time or two if you only use grain to catch the horse for a ride. You must go out on random occasions and feed

Gentle handling will encourage a horse to accept the halter.

the horse while you stand holding it, then turn it loose. Again, this will help your horse associate capture with pleasure instead of just work, thus encouraging cooperation.

Once in while you will come across a horse than can be approached but will not let you halter it, or perhaps even touch it. Every time you think you've caught it, it bolts away. If your horse is like this, you can use a little cheater method for catching it. You can either leave a leather halter on the horse, with about five feet of rope attached, or you can tie a rope of similar length around your horse's neck, using a nontightening knot, such as a square knot, that won't strangle your animal if it steps on the end of the rope. This rope will give you something to grab without reaching too close to the horse's head, which is generally what causes a horse to bolt.

Keep in mind if you leave a halter on your horse that the halter can get hung up on something and injure your horse, even if it eventually breaks. For this reason I prefer the simple rope around the neck, and I actually use baling twine rather than rope because I know it will break easily if it catches on something. Do not use a rope or twine longer than five feet because of the risk of entangling your horse's legs and feet in it, not to mention the greater chance that the rope will be caught and tangled in a fence line or some other such thing.

If your horse is turned out with others, you must deal with the herd as a whole when singling out the one you want. If they all come when you call, make sure the horse you're after is in a clear position before you approach it so you don't get trapped between two or more horses. If the gang runs away when they see you, stand back and let them get their running over with, as they will make a game of this. Wait until they've stopped or decided to come to you. If the herd is scattered and ignoring you, just go after the horse you want. Catch it as if it were alone, following it if necessary.

Be careful about bribing with food when there is a herd of horses involved. This will invariably set off a scramble of competition and bickering. You don't want to be in the middle of this and are probably better off using some other method.

Haltering

When you can stand by your horse, either in a stall or out in the open, go to the left side of the horse and lay a hand firmly on the horse's neck before trying to halter it. This is a simple signal to tell the horse you are in command now. If you believe your horse might not fully respect your authority and suspect it will dash away before you've haltered it, you can use your lead line to convince the horse to stay by looping it around the horse's neck just behind the ears.

To halter your horse, attach the lead line to the bottom ring of the halter nosepiece and let it trail on the ground, unless you're using it to hold the horse still. Make sure the headstall strap is unbuckled. Hold the nosepiece with one hand on each side and place it around the horse's muzzle. Slide the headstall strap up and behind the ears and buckle it into position on the left side. When adjusted correctly, the halter should not be tight under the horse's throat or around the nose, and the side rings of the nosepiece should lay about an inch or a little less below the points of the cheekbones.

When the halter is secured, pick up your lead line. Hold it about a foot below the horse's chin with your right hand—the control hand. Your left hand should hold the slack with any excess laid in folds, gripping the folds in order to hold them in a bunch.

Do not coil or loop the excess line. If you are holding onto a coil and the horse jerks away suddenly, the coil will tighten around your hand before you can even think to let go. Your hand will be trapped and you may be jerked or dragged. This is a good way to break a bone or lose a finger, as countless careless horsepeople can attest.

Methods for Tying

What you tie your horse to and with is as important as how you tie it. Make sure your halter and lead line are in good shape, made of strong material, and fitted with good hardware. Remember not to use leather to tie with unless you are in an enclosed space and don't mind sacrificing your halter or lead line if a struggle ensues. This is not a facetious statement; most would rather see their equipment break than a horse injured while fighting the tie.

If you tie or snap onto a metal ring or eyebolt, make sure it is bolted with a nut to a solid post, not just screwed into a board. The only place you can get away with tying to an eyebolt that is simply screwed into the wall is in an enclosed space, such as a stall; if your horse pulls the eyebolt free, it has no place to go.

If you are tying your horse to a fence or wall, use only a vertical post set firmly in the ground. Never tie to a horizontal fence board. Not only is the board breakable, it is held by nails, which are easily pulled loose. Once a fence board is pulled loose, it is still attached to the horse by the tie line—exposed nails, jagged edges, and all. I

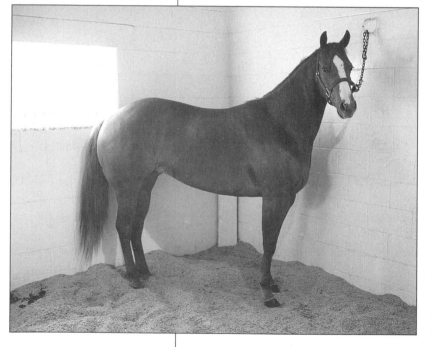

Always tie your horse high and short to prevent entanglement.

have witnessed a horse running loose dragging a board. The faster the horse ran, the more the board cracked the horse in the legs, causing the horse to race in blind panic until it had severely injured itself.

Never tie your horse to anything movable or removable, including wheelbarrows, unsecured horse trailers, truck side mirrors, clotheslines, door handles, or ground stakes, as any of these can be moved or torn free and cause injury.

Never tether your horse out to graze. Yes, I've seen it done a lot of times, too, but it's just not worth the risk. Tethering is the perfect way to tangle your horse in a line and can cause permanent injury to a horse's legs. In addition, if a horse steps on the line and finds it can't raise its head, it may panic and throw itself down. Finally, if a horse starts running and hits the end of the tether, it will either yank the tether loose or get jerked to a hard stop, possibly falling.

Your horse should be tied at the level of its chest or higher to prevent it from stepping on or getting a leg caught over the tie line. The length of the tie line should be no more than thirty inches from the horse's halter ring to the post. The lower you tie your horse, the shorter the tie line must be; twelve inches is not too short at chest level.

The ideal and safest tying method is cross-tying. Cross-tying gives you easy access to move around the horse, prevents the horse from moving much in any direction, and ensures it can't get a leg over the line or pull back against an anchor directly in front of it.

When cross-tied, your horse is tied with two lines, one fastened to each side ring on the halter nosepiece. The lines are then secured, at or above the level of your horse's head, to two posts or two bolted rings set eight to twelve feet apart, such as on each side of a shedrow, washrack, or stall. Cross-tie lines are generally a little longer than the thirty-inch maximum mentioned for a standard tie line so they can reach the posts, but the lines are not meant to have much slack.

No matter how careful you are about tying your horse there may be a time when you have to untie your horse quickly; it can rear and get a leg over the line or panic for some reason and start struggling against its tie. If your horse is attached with a snap, you probably won't be able to unsnap it because of the tension put on the snap during the horse's struggle.

If you make a habit of carrying a pocketknife around the stable, you will be able to cut your horse loose. Try to grab the line and cut as far away from the horse as you can to give yourself as much lead line as possible. In this way your horse won't be turned loose after you cut the line.

If your horse is attached with a rubber tie or bungee cord, don't hold the tie—hold the halter if possible, or nothing. Cut as close to the halter as you can so that the longest part of the tie snaps back away from you and the horse. *Watch out for the rebound of a snapping tie!*

If your horse is tied to a post, always use a quick-release knot that can be untied by pulling on the end. Have someone that has used this knot show you how to tie it. Remember, though, that if you can untie the knot by pulling on the end, so can your horse. Always run the end of your tie line loosely through the loop of the knot so you can pull it out and yank on it to free your horse if you need to, but if the horse pulls on the end, the loop will tighten rather than release.

Anytime you release a horse in an emergency situation and are still holding on to it, be prepared to be jerked suddenly when the horse finds itself with no more resistance from the tie. Don't pull back against the horse and try to stop it; instead, follow it back until the horse stops itself. Keep slack in the line if possible so the horse has nothing to pull or fight against, and avoid screaming, yelling, or arm-waving.

If you can't follow the horse fast enough or are being yanked off your feet, let the horse go. I admit it's no fun trying to catch a frenzied horse, but it's better than getting yourself dragged, rope burned, or otherwise injured.

If your horse is fighting frantically while you are trying to free it, and you feel you are in danger of being knocked down or struck by flailing legs, get away from the horse. Your horse may wind up injured in its struggle, but if you ever need to make a choice between yourself and your horse, choose yourself. *Your horse is replaceable—you are not.* The horse will eventually stop fighting, one way or another, or it will fight hard enough to free itself.

Leading Techniques

The proper way to lead a horse

Leading horses seems very simple, but if you don't do it right you will end up turning horses loose, running over people and other things, and getting yourself dragged, stomped, and kicked.

The ideal way to lead a horse is with a halter and lead line. I wish this were more obvious to more people. No matter how inconvenient it is to find a lead line, don't lead a horse around by the halter. Your arm makes a lousy lead line, as it has no give (well it does, actually, but it comes with some serious injuries).

Don't lead a horse around with just a rope wrapped around its neck or a hand hooked in its mane unless you don't mind if the horse gets loose. No matter how much you trust your horse to loyally follow you, any surprise situation, such as another horse passing by or an unexpected horn honking, could set your horse off and cause it to flee. Once a horse learns it can depart at will, this often becomes habit.

You can lead a bridled horse by the reins, but only if the reins are pulled off over the horse's head. If you leave the reins up and try to lead it by holding on to one or both reins near the bit, you will have limited maneuverability and no slack. If the horse pulls away from you, there is little you can do about it.

If you want to lead a horse with a rider on its back who (understandably) doesn't want to give up control of the reins, hold only the left rein under the bit with one hand, with the expectation that you will turn the horse loose and the rider will take over control if the horse pulls away. If that's not satisfactory, place the horse's halter under the bridle, attach a lead line to the halter, and lead it by the lead line, leaving the reins to the rider.

The Handler's Position

Horses are traditionally led from the left side, which makes your right hand the one you will use to control the horse most of the time. Hold the lead line in your right hand about a foot or a little less below the horse's chin. Never hold the line at the halter ring, as this tight hold will often turn into a pulling or dragging match (most horses resist that sort of stifling pressure). At the same time, never lead a horse on a long or sloppy slack line, which will allow the horse too much free movement and can set you up to get kicked.

The left hand is used to hold the excess line and to retain control if you lose your grip with the right hand. You will also lead the horse with your left hand on occasion, such as turning the horse sharply to the left or backing it. Also, if you are turning it to the right in a tight circle you will frequently have to move to the right side of the horse and will probably use your left hand to maneuver the animal.

Moving Forward

To signal your horse to move forward, stand near the horse's head and push forward on the lead line as you step forward. The horse should move along with you, ideally because it's following your motion rather than obeying your hand signal. The horse's head should remain parallel to your body. Don't get in front of your horse or let it trail behind you, as you will be setting yourself up to be stepped on, knocked down, or jumped on if the horse surges forward suddenly.

By the same token, don't let your horse get too far in front of you. It won't be able to do this if you keep a short hold on the line and your arm near your side. A horse that gets too far forward has an increased chance of taking off and dragging you. An additional hazard of letting your horse move too far forward is being kicked. If it gets far enough in front of you a horse can actually kick you in the leg or stomach by kicking forward and out with a hind leg (cow kicking). I must admit to having allowed myself to be kicked in the stomach this way. It hurt.

Reluctance
If your horse refuses to follow you, first try to find out why. Perhaps you've asked it to leave its buddies or walk into or on something unsteady or noisy. Maybe the horse is frightened of something you are leading it toward or by. Assess the situation and decide if your demands are reasonable and how important it is that your horse obey you. Most certainly a horse unwilling to leave its mates should not be allowed to have its way, nor should a horse that is frightened of a puddle of water or an unfamiliar but safe area such as a washrack.

If there is no justifiable reason for your horse to refuse, cluck or chirp first to signal it verbally. If you get no response, don't move forward and start dragging; this will only encourage your horse to pull back. Instead, take the excess line in your left hand and use it as a whip. Swing your left hand behind you and swat the horse with the line on the rump. Keep yourself facing forward to maintain control over the horse's front end. Be prepared for the horse to move its rump away from you when you swat it, or to jump forward in surprise.

If swatting with the lead line fails to intimidate your horse into action, try carrying a medium-length whip in your left hand to tap the horse. Aim for the haunch or the lower hind leg and keep your whipping to a tap or flick; don't get aggressive or you will chase the horse away from you rather than encourage it to cooperate and move forward.

As a last resort to convince your horse to follow, have someone trail the two of you at a safe distance, off to the left or right in the horse's field of vision (horses have a blind spot directly behind them). The person following can wave hands and shout to scare the horse forward or can tap its hind legs with a long whip to urge it on. The horse may try to kick at the follower, especially if it can't see clearly, so it is important the person not get too close.

Overeagerness

If your horse is overly eager to go and tries to get ahead of you or take off running, jerk the lead line quickly and intermittently so the horse doesn't have any steady pressure to pull against. Use the verbal command "Whoa!" in a sharp tone as you jerk the line. Your horse will learn the command quickly if you use it consistently.

Keep rattling the lead line even after your horse comes back to you to remind it not to pull forward again. If this is not enough to slow the horse, especially if it habitually tries to drag you around, you may need to resort to a lead shank for stronger restraining measures.

Turning

A gradual, easy turn can be done in the same position as you would lead a horse in a straight line. When turning to the left you simply pull the horse toward you as you move away from the horse into the turn. To turn right, push your lead line under your horse's jaw until the horse feels a right-hand pull. At the same time, walk toward and into the horse with your shoulder to push it away from you and into the turn.

To turn a horse in a very tight circle move to whichever side you want the horse to turn. Back away from your horse toward its flank as you pull the horse toward you, this time using your left hand on the lead to control if you are turning left and your right hand on the lead when turning right. You will end up with the horse facing you. Immediately move to the left side of the horse's head, switching hands if necessary so your right hand is back in control. Be careful not to remain directly in front of a horse in case it decides to move forward quickly.

If you try to turn a horse too tightly, it will sometimes bend at the neck but not move its body. You'll wind up with a bewildered horse looking back at you.

To correct this, you can place your free hand against the side of the horse's rump and literally push the rump away from you, continuing to pull its head toward you to complete the turn. This sounds scary but with the horse already bent toward you all its momentum in the rear is toward the off side. It is easy to push the horse over and very hard for it to balance itself enough to try to kick you. If you don't surprise the horse or slap at it, it has no reason to kick you anyway.

Backing

To back a horse with the lead line, face your horse but remain beside the horse's head—not in front of it. Switch hands so your left hand is in control of the lead line. Push back on the lead line toward your horse's chest. Use intermittent pressure if the horse resists. Ideally, the horse will tuck its chin toward its chest and walk back with you following, always beside its head.

If your horse resists and raises its head against the backward pressure, you will lose your ability to push it back with the lead and will find yourself pulling down instead. If this happens, or if the horse's head is down but it still refuses to budge back, take your right hand and press the middle knuckles of your fingers into the hollow just above the chest and just inside the left point of the shoulder. This area is soft and somewhat sensitive, so the pressure of your knuckles should be sufficient to move the horse back.

Slapping at a horse's chest or head to get it to move backward is usually not successful in forcing the horse to move back and is more likely to make it fling its head up or at you, rear, or dance around in confusion. You will receive a similar reaction if you try to force a horse backward by jerking on the lead line or shank. Stick with pushing from the chest, increasing force if necessary.

Trotting

To retain maximum control, leading is best done at a walk. To trot a horse on the lead, you must give it more slack to avoid having your feet tromped, but this gives up some of your control.

A horse asked to trot on the lead often reacts with either excitability or laziness. If your horse is excitable, it's more likely to try to bolt or frolic while trotting, possibly kicking at you. With the added slack it has a greater chance of success. If your horse is lazy, you will probably end up dragging it along, which will put you in front of it. Again, this is not a safe position because you will be in the direct path of the horse if it comes forward quickly. Even a lazy horse can have an unexpected burst of energy.

If you must trot your horse on the lead—for your vet or shoer to observe its motion or for showing purposes—give up as little slack as possible, extending your arm toward the horse so you are not in its tracks. Stay parallel to the horse's head, no matter the pace. If you can't keep up, slow the horse.

If the horse stops, whether under your command or of its own accord, you must stop with it simultaneously to keep your position. If stopping wasn't your idea, verbally urge the horse to resume trotting or slap its rump with your excess line. If the horse surges ahead of you, snap at the lead line in quick jerks to get its attention. Don't pull straight back against the horse, as it can brace itself against the pressure and pull harder away from you. Try to keep pace with the horse until it stops or you will end up too far behind it in a dangerous position. If you lose control or can't keep up long enough to stop the horse, turn it loose; this is preferable to being kicked or dragged.

If your horse becomes fractious at any time while trotting, stop the horse immediately, using the same snapping action on the lead, and forget trotting it. Furthermore, if your horse shows a tendency to bolt or try to pull away from you when you increase the pace, you must get the horse slowed and back under control before you lose it. Any such out of control situation can only lead to a mishap or disaster.

∩ ∩

The faster you allow a horse to move on the lead the less control you will have. Cantering or loping a horse on the short lead is downright stupid and I don't feel there's any sense in discussing methods of doing so.

I discussed in the section on tying horses the following information concerning what you do when you need to free a horse that's fighting the tie, but it's so important I will repeat it in regard to leading horses.

If you are leading a horse that backs or bolts away from you, *don't pull against the horse to try to stop it.* This panics the horse (which was probably somewhat panicked or excited already or it wouldn't have tried to get away) and will make the animal fight harder to get loose.

The best thing you can do is follow the horse with as little noise and commotion as possible so as not to further alarm it. Let out as much line as possible and keep as much slack in the line as you can so the horse has nothing to fight against.

If you must, let the horse go. Catching it afterward when you are still in one piece is a lot easier than trying to catch it after you've been dragged, burned your hand on the rope, or pulled your arm out of its socket.

Using the Shank

A lead shank is a chain about two feet in length, similar in appearance to a dog's choke chain. It is sewn, riveted, or snapped to the end of a lead line. The shank enhances control when used properly.

Nose Shank

For use while leading, the chain should be run through the left side ring of the halter nosepiece, outside to in. The chain is then pulled over the bridge of the horse's nose and slid under the halter nosepiece. Then the chain is run through the right ring of the nosepiece, inside to out, pulled under the jaw through the bottom ring, and snapped back to itself at the end, where it is attached to the lead line by a triangle-shaped ring.

When the horse pulls against the shank, snap the lead line intermittently. The chain will bite into the bridge of the horse's nose and cause it to slow down and pay more attention. Don't jerk hard on the shank, as any excessive pain will cause a horse to overreact, possibly rearing. Don't pull steadily on the shank because the steady pressure is easy for a horse to brace and pull against. For best effect, stick with give-and-take pressure and snapping movements with your wrist to rattle the chain.

A quick, frequently used application of the shank is to run the chain through the left ring of the nosepiece and over the nose, then snap it to the right ring. It is hard to rattle the chain when it is fitted this way, and the shank has a tendency to be pulled tight, pinching the nose and pulling the halter over too far to the left. It is not nearly as effective as fully encircling the horse's nose and jaw.

Another poor method of setting the shank is to bring the chain around through both side rings and snap it to the bottom ring or the top ring on the right. Again, the chain tends to get stuck in a tight position when pulled, removing your give-and-take and pinching and misshaping the halter on the horse's head.

Jaw Shank

A shank can be set so it rests against the horse's jaw. This is an especially popular application for halter class performance. The idea behind the jaw shank is that the chain, when pulled, will apply pressure to the horse's jaw, thus lifting the head and urging the horse forward. When used properly, especially with a very light show shank, the jaw shank is effective. When it is jerked or pulled tight, a horse commonly will offer resistance, sometimes to the point of running backward or rearing.

To set a shank under the jaw, run the chain outside to in through the left side ring of the nosepiece. The chain then goes under the jaw and attaches to the right side ring. If the chain is long it can be run under the jaw through both side rings, then snapped back to itself. This method is probably preferable in that it provides more even pressure. The chain is meant to be kept slack, with slight intermittent pressure used to encourage the horse to move forward or raise its head.

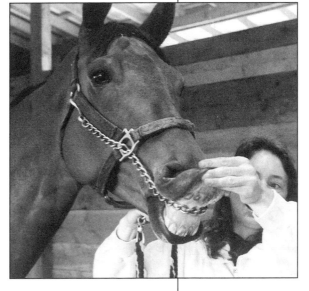

The lip chain

Lip Chain

A more severe use of the shank is as a lip chain—a shank set under the horse's top lip against the gum. Although the lip chain is irreplaceable in certain situations where maximum control is needed, it is not meant for casual use and should not be used by anyone with a hot temper or heavy hands.

To set a lip chain, the shank is run through the left side ring of the nosepiece, outside to in, then snapped to the right side ring. If there is a lot of excess chain, it is run through the right side ring and snapped to the top right ring. The chain is then placed under the horse's top lip, over the gum as high as possible. The chain must be kept firmly in place by the handler or it will simply fall off.

The lip chain is a potentially cruel form of restraint meant to be used with steady pressure—never yanked or rattled. The pressure on a horse's gum is irritating if held firmly, painful if pulled, and just about unbearable if jerked, which will cut and bruise the gum. If your horse is rank enough to necessitate the use of a lip chain on more than the rare occasion, such as receiving an injection from the vet, you may need to find a more docile horse.

Lunging

I have stated that I don't think a novice should try to lunge a horse without hands-on instruction, especially if the horse has not been trained to lunge. I say this because lunging allows the horse out on a very long line, which gives it the freedom to roughhouse or kick the handler. The long line also provides the handler very little control if the horse decides to bolt or take off running. In spite of my belief, I cannot deny that lunging is quite popular and you may want or need to exercise your horse in this manner, so I will provide some instruction.

If you decide to lunge your horse, do so in a small, enclosed area to prevent the horse from getting too far out of hand. A round corral is perfect, but an arena or small paddock will do. Avoid grassy areas that might tempt your horse to eat rather than cooperate, or any area with many distractions.

Your lunge line should be fitted with a strong snap and should have a thick knot tied in the end of it. If you make your own line, use a length of cotton or nylon rope at least twenty-five feet long. Additional supplies you will need to lunge your horse include a long whip, such as a buggy whip or one made for lunging, and gloves. Your horse can wear its own halter or you can buy a special halter with a ring attached to the top of the nosepiece with which you attach the lunge line. When using a normal halter, attach the lunge line to the side ring of the halter on the side you will lunge from. When changing directions, snap the lunge line to the opposite side ring. This will prevent the halter from being pulled uncomfortably off to the side and will increase the responsiveness of the horse. Some people also use nose shanks to lunge a horse for stricter control. The nose shank must be placed properly—run completely around the nosepiece of the halter and snapped to itself—in order to be both effective and humane.

Verbal commands are very helpful when lunging a horse. Be prepared to use clucking or chirping sounds to

Lunging allows the horse a great amount of freedom, so it should only be done in an uncluttered, enclosed area.

encourage the horse to move forward and a sharp "Whoa!" command to stop the horse. A horse can also be moved to a faster gait by the sharp or excited tone of "Get up!" and can be slowed by a soothing tone of "Easy." How do you know if your horse is trained to respond to these commands? It doesn't really matter. If you use your verbal commands and intonations consistently, your horse will quickly pick up on their meanings.

If your horse is trained to lunge you should have little problem getting it started. Lead the horse into the center of the area where you will be lunging. Make sure your excess line isn't tangled, then drop it to the ground. Hold the horse with the line in your right hand if the horse will be moving clockwise and the left if it will be moving counterclockwise. Hold the whip in your other hand, pointed down toward the ground.

To move your horse away from you, back up a step while you let out some slack and chirp at the horse. The horse should move forward. As it begins to move, back away a little, but let the horse do most of the moving out or you will find yourself backed against a wall or fence. Keep letting out slack gradually, but never let out so much that the line touches the ground.

When your horse is at a distance from which it couldn't easily kick you, raise the whip or thump it on the ground to encourage the horse to move out to the end of the line and circle around you. Once the horse is circling, you can *gradually* increase its speed to a canter by waving the whip low to the ground and clucking or chirping to the horse. Be very conservative about increasing your horse's speed until you feel you have good control. This may take days or weeks rather than minutes, so don't get in a hurry or feel like you are failing if you only feel comfortable trotting your horse.

To slow your horse, stop all signals and say "Whoa!" If the horse does not respond, start pulling the line in, walking slowly toward the horse to decrease the slack and length of line. Expect the horse to keep trying to move away, but keep advancing toward it until, if necessary, a wall or fence stops its retreat.

If your horse gets out of control while lunging and tries to run off or bolt, follow it as best you can, holding on by the knot at the end of the line. If you must, let the horse go. You are, of course, working inside an enclosure so your horse will be relatively safe if turned loose.

If your horse bucks or kicks on the line, stop it as soon as possible, giving a sharp command of "Whoa!" Start over, with less line. Keep the horse at a walk or trot until it is less playful. Don't whip the horse for playing, as you will only encourage a violent reaction or attempt to escape.

If your horse responds to your attempts to lunge it by stopping and facing you, it has probably never been properly trained to lunge. If this sort of exercise is important to you, it is possible for you to train your own horse. Most horses enjoy the freedom a lunge line affords, so they are not very resistant to training once they get the hang of it.

The most difficult concept of lunging for a horse is accepting the fact that it's okay to move away from the handler. All previous handling has taught the horse to stay by and move parallel to the handler's side. The simplest way of encouraging a horse to move out and around the handler is to enlist the help of a second handler. While you take up the position for lunging, your helper should lead your horse forward on a separate lead line until it is circling you at an acceptable distance. As you begin to take control with verbal, hand, and whip cues, your helper should remove the short lead line and begin to move just forward of the horse so it is following your helper but under your control. When a decent distance is made between your helper and the horse, your helper should exit the enclosure. If you've been successful in capturing your horse's attention with cues, your horse should naturally move into the lunging pattern.

If your horse stops and faces you again or you have no help, use your hands and whip to wave the horse out from you while simultaneously backing away. The moment the horse starts to move out use your whip to tap the ground or flick at its hind heels to encourage it to keep moving in a forward direction. If the horse starts to come back to you, turn the whip and push the horse out from the shoulder with the handle.

When lunging your horse, be careful to keep its head off the ground, where it can step on the line, and its attention on you. Constantly use your whip and your voice to keep the horse focused. Your whip is most effective for dramatic show and snapping sound effects. Do not actually touch the horse with the whip unless you absolutely can't make it go without doing so, then flick the whip or snap it against the horse's lower hind legs.

Often a horse will kick out at the feel of the whip. This type kicking is not usually directed at the handler, but it is still not acceptable. If your horse kicks at the whip, pop it again immediately and continue to do so every time the horse kicks until it realizes kicking won't rid it of the whip. Persistent popping is more effective than an aggressive slashing attack with the whip, which can cause terror on the part of the horse and lead you to lose control.

Trailer or Van Loading

The ideal loader is a horse you can face at an open stall of a van or trailer, toss the lead line over its neck, and stand back as it steps in on its own. You are then free to latch the gate behind the horse, go up front to secure the horse's head, then drive away with a big, cheesy grin on your face. If your horse is not quite that cooperative, you will need help loading, preferably from a level-headed, experienced horseperson that has loaded many horses in the past.

Some horses will step right in the van or trailer if you lead the way. You will be walking in directly in front of the horse, which is a dangerous position, so make sure you have an escape door or route to duck out when the horse comes forward at you. Your helper should be standing back, ready to latch the hind gate as soon as your horse steps in so it cannot back out again.

Most trailers and vans have butt straps in addition to the rear gates; they are meant as an added safety device in case the tailgate breaks or swings open unexpectedly. Don't use the butt strap to try to stop a horse from backing out because the force of a horse can easily break the fastenings. Latch the tailgate first, then snap the butt straps in place.

Always make sure your horse is tied securely with a tie positioned high in the trailer. You can use your lead rope or a tie provided in the trailer. If left untied, the horse can get its head down or turned back while you are traveling. A horse often is unable to get its head back up or around due to the tight quarters and will panic and start fighting, very likely injuring itself.

If your horse balks at loading, it may be because of the trailer or van you are using. Make sure the ceiling is tall enough for your horse's head to clear, even when its head is raised high. Most horses won't think to duck, and if they bump their heads, they will be very unenthusiastic about coming forward again.

Tight, dark quarters are another factor in a horse's unwillingness to load. Some trailers and vans have a divider that can be swung aside for loading, then set in place after the horse is secured to give the horse a sense of space when loading. Often the use of an open stock trailer or four-horse trailer rather than a crampy two-horse will prove horses much more willing to load. Opening windows and roof vents can allow more light, and of course, you can illuminate the interior with a shop light. Even painting the interior white can improve a horse's attitude on loading.

The ramp may also be offensive to your horse if it is noisy or wobbly when the horse steps onto it. Make sure your ramp is lying level so it doesn't move, and try covering it with some straw, shavings, or a heavy rubber mat to muffle the clomping sound. Also try parking your vehicle so the ramp has as little slope as possible.

Many trailers and vans have no ramp. The horse is either expected to step up a short distance or walk in from a loading platform. If your vehicle is the step-up type, expect some horses to be reluctant to do so, especially if the step up is so high as to force the horse to jump to get in. A hesitant horse often takes the first step, hears the clump of its hoof on the wooden floor, and quickly changes its mind. If your horse proves unwilling to step in without a ramp, try parking the trailer on a decline so the ground behind it is level with the floor of the trailer. You can also make a sort of ramp by laying flakes of straw or other dense bedding behind the opening of the trailer.

If you've done your best to create an acceptable situation for loading and your horse still stubbornly refuses, there are some pretty effective means of coercion you can use. One of the best ways to load an unwilling horse is to back the trailer or van right up to an entrance in your barn. Close the

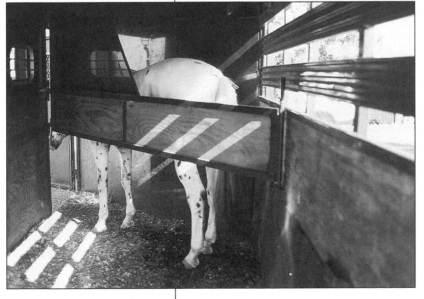

A bright interior and high ceiling will encourage your horse to load. The horse should be closely contained, however, with a gate or divider for travel to help it keep its balance.

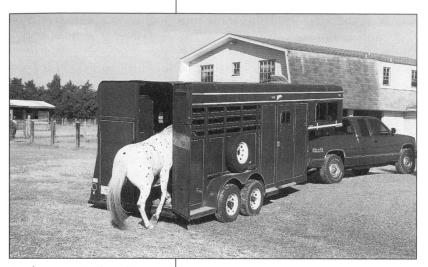

Few horses want to jump into a trailer. Minimizing the step up will give a horse less reason to refuse.

barn doors so they meet the sides of the trailer, or open the tailgate doors wide to block off any side gaps. Clear the shedrow you will be working in of any equipment the horse could step on, knock over, or become tangled in. Lead the horse up to the trailer with your helper(s) following at a safe distance. Gently urge the horse to load. The quieter the experience this time, the more willing your horse will be next time.

Don't get in a pulling match with your horse by attempting to drag it into the trailer; you will lose. Use light, intermittent pressure on the lead line and a lot of soothing vocal encouragement. Try bribing the horse forward by rattling a can of grain. If the horse puts a foot on the ramp or in the trailer, pause and encourage it with verbal praise to stay there or come forward.

Often a horse will back off at the first feel and sound of the foreign surface. If this happens, stop the horse as quickly as possible, give it a moment to calm and think, then move it forward again.

If it seems clear your horse is making no attempt to cooperate, have your helper wave a long whip at the horse's hind legs and tell it sharply to "Get up!" You must stay quiet and soothing—only the helper behind the horse should come across as threatening. This will convince the horse the best direction is forward.

A common evasive reaction of a horse is to swing sideways away from the entrance. This is where being in a shedrow is very helpful, as it limits the horse's swinging area. Ignore its sideways stance and continue to have your helper get after it from behind, moving the horse over by flicking its heels with the whip if necessary.

If your horse begins to show signs of panic or anxiety and kicks, rears, or starts sweating, back off for a moment and try to calm the horse. You don't want this to become a traumatic experience in your horse's mind.

If, by this time, you've had no success in loading your horse, stronger measures might be in order. If you have two capable, strong helpers available, move the horse as close to the opening as possible. Have your helpers lock arms behind the horse's rump and try shoving it into the trailer. This is often surprisingly effective. The horse can't kick with the pressure placed on its rump because its hind legs will be drawn under its body. Some horses will brace themselves, though, on their front legs so your handlers will only be pushing the horse's rear end up in the air and will not be able to move it forward.

If you have not been successful in any of these methods, and you have been trying for a good amount of time, you may have to give up for now, especially if your horse (or you) has become sweat soaked and frazzled. Even the best horsepeople have come across horses that won't load. The smartest won't make a battle of it. The greater the fight you get in with your horse, the more chance of injury for either you or the horse and the more traumatized the horse (and you) will be.

Your personal failure in loading your horse does not mean you can't transport the horse at all. There are two almost surefire alternatives to any of the above-mentioned methods. First, you can hire a professional horse transport service. Be honest and tell them about your inability to load your horse; if they are willing to take on a difficult loader, they are almost sure to be successful in loading. Second, although I rarely recommend the use of drugs on horses for any reason other than treating illness or injury, I believe tranquilizing a difficult horse to get it into the trailer is worthwhile. Tranquilizing will calm the horse and make it more pliable and willing to cooperate. If you can use a tranquilizer one time to give a horse a good, or at least tolerable, experience loading and hauling, you might save yourself future battles and trauma.

If you choose to use a tranquilizer, have your veterinarian administer it, even if you have a helper available that swears he or she has given tranquilizers dozens of times. It's vital to use the right dose on your horse. Too little will be ineffective and too much will cause your horse to be too weak to travel and may even cause it to collapse.

Don't make a habit of tranquilizing. You should only need to use it once or twice. If you are still having trouble loading after this, you may need to recruit the help of a trainer, hire a professional horse-hauling outfit, or avoid hauling the horse.

Hotwalking

The hotwalker consists of a machine base with four overhead arms extending from the base. A horse is attached to a tie, which in turn is attached to the end of an arm. The hotwalker serves to exercise horses at a walking pace by pulling them around a circular path. Hotwalkers are heavily used at racetracks but are also becoming common fixtures at boarding and training stables, as well as private horse facilities.

Most hotwalkers are wired with a switch on a post or wall at the entrance to your hotwalking area. This enables you to turn the machine on and off without having to duck under the arms and use the switches on the motor.

To put a horse on the hotwalker when there are no horses using it already, turn the hotwalker off. Walk your horse up and attach it to a tie, snapping the tie to the bottom ring or inside nosepiece ring of the halter. Use only a nylon halter for hotwalking, as a leather one can break and a rope halter can be pulled off the horse's head.

When you step away from the horse, walk forward quickly so you are leaving the horse behind. This gives the horse minimal chance of kicking you since it would have to wheel all the way around to take aim. Turn on the machine as quickly as possible to prevent the horse from pawing or playing while waiting.

If other horses are already walking, you may still stop the hotwalker, but this makes the other horses restless or rambunctious and they may shuffle around on their ties until they can reach each other to kick. The best method is to keep the walker moving, but this is not the easiest method for you.

Wait for an empty walker tie to come toward you. Approach it and walk beside it until you are at the proper pace. If you fall behind, pull your horse out and start over when it comes around again. Once the horse's head is even with the tie, attach the tie to the halter ring. Walk a few steps with your lead line slack to make sure the horse understands it is under the command of the machine. Unsnap your line and move immediately forward. If there is an unoccupied space, duck out there. If not, you must cross between two horses. Watch the horses and pick the two that appear most docile. Walk quickly between them and out of range. Don't run, wave your arms, or otherwise startle the horses.

To take a horse off a stationary walker, always approach the horse from the front. If the horse turns away from you, back off and reapproach from the front again. Before detaching it from the hotwalker tie, attach your horse to your lead line and hold it firmly so it understands you are in control.

To take a horse off a moving hotwalker, move to the inside of the hotwalker near the motor. Go in through an unoccupied spot if available or cross in front of the most docile horse. Walk toward the horse you want to remove with your hands at your sides so as not to startle it.

Keep your arms near your body and reach quietly toward your horse's jaw. Snap your lead line onto the bottom ring of the halter and begin leading the horse so it understands you have control of it. Unsnap the hotwalker tie and push the horse out, leading it immediately away from the walking path and the other horses.

Always be cautious when moving horses on and off the hotwalker. It is better to be conservative than to get in a hurry and get kicked or struck. If you are fearful of putting a horse on a moving hotwalker, go ahead and turn it off. If

Thoroughbred fillies enjoying a stroll on the hotwalker

you are worried about a safe escape route when all the hotwalker arms are occupied, wait until an extra space opens up or hand walk your horse.

If you use a hotwalker to cool your horse, your horse should cool sufficiently with twenty minutes or a half hour of walking. Don't leave any horse on the walker for more than an hour. Time on the hotwalker is often tedious for the horse and uncomfortable due to the sometimes awkward positioning of the horse's head. If left too long a horse will develop bad habits such as stopping, pulling back, biting the tie, or trying to roll.

If you need to give your horse a drink of water during the cooling process, take it off the walker and out of range of the other horses walking. Don't water a horse attached to the hotwalker even if it is the only horse there. This gives the horse too much freedom to move around and bump or kick you.

If your horse pulls back to stop the hotwalker, you can sit and watch the horse, yell at it constantly, or throw pebbles at it to keep it going. If you do this, you might as well be hand walking it. A better way to keep the horse moving is to have it wear a jaw shank. Wrapping the chain around the nose is the least harmful way of applying the shank, but a chain run from side ring to side ring under the jaw is more effective in pulling the horse forward. Attach the hotwalker tie to the end of the chain instead of the halter so that when the horse pulls back the chain bites it on the nose or under the jaw.

Turning Horses Loose

Turning a horse loose is never difficult, and should not be hazardous or harmful if done properly. I didn't plan to include the techniques until I recently watched a person knocked to the ground and stepped on by a horse he'd just turned loose.

The guy led a horse into a pasture occupied by six other horses, left the gate slightly ajar, and took the halter off his horse while he and his horse had their backs to the gate. One of his horse's pasture mates took the opportunity to try to force its way out the open gate. At the same time, the man's horse wheeled to face the playful charge of another mate, knocking the man to the ground and underneath the hooves of the would-be escapee he was trying to shoo back.

This scene could have been prevented with no real effort. The first rule for turning a horse loose in any situation is to secure the gate or stall door behind you while you are still in control of the horse. You don't need to latch it and probably shouldn't since you need an escape route, but you must close it so it appears firmly shut to the horse or horses.

Before letting go of the horse, turn so you are standing at the gate or door. When you remove the horse's halter you should be one quick step away from exiting in case the horse whirls and kicks as it takes off. This is especially important in a stall, where you will be hopelessly trapped if the horse acts against you once it's loose. If you know or suspect the horse will quickly wheel and kick, you can take extra steps to ensure your safety by standing outside the gate and removing the halter from there. This is not totally hazard free, though, as the horse could bolt away before you've removed the halter. From outside the gate you'll be unable to follow the horse to prevent its escape and will have to enter the enclosure to catch the horse and remove the halter and lead line.

Take extra precautions when other loose horses are hovering around the area where you want to turn your horse loose. A new arrival often sparks the interest of the herd, and they will commonly approach and pester both you and your horse. Your horse may react aggressively or defensively; in either case you'll be stuck in the middle of the fray. To prevent a situation such as this, you can distract the other horses by setting out some food for them away from the gate you will be entering. If this is not convenient or possible, you can chase the herd off by shouting and waving your hands or by throwing clods of dirt at them. This won't work for long with most horses but will give you the time to quickly enter, turn your horse loose, and get out.

There is a display of lunacy I will never understand, but I have seen it too often to believe it to be uncommon and so find it worth mentioning. For some reason, some people are compelled to slap their horses on the rump, with a hand or lead line, as they turn them loose. Is this to tell the horse to go away? Is there a belief that a horse won't know it's been turned loose until it's forced to run off? Perhaps a gesture of affection? I don't know. All I know is that slapping a loose horse on the butt is an invitation to be kicked in the face. No matter how gentle and well trained a horse is, I can't think of any sound reason for slapping it so and many reasons for not.

7

The Beast in Hand

Dealing with Unacceptable Behavior on the Ground

There are certain behaviors that cannot be tolerated while you are handling your horse on the ground. The actions of a spoiled, incorrigible, untrained, or undisciplined horse can be detrimental to your health, lead to injury of the horse, interfere with the well-being of others, or damage equipment.

Unacceptable behaviors include biting, kicking, striking, rearing, bucking, or bolting while being led, and habitually pulling back while tied. None of these behaviors is easy nor impossible to correct.

Biting

Horses bite when they are angry or frustrated but also when playing or bored. You may be bitten just because you are near and convenient or because you've caused your horse pain—perhaps pinched it with the girth or brushed too hard in a sensitive spot. If you turn your back as if to leave a horse you've been petting or feeding, it may attempt to bite you to get your attention back.

Horses don't necessarily single out people for biting, although people *are* common irritants to horses and tend to make themselves so very convenient.

horse is also a common target, but a bored or frustrated horse will sometimes bite walls, fences, any equipment within reach, and even itself.

Stallions, even immature ones, tend to bite more than other horses, often just for fun but with results no less painful or harmful than an act of aggression. Stallion biting is motivated by hormones, testosterone particularly, that bring about aggressive urges. Many stallions that habitually bite become geldings that would never think of biting. In addition, an otherwise gentle gelding or mare injected with testosterone can turn into an aggressive biter overnight.

Biting is a habitual act; the more a horse bites, the stronger its tendency. If you let your horse bite, even gentle playful nips at your shirtsleeve, you are enforcing a habit that will become harder to break with every bite.

Horses can bite quickly, without warning, and this is how they best get away with it. You can't effectively correct a horse by scolding it or swatting it after the fact; you must stop the bite before it happens. If you can make your horse understand it must not bite and any attempt to do so will meet with an instant reprimand before contact is made, it will quickly learn biting is not worth the effort.

The best deterrent for biting is a sharp backhand punch or elbow jab to the horse's muzzle *the moment* it takes a bite at you. This means never turning your back or taking your eyes off a potential biter's face so you can anticipate the bite and act immediately.

I normally would not recommend hitting a horse around the head for any reason, as this tends to cause an animal to become head shy—to flinch away from or resist any handling of its head or ears. The problem with biting is that its source *is* the head of the animal. If you don't reprimand the horse at the mouth, you may not get your message across. This is why technique is so important. If you slap at a horse's face or try to smack it with a forward punch, your extended arm and exaggerated motion will frighten the horse and cause it to throw its head back and away from you. It's likely that your punch will miss its mark and you will have achieved nothing more than a newly head shy animal. If you use an elbow jab or a backhand, your arm stays close to your body and the horse gets little warning. What the horse experiences is an immediate sharp blow directly to its mouth at the moment it reaches to bite. This leads to a direct association of the attempt to bite with the blow.

Don't bother striking out at your horse if you are slow to react or too far away to effectively make your target, even if you received a painful bite and are angry. The reprimand has no effect if it is delivered after the fact, except to confuse and terrorize the horse.

If hitting your horse is unacceptable to you or you don't think you can do it right, you can use restraint methods to prevent the horse from biting. Restraint devices don't teach a horse not to bite, but they do prevent biting and are effective over an indefinite period of time, provided you can get the restraining device on and off the horse without being bitten.

A shank can be used to deter a horse from biting. Nose and jaw shanks are not extremely effective. You must jerk the shank hard to stop a horse from biting, and this will usually cause the horse to throw its head up and shy away from you. A lip chain is most effective on a horse that bites because it occupies the horse and gives you an enormous amount of control over its head movement. You must be firm and confident with the lip chain or it will be ineffective, but you must also be gentle and steady or it can become a weapon of torture. Always consider the lip chain an extreme measure of control. If your horse is not a serious biter or if you are not sure of your ability with the lip chain, don't use it.

If your horse bites only during grooming and saddling, you may be able to avoid the issue just by tying it short enough that it can't reach you. This would be a good time to consider why the horse is biting at you. Are you too rough with the brushes? Are you tightening the cinch or girth too fast? Does your horse have untreated sores or galls? We will get into grooming and saddling techniques in subsequent chapters.

You can also buy a muzzle to prevent horses from biting, similar to those used on dogs. Muzzles come in leather, plastic, or wire mesh and attach to the nose-piece rings of the halter, surrounding the entire muzzle area of the horse. The muzzle should be used only while you are actively working with or around the horse, as the horse cannot eat and has considerable difficulty drinking water while wearing one.

Kicking

A horse will kick out of anger or irritation, as a reaction to pain or fright, and occasionally in play. It will also kick in an attempt to establish dominance; this type kicking is seen not only in a herd setting, but also when dominance has yet to be established between a handler and a horse.

The People Kicker

Biting is a nuisance and can hurt a lot if the horse makes its mark; kicking is pretty much always painful and extremely frightening. Kicking can cause serious injury or death. A horse that kicks must learn to control itself around people.

Some horses will do a fake kick while you are working with them. This is a threat—an experiment in dominance. If you ignore the kick or simply scold your horse for bad manners, even if the blow was obviously not meant to connect, you will reinforce your horse's show of dominance and lead it to believe kicking is an effective way to get what it wants. No aggressive kicking, whether fierce or fake, can be tolerated. Treat any such kick as if your life has been threatened.

A common reaction to kicking is to yell at the horse, slap it, or kick it in the belly. To me, this just isn't good enough. The horse will stop kicking for the moment but will kick again another time. The best way I have found to stop the kicking habit for good is to horrify the horse. You need to make the horse think it died and went to hell.

The first time a horse kicks at you, you won't be prepared. Sharply yell "NO!" or "QUIT!" in your most monstrous tone of voice. If you have control of the horse, either on a lead line or tied, boot the horse in the belly, stepping back toward the horse's front end immediately after. Then prepare yourself for the next kick.

Tie your horse securely in a stall, corral, or inside shedrow. If you use a stall, anchor your tie to something solid in a front corner or on a side wall. Don't use a rubber tie or bungee, and don't allow the horse more than twenty inches of slack.

Get a lawn rake (the kind with flexible tines) and place it within grabbing distance. Work with your horse as usual, grooming and such. Keep yourself between the horse and the exit. When your horse kicks, grab that rake and beat and rake the tine end on the horse's rump and side in a wild manner. Jump up and down and scream and yell as fiercely as you can, keeping yourself a rake's length away. Although the horse should be too terrified to go after you, this will protect you from being kicked.

Continue your wild behavior for about half a minute. This will seem like a *long* time. When you stop, back away, lay the rake down quietly, and wait for your horse to cease all movement and stand facing you. You should have your horse's full attention.

When your horse is standing still, approach quietly and stand with a hand placed firmly on the horse's shoulder. Don't move, pet, or talk to the horse. You are not its friend at this moment—you are establishing your dominance while reassuring it you are no longer an aggressor.

What you can expect from the horse during the rake attack is an all-out effort to get away from you. The horse will hunker down, move as far away as possible, and likely fight the tie. This is why a strong tie and post are essential. If you don't trust the snap on your lead line, tie the line on to the halter, bypassing the snap.

Don't stop your attack just because your horse is putting up a fight. If the horse breaks loose, get out of the enclosure, or if the horse is in a shedrow, get into a stall or tack room. Leave the horse alone until it settles, then catch it and start over with a stronger tie. You may not have to repeat your performance. Your horse may very well have already decided kicking is hazardous and not worth the trouble.

After the attack, expect your horse to cower from you. It should flinch and be nervous when you approach, so you must move quietly and smoothly. Stop if your horse jumps away from you as you approach, then continue your approach as soon as it stops movement again. The horse may flinch when you reach to touch its shoulder. You will do better if you are close enough that your arm isn't fully extended, as an outstretched arm looks more threatening to the horse. When you place your hand on its shoulder, the horse may still flinch. If it begins fighting, back away to a safe distance and stand quietly, waiting it out. Then start over.

This method of kicking deterrence may sound unpleasant and cruel to you. The reason I use it is because I don't have to do it often—one thirty-second session is often enough to cure a horse from kicking for life. Traumatic experiences (and this certainly should traumatize the horse) are instantly ingrained in a horse's memory. If the horse does have a momentary memory lapse in the future and kicks at you, a quick reminder of raising your voice and your rake should be enough to quell any further attempts.

Make sure you have a rake on hand every time you work with your horse until you are fairly certain it won't kick anymore, but never use the rake to tease or threaten the horse. It should only be picked up if the horse actually kicks.

Why a rake? Why not a whip or a rag mop with a floppy, soft end? Well, a rag mop does have a soft and kind-looking end that could be used to discipline the horse. The problem with the mop is that the rag part is *too* soft. You are likely to aim for the horse with the rag ends and wind up hitting the horse with the handle instead, which would be painful and cruel. There is nothing really wrong with using a whip, provided it's long enough to protect you. I choose not to use a whip because I don't want the horse to associate the tool with any other activity. I still want to be able to carry a whip when lunging or otherwise schooling a horse without it cowering in terror. As far as the lawn rake goes, it's not nearly as cruel as it looks or sounds. The tines are flexible and dull edged. They don't do any real physical harm, even when you beat the horse, as long as you touch the horse only with the tines. You can assure yourself of this by using a plastic-tined rake. What really gets through to the horse and makes the rake effective is the noise, the peculiar feeling of the tines bouncing off its hide, and the sight of this big THING coming at it, brandished by some lunatic creature your horse previously thought it could bully around.

If you don't think you're up to this sort of corrective measure—it frightens you, you think it's too harsh, or you don't think you can control your temper or patience enough to do it correctly and humanely—that's okay. But it's not okay to ignore the problem. If you allow your horse to kick even once, it will kick again. It may kick only at you, but there are times when its kick will be directed at an innocent passerby—a young child perhaps. Have a trainer work with your horse to get it over the kicking habit. Another trainer might have different methods than mine that are more acceptable to you. In addition, hiring a trainer gives you the choice to watch or not watch your horse being schooled.

The Horse Kicker

You really can't prevent horses turned out together from kicking each other; this is one of the methods they use to establish and maintain a herd hierarchy. If you have a horse that kicks incessantly or severely, however, you may have to break up the herd to protect the other horses from injury. Separate and isolate the bully. Although you should avoid turning this horse out with others, you can still provide it with some degree of companionship by placing it in a paddock or pasture within sight of or across the fence from other horses.

Additionally, any horse that is getting picked on to the point of being injured or deprived of food should be separated, but in this case it's best to try to find it a meek companion such as a passive horse, a weanling, or a goat. The right companion will not only prevent loneliness, it will help teach the horse stronger social skills.

If a horse kicks at another while under saddle, the rider should discipline the horse by yelling a sharp "No!" at it and smacking it with the reins or a whip on the side of the flank the horse kicked from. This is not terribly effective. It will stop the horse at that moment, but the horse will likely try to kick again.

If a rider knows a horse has a tendency to kick others, he or she should keep the horse in such a position that it can't reach another horse. Many people tie a red ribbon in their horse's tail to let others know they have a kicker. Although this is a good idea, don't think a red ribbon lets you off the hook. Not everyone understands or heeds the warning. It's still your responsibility to keep your kicker away from others.

The Stall Kicker

A horse that kicks in the stall is difficult to correct because it spends so much time alone with nobody around to enforce any sort of discipline. If the horse is a mild kicker and is not causing any harm to the stall or itself, you may choose to ignore the habit. Too often, though, a stall kicker will dent, crack, or knock boards off the wall, tear off its hind shoes, and cause chronic swelling and possibly lameness in the hind legs.

Since stall kicking is so often a habit of boredom or frustration, you might be able to cure the stall kicker by giving it more time turned out or leaving it turned out all the time. If the horse must be kept inside or turning it out does no good, you can let the horse go on kicking but protect it and the stall by padding the walls with gymnasium mats, or you can try to teach it not to kick.

The most effective method I have heard to stop stall kickers is to attach a short, heavy length of chain to a leather dog collar which is then strapped around the horse's hind pastern. It is best to have one on each hind leg. When the horse kicks, the chain will whip around and hit the horse on the hind leg, instantly reprimanding the animal and deterring further kicking.

The chain should not cause injury, but if you are worried, you can attach a length of soft cotton rope to the dog collar instead, with a small, dense rubber ball secured to the end of the rope. Some tack shops also carry ankle rattles—large wooden beads strung on a leather thong. The thongs are placed on a horse's hind pasterns so that when it kicks the beads rattle, bump, and irritate the horse.

If you use any of these methods, stop use only when you're fairly certain the horse has stopped kicking for good. Resume using whatever device you've chosen if the horse resumes its habit.

When using dog collars, make sure the collars aren't so tight they chafe the horse's tender heels. As a preventive measure, you can coat your horse's pasterns with a zinc oxide ointment or bag balm before putting on the collar.

Forgivable Kicking

Although I previously stated no kicking should ever be allowed, there are a few exceptions. Kicking is a defense mechanism for a horse, and if the horse has just cause to defend itself, it is difficult to reprimand the animal for doing so.

There are occasional instances in which a horse will kick at a person and deserve no punishment. For example, a horse might kick out of irritation from a fly or bee; if you're standing near its hindquarters, you might mistakenly believe the kick was aimed at you. A horse will often use a kicking motion to pull a hind hoof away from you if it's not accustomed to having its feet handled or cleaned. You are in a vulnerable, awkward position at this time and might accidentally be kicked in the knee, shin, or thigh.

Certain circumstances created out of carelessness will provoke an otherwise well-behaved horse to kick. If you surprise a horse with sudden noise or motion, the horse's reaction may be to kick out. I was once kicked in the knee by one of my oldest, gentlest geldings when I unexpectedly ripped open the snaps of a raincoat as I was passing behind him through his blind spot.

If you invade your horse's space while it is eating, it may kick in defense of its food supply. Although a horse should understand you are not there to steal its food and kicking a person over food is not really acceptable, certain horses, especially those that have been deprived of food in the past, cannot easily control themselves in such a situation. It is better to recognize this and respect the horse's need for isolation while eating than to make a battle of feeding time.

If you tease your horse by clapping, slapping, or tickling, you will probably eventually get kicked. A horse may also kick if irritated by improper grooming, such as being curried hard at the flank or underbelly.

If you blast a horse with a hose, especially cold water, without fair warning, it may kick out—I'm sure you can imagine what a shock that would be and how a horse, or any creature, may react violently.

If you strike or tickle a horse with a whip, especially if the horse is unaccustomed to a whip or does not see it coming, the horse may kick to rid itself of the irritation. Again, it is questionable whether the horse should be punished for this. Most of the time I will reprimand a horse for kicking at the whip, the exception being if I carelessly surprise a horse that has never been handled with a whip before.

A rider that surprises a horse with a hard jab of the spurs, or one that constantly rakes, pokes, and jabs at a horse's sides with spurs, will often cause a horse to kick. The rider might perceive this as bucking, but the horse is almost always kicking to rid itself of the irritation. I would do the same if my sides were getting poked. I recently witnessed a trail class competition in which several very well-trained horses swished their tails and kicked because of the spur jabs they were receiving as the riders tried to force them through the obstacles up, down, sideways, and backward. Some hung in there quite a while before they were irritated to the point of kicking.

Treatment of a painful injury can cause an otherwise docile horse to kick, especially if the injury is new and the horse is suffering from trauma. In a case such as this, a horse may not even recognize its regular handler, much less consider discipline and manners.

Finally, as I mentioned before, if you slap a horse on the rump as you turn it loose, you might as well put a sign around your neck reading "KICK ME!"

Striking

Striking occurs when a horse throws a front leg forward in a deliberate attempt to strike something. Striking is often done as a horse rears, but a horse can also strike quite effectively from a standing position. Striking is most commonly a trait of stallions and ungelded colts, probably because striking is considered an act of challenge—an invitation to fight. I have rarely seen a gelding strike; a gelding that does strike is usually either a recently gelded colt still under hormonal influences or a young gelding in play with another of its kind. Mares and fillies are known to strike, most commonly when greeting an unfamiliar horse or facing off a stallion. It is far more common for any horse to strike out at another horse than it is for one to strike a person, but if a horse does strike at you, you can be severely injured, so this nasty behavior cannot be ignored.

To prevent yourself from being struck, the first thing you want to do is make a habit of never standing or walking directly in front of a horse, as this is the direction in which the horse will strike out. A deliberate strike from a horse should be considered an act of aggression or a test of dominance; it's no different than kicking except it's done with the front legs.

You can often tell when a horse is about to strike, and this can help you stop the action before it takes place. Signs to look for are a raised head and flinching nose or an arched neck and overly bold expression, as if the horse is challenging you (it probably is). The horse will often be light on the front—squatted down slightly in the hindquarters and prancy or high-stepping with the forelegs (also often a prelude to rearing).

When a horse strikes at you, your best reaction—besides getting out of the way—is to yell sharply, "NO!" or "QUIT!" Take a good hold of its head by the lead or tie line and slap the horse under the belly with an open hand, pulling its head toward you in order to push its hindquarters away and prevent yourself from being kicked. This should stop the horse from striking momentarily, but don't expect such a reprimand to cure the horse. In the case of striking, deterrence is often more effective than discipline in creating a safe animal.

If you suspect your horse might strike, a pretty effective deterrent can be found in the lead shank. If the horse is tied, use your lead shank as a second line. If the lead shank is worn around the horse's nose, yank on the shank line sharply when the horse strikes while simultaneously stepping back to the side and slapping the horse under the belly. This action will pull the horse's head down and in toward you while your slap will turn and raise its hindquarters, forcing the horse's front legs down to discourage further striking or rearing.

If you choose to use a lip chain to deter your striker, the moment your horse strikes or you sense it's preparing to, tighten the pressure against the lip chain as you yell "No!" then pull the horse's head in toward your chest and slap the horse. As long as your horse is wearing a lip chain, however, you may never need to discipline it in any way. A lip chain is a rather humbling device and will often deter a horse from ever trying to strike.

Rearing

Rearing occurs when a horse stands on its hind legs. A horse that rears may simply hop straight legged a few inches off the ground in front, or may rise so high that you are staring at the bottom of its hooves. In extreme cases, a horse will rear so violently as to throw itself backward—this is actually called flipping. Although any horse may rear, rearing, like striking, is most common among stallions. You could avoid the need to ever deal with rearing and striking by simply avoiding stallions or gelding your colt early.

If a horse that normally wouldn't do so rears because something frightened or startled it or you've been severe and heavy-handed on a shank, there may be no need to discipline the horse; it is acting instinctively, albeit in an exaggerated manner, to defend itself from an unexpected or painful experience. If such a horse is tied, back out of harm's way and try to calm it with your voice. Rearing while tied often leads a horse to fight to free itself. Stand back and let the horse fight the tie until it gives up. If you are leading the horse when it rears, let as much slack out of the line as you can so you can get out of range of the horse's front legs. Follow the horse back, moving smoothly and talking soothingly until the horse calms and stops. If the sight of flailing hooves frightens you, don't hesitate to turn the horse loose; this is preferable to being struck on the head or knocked down.

If your horse rears out of play, aggressiveness, or to try to intimidate you, you need to deal with the rearing in a strict manner so it won't become a habit. Reactions in a rearing horse are a bit different than those of a striker; if you try to correct the horse by jerking on a shank, yelling, or slapping at it, especially from the front, you will likely cause it to rear again or try to pull away from you.

Your best bet for preventing rearing is to use a lip chain whenever handling the horse. If the horse is a confirmed rearer (if it has reared with you more than once), put the lip chain on it every time you handle the horse or lead it. Use a firm, steady grip so the horse can't forget the chain is there. If your horse has the tenacity to try to rear while wearing the lip chain, tighten your hold, putting extra pressure on the horse's gum until you've gained your horse's attention and cooperation.

If using a lip chain on a regular basis doesn't appeal to you, or if your horse rears despite the lip chain and you are positive you've been strict enough with the shank, get rid of the horse. Rearing is not a common habit for a normal, decently trained horse and there is no reason for you to put up with such vile, unnecessary behavior.

A stallion rearing in play. The danger is in the flailing legs and hooves.

Frolicking

Horses that dance, buck, and kick up while being led are generally more excited or playful than aggressive and are simply releasing pent-up energy. A good way to prevent this behavior is to give your horse more exercise or room to play on its own time. If, however, you must lead around a horse that's still so happy it can't keep its feet on the ground, you will do best to resort to the lead shank for control and deterrence.

A chain around the nose should be enough to remind your horse of its manners. When the horse begins to jump around, yell sharply and jerk down quickly with the lead line. Rattle the line off and on as a reminder. If your horse doesn't yield to the nose shank, switch to a lip chain. As usual, hold the line so the chain is firm against the horse's gum. If the horse starts to buck, tighten the shank, pulling the horse's head down and toward you. The closer the horse's head is to your body, the less freedom of movement you will allow it. If your horse continues to try to buck, you are either being too meek with the lip chain or this is far too much horse for you.

Bolting or Pulling Back

If a horse bolts away from you while you are leading it or pulls back on its tie because something truly startled it, you can forgive the horse. If, however, your horse bolts or pulls back because it has figured out this is a good way to get loose, you must quickly convince the horse it cannot get away with this behavior and attempts to get away will only result in grief.

Bolting

It's easy for a horse to get loose if it bolts unexpectedly. A horse's lightning-fast reflexes enable it to move from a standstill or dull plod to an out-and-out rampage with no warning whatsoever. If you are caught unaware, the line will be pulled through your hand and burn your palms. Even if you are able to keep a good grip on the line, you can be jerked hard enough to injure your shoulder or knock you off your feet. Again, the lead shank is the most effective deterrent.

When using a lead shank on a horse you believe might bolt, keep a firm grip on the lead line with both hands. The shank won't work if you let go of the line. When the horse bolts, whether wearing a nose shank or a lip chain, the chain will bite the horse hard as it hits the end of the slack. This should stop your horse momentarily, long enough for you to give the nose shank a couple of sharp yanks or increase pressure on the lip chain to stop the horse from pulling away farther. If you've startled or frightened the horse by not giving in as it expected, your horse might continue to back or pull away from you, even against the pressure of the shank. If this happens, let out as much slack as possible and follow the horse. Try to aim the horse for the nearest fence or wall to stop its backward or sideways movement.

Practice leading your horse in an enclosed area near a wall or fence so the horse's bolting space is limited. You will need to gradually move away from fences and walls because the horse will be just as aware as you are of the limited space and may resume its attempts at bolting once you are in an open area.

Once you start using a shank on a habitual bolter, use it every time you lead the horse. The horse will know when you've taken the chain off, and if the animal is crafty enough to try to get loose by bolting in the first place, it will certainly be crafty enough to try again once it feels the resistance is no longer there.

Pulling Back

It only takes one episode of pulling back against a tie and breaking loose for a determined horse to form a habit. In this case you do not want to use any kind of chain shank to correct the horse since the chain will likely break with the force. If the chain does not break (and even if it does) it can injure the horse by fracturing facial bones or cutting and bruising flesh.

To cure a horse from pulling back to free itself, you must create a situation in which it is impossible for the horse to succeed. Find something stout to tie the horse to that absolutely won't break or bend. A heavy post, such as a railroad tie set firmly into the ground or a sturdy tree trunk, is ideal. A four-by-four post or a steel chain-link fence post will not be strong enough. Make sure any vertical post or trunk has a notch, horizontal board, branch, or peg you can set your tie above to keep your tie line from dropping to the ground. If you prefer a cross-tie over a straight tie, tie your lines around the posts only; do not snap or tie to bolts to anchor your horse.

Use a nylon halter. Adjust it on your horse's head tight enough so it can't be pulled over the ears (test it by trying to pull it over yourself), but not so tight that it squeezes the horse's windpipe or you can't get your hand under it. Use rope of at least one-inch diameter with no snaps. Tie a secure knot under your horse's jaw at, but not through, the bottom ring, or at the side rings for a cross-tie. Tie the other end of the rope, using a quick-release knot, to the anchoring post five to six feet above the ground, leaving no more than two feet of slack in the line for a straight tie, and almost no slack for a cross-tie.

Let the horse stand tied, but stick around and watch. Keep a pocketknife handy in case you need to cut the horse free. When and if the horse pulls back, don't interfere. Let the horse fight it out with the tie until the horse gives in to it, no matter how ugly the struggle appears. Release the horse only if it gets down on the ground and can't get back up (its head would be stretched up because of the tie) or somehow gets a leg caught over the rope. It may take a few struggles, but the horse will eventually accept that it can't get loose by pulling back.

If your horse somehow breaks free during the struggle, don't let yourself give in to the belief that your horse cannot be taught to tie. You've obviously not used strong enough equipment or anchors or have adjusted the halter too loose on your horse's head. Make some improvements and try again. Only if a horse out-and-out tries to kill itself fighting would I give up on trying to teach it to tie. It is just too hard to work with a horse if you feel you can't let it stand tied safely.

I have seen horses schooled to tie by wrapping a rope around the horse's barrel and running the rope through the horse's front legs and the halter rings to the tying anchor. This method ensures the horse can't get loose since it simply cannot pull the rope off in this position. The problem I have found with this method is that in a real struggle the rope will often cause severe burns under the horse's elbows and chest, even if the rope is padded. In addition, it is unrealistic to think you will use this method every time you tie your horse, so the horse must still be taught at some time to give in to pressure from the halter only.

Don't get lazy in the future about tying your horse, even if it no longer shows signs of pulling back. Always tie your horse, and for that matter any horse you work with, to a solid anchor with a short, strong tie line and a nylon halter.

Vices

There is a significant difference between misbehavior and vices. I consider a vice a form of habitual behavior that is not affected by training or handling. A vice may be irritating to you or harmful to the horse, but it is not a deliberate thwarting of learned rules.

Cribbing

Cribbing is an odd little habit unique to horses. A cribber will latch on with its teeth to something firm, such as a board, rail, or feed tub rim, and will suck air in great heaves into its belly. The horse will normally belch back some of the air, but a considerable amount of air will remain in its stomach as gas to be passed or trapped in the intestines.

Cribbing is potentially harmful to a horse in three ways. First, if the excess air that is swallowed reaches the intestinal tract it may be trapped, leading to painful distention and symptoms of colic. Most commonly, the gas eventually makes its way through, but on rare occasions surgery is required to relieve the gas. Second, a chronic cribber will, with time, wear its front teeth down to the nubbins. Third, a serious cribber will bypass eating for cribbing and will lose condition.

You cannot teach a horse not to crib because you cannot enforce rules when you're not around. There is a small possibility that you can stop the habit early on. If cribbing develops out of boredom or frustration when the horse is stalled, turning the horse out on pasture could cure the habit, as the horse will occupy its time more favorably with grazing and play. A determined cribber, though, will crib as heartily in a pasture setting as it will in a stall.

Truly the most effective method for preventing cribbing is to use restraint. A horse must arch and expand its throat in order to create an airway into its belly; it can't do this while wearing a well-fitted cribbing strap. There are several types of cribbing straps, all with the same purpose. The cribbing strap lies just behind the ears and is fitted tight against the throat. The throatpiece of the strap may be a simple leather thong or a jointed aluminum cup molded to the shape of the horse's windpipe. A severe cribbing strap will have bumps or short, blunt prongs set against the throat to cause the horse pain if it attempts to swell its throat.

You can also try removing any horizontal objects from the horse's stall that the horse might use to crib against. This would mean barring or boarding up ledges, door tops, and partial walls and removing food and water containers. This can be expensive and inconvenient and not all that effective. A creative cribber will press its teeth against a vertical wall to crib if nothing better is available. Besides, if cribbing stems from the boredom or frustration of confinement, taking away the horse's ability to eat and drink at will or hang its head out the door or over a wall will only increase the horse's neuroticism.

Wood Chewing

Wood chewing should not be mistaken for cribbing; they are completely different vices. A horse will chew wood out of boredom, to satisfy the urge to graze, or because it is starved and can find nothing else to eat.

Eating wood is not good for your horse. A horse will often get slivers in its mouth or throat from eating wood, which will become infected and abscess if not removed. The wood has no nutritional value for a horse and is hard to digest. Pieces of wood trapped in the intestines can cause a life-threatening impaction. Even if your horse is lucky enough to escape harm by ingestion, your stable and fences will suffer, along with your pocketbook.

If your horse chews wood because it is hungry, *please* increase its food supply. If your horse needs more grazing time, turn it out to pasture more often or supplement its hay or grass supply with a dry grass hay, which takes a good amount of time to eat but won't bloat or overfatten your horse.

There are several things you can do to prevent a horse from chewing wood. You can cover the tops of your fence boards, stall walls, and doors with a metal rim and attach sheet metal to the walls just outside your stall doors. You can paint a nasty-tasting solution on your wood surfaces. Most tack supply or feed stores have such a product. You can string a line of electrified wire or tape just inside your fences to prevent your horse from touching the wood. You can also, of course, avoid the problem altogether with the use of nonwood products for fencing and gate materials.

Pawing, Pacing, Weaving

Horses that paw, pace, or weave are almost exclusively stall-bound horses. These vices are developed out of boredom, frustration, loneliness, and possibly claustrophobia. Giving a horse a permanent or daily turn out can often stop these habits instantly, but they commonly return when a horse is returned to a stall.

Horses most often paw when they want something. Whether it is attention, food, or freedom, the pawing usually stops when the horse receives what it wants. If you are unwilling or unable to satisfy your horse's needs or wants, or it continues to paw just for the pleasure of it, you can prevent most damage by placing heavy rubber mats in its standing area. I've known horsepeople to hobble horses to prevent pawing, but I believe this is cruel and unnecessary. It's best just to improve the horse's conditions and to lay mats.

Pacing and weaving are neurotic behaviors wherein a horse will either walk circles in the stall or a repeated back-and-forth pattern along a fence line (pacing), or will stand and sway, swinging its head and shifting from one front foot to the other (weaving). These behaviors can go on for hours at a time and will often cause a horse to lose weight, unnecessarily wear down its shoes, and lead to stress injuries.

The surest cure for pacing and weaving is to get the horse out of a stall and into a pasture or paddock and give it a companion—the more the better. This will not stop all horses from pacing and weaving but works for most, although some will take weeks to readjust and forget their neurotic behavior.

If a pacer or weaver must be kept in a stall, you may be able to control the vice by giving the horse a small goat or pony to share its stall. If this is not possible, a window opened into an adjoining stall may provide some companionship and comfort. I have also seen pacers and weavers hobbled, tied for hours on end, or kept in stalls packed with as many as five bound bales of straw to prevent movement—all of which are cruel and will only add to the horse's distress, which was the cause of the vice in the first place.

Bucket Bumping

Bucket bumping is, again, almost exclusively a stall problem. The small space and lack of activity make feed tubs and buckets handy toys and awkward obstacles. A large or clumsy horse may continually bump into its bucket. A playful or bored horse may paw at, chew on, or bump its buckets just for fun. A hungry horse may rattle its bucket in the hope of magically bringing forth some fresh grain. Other times a horse will use a bucket or feed tub to rub against or lean back on.

Bucket bumping can be noisy and disruptive, can cause injury to your horse if the bucket has sharp edges or exposed bolts or screws, or can damage or destroy your buckets. Horses also have been known to poop in their buckets while leaning or rubbing against them and contaminate their food and water supplies.

Try building a corner feeder out of a triangular piece of plywood rimmed with one-by-fours. You can also hang a corner-shaped bucket and nail a one-by-four to the walls across the front of the bucket to prevent it from being lifted or bumped. Perhaps the most effective method is to remove the buckets completely from the stall and hang them just outside the door within easy reach of the horse.

By the way, if your horse is using its bucket to scratch its hind end or tail against, you need to find out what's causing the incessant itching, as this is not natural for a horse. Shedding, baths, and drying mud or sweat can cause itching, but most often itching is a result of worm, lice, or mite infestation.

∩ ∩

I have spoken throughout this chapter of problems concerning misbehavior on the part of the horse. To be fair to the horse, I must say there are some human behaviors that are also unacceptable and may cause a horse to develop bad habits and a poor, unmannerly temperament. Most horses are not deliberately bad—they develop bad habits and manners because of the treatment and handling they receive. Whether this treatment is exaggerated kindness, cruelty, or simple unthoughtfulness, a horse's behavior cannot be changed permanently unless the handler is willing and able to assess his or her own behavior and make any necessary changes. A hot, quick temper, impatience, ignorance, laziness, slovenliness, poor timing, cutting corners, and disregarding safety rules and the basic needs of the horse all have detrimental effects on the quality of a person's horsemanship and the quality of the horse's behavior. This is true not only for ground handling, but for all phases of horsemanship.

8

Brushes and Bubbles

The Ways and Whys of Grooming and Bathing a Horse

Grooming is essential in order to keep your horse's coat and hooves clean and its mane and tail detangled. If done routinely, it is also an excellent opportunity to keep an eye on your horse's condition and quickly discover any skin or hoof problems, cuts, infections, or swelling. This is not all that grooming is good for.

The time you spend grooming your horse is time in which you will get to know one another and become familiar with each other's body language and signals. Proper, conscientious grooming done with patience and kindness can turn a distrustful horse into a friend and can increase your confidence in handling horses.

Preparations for Grooming

Supplies

Before beginning, assemble the supplies and grooming tools you will need so you will not run back and forth gathering as you go. Use a bucket or a plastic box with a handle to carry your supplies and keep them out of the dirt and bedding.

Ideally, each horse should have its own set of clean brushes and rub rags to help prevent the spread of skin diseases, lice, and mites. If this is not possible, clean any shared brushes and rags in a bleach solution each day they are used, no matter how healthy the horses you are grooming appear to be.

The basic ingredients of your grooming box should include a soft-bristled brush, a stiff-bristled brush, a rubber curry, a mane and tail curry or comb, a hoof pick, hoof brush, and rag. You will surely add to this list as you see the need with items such as hoof ointment, fly wipe, and rubbing alcohol.

Tying

Your horse should be tied or cross-tied securely for your grooming session. Never groom a horse that isn't tied. You will wind up following the horse around as it moves at will, and if you are in a large enclosure the horse might just leave you. Grooming a loose horse also sets you up to be kicked, stepped on, bitten, or trapped against a wall or in a corner. In short, you are inviting mishap and injury.

Tying the horse while grooming also keeps the horse from pawing at, chewing on, or taking things out of your brush bucket. I saw a woman badly injured after an untied horse she was brushing pulled a rub rag out of her brush box with its teeth and became frightened of the rag waving in the air. The horse didn't think to drop the rag but panicked and flailed around the stall until it had trampled its groom.

When moving around the horse you are grooming, use caution never to startle it, which could cause a defensive and violent reaction. A horse may be startled if you bump it suddenly, make an unexpected noise, touch it without warning, or approach from its blind spot.

Safety Rules

When working closely with a horse, try to keep one hand on it at all times and speak softly and constantly to the horse. This will help your horse keep track of you and reassure it as to your intentions.

When grooming the head, tail, or hindquarters always stand to the side very close to the horse. Never get in front of the horse where you may be bumped, shoved, or struck, and never stand behind the horse where you may be kicked or where the horse cannot see you.

When crossing to the opposite side of your horse, never try to go around the front end by ducking under the horse's neck. Again, you will be setting yourself up to be knocked over, bumped on the head, or struck in this position. Nor should you walk around the back of the horse with any distance between you and it. This places you in the horse's blind spot where any noise you make could cause the horse to try to move away from you or kick at you.

The safest way to cross to the other side of a horse is to pass closely behind it. Stand at the horse's flank, facing its rear. Place your near hand on top of the horse's rump and cross behind the horse right up against its tail and hocks. Keep your hand on the horse's rump until you have crossed to the other side, allowing your outstretched arm to brush along the rump and tail. This gives the horse an indication of where you are even when you pass through its blind spot.

Crossing so close to a horse's hind legs may seem foolish to you, but is actually the safest method of walking behind a horse. When you are close enough

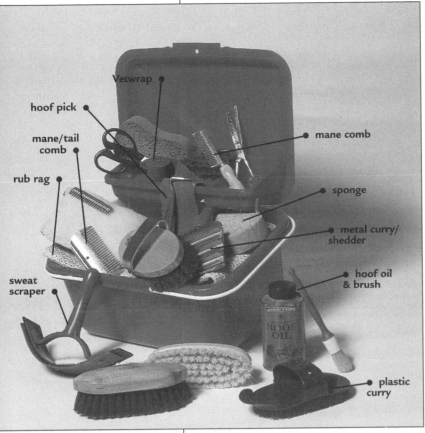

hoof pick

mane/tail comb

rub rag

sweat scraper

Vetwrap

mane comb

sponge

metal curry/ shedder

hoof oil & brush

plastic curry

Grooming supplies

to brush up against the horse's hocks it cannot easily kick out at you, as your legs will be in the way and the horse doesn't have the room or freedom to lift a hind leg without interference.

Off and on you will need to move your horse while grooming or bathing it—for instance, if your horse is standing crowded against a wall. You'll have no luck if you try to pull the horse over by the tail—it will resist and pull away from you. Shoving the horse is also rather pointless; horses have a tendency to resist being pushed and will usually push back rather than move in the direction you want. You will need to get on the off side of the horse if there is room, or behind it close to its hindquarters if there's no space. Raise your hand so your horse can see it, snap your fingers, and chirp or cluck to the horse. If it doesn't move over, continue clucking and wave your hand toward the horse's hindquarters to shoo the horse. If you still get no response, lightly slap the horse on the rump, again chirping, to move the horse over. Once the horse understands what you want, simply chirping and raising your hand will usually convince it to move, no matter where you're standing.

Hoof Care

Everyone has his or her preferred sequence for grooming tasks, and the sequence is really not important. I like to get the least pleasant jobs out of the way first, so I always start with hoof care.

The first thing you must do is pick up your horse's foot. Start with a front leg. Stand near the horse facing toward the rear. Run your near hand from your horse's shoulder down the leg to the ankle; grip the back of the horse's ankle at the fetlock and pull up, pressing your shoulder against the horse to set its weight on the off side.

If your horse refuses to lift its foot, first try squeezing the ankle with your fingers as you pull up. If you get no response, press against the backside of the horse's knee with your near hand as you try to lift at the ankle or pastern with your other hand. If you've still had no success, take your hoof pick and press (don't jab!) the pick end into the horse's fetlock just below the ankle until the

Picking dirt out of a hoof

horse picks up its foot. Use the lightest pressure you can get away with when using the pick to urge a horse to lift its foot—a hard jab or grinding pressure will be painful and cause the horse to overreact by flinching away or perhaps hitting you with a quickly raised hoof.

Lift the back hooves in the same manner, standing at your horse's flank and running your hand from rump to fetlock. You run your hand down the leg, rather than simply reaching down and grabbing the ankle, to avoid surprising the horse and causing it to flinch, kick, or strike out.

Be conscious of where you stand when you are working with a horse's hind foot. It's tempting to stand far enough back to best see what you are doing, but that's a great way to get kicked in the face. Your body should remain at the horse's flank and your head and shoulders should stay level with your horse's raised hock. If you rest the hoof in the palm of one hand, you will place it at a visible angle.

Once in a while a horse will try to set its foot back down after you've lifted it. This is a good time to double-check that you are holding your horse's leg at a comfortable angle. If you are overextending a joint or causing the horse to lose its balance, it may have good reason for wanting to set its foot on the ground. If this is not the case, your horse must learn to stand quietly and cooperate while you clean its hooves. Not only will it make your task simpler and quicker, it will also teach your horse manners that will be appreciated the next time your farrier visits.

If your horse tries to pull its foot away from you, hold the foot firmly with both hands as long as it is comfortable to do so, and speak sharply to the horse to let it know it's misbehaving. If the horse is jerking you off your feet or you feel you might be kicked or struck, let go. Start over and make sure the horse is standing with no resistance before you begin to clean the hoof. Be patient and don't resort to yelling or slapping at the horse because you are in a vulnerable position if the horse jumps. I once slapped a filly under the belly after she'd yanked her foot away from me three times in a row. She promptly reared and stuck a toe grab from her shoe into my skull.

If after some effort you've failed to get your horse to cooperate and hold its foot up quietly, ask someone to hold the horse for you, using a shank if necessary.

Be gentle with the pick while you are cleaning the bottom of the hoof, as some areas are quite sensitive. Hold the pick facing away from you and pick from heel to toe to prevent poking yourself or your horse with the hoof pick if it slips. Pick the bulk of the material out of the hoof gently until you can see the outline of the frog. Remove any matter in the cracks and crevices in and around the frog (the spongy, triangular part of the sole). The frog is tender, so make sure you don't jab it or press too hard with the pick.

Use a hoof brush to polish off the bottom and outside of the hoof. If mud has caked and dried on the outside, you may need to use the side of your hoof pick to scrape it off. Don't ignore the mud, as it will promote drying of the hooves.

It is never a bad idea to use hoof dressing or ointment. Hoof dressing will help keep the hoof supple and resistant to cracks and chips. You will get results by painting your horse's hooves once a week or so, but once a day is useful in an especially dry or muddy environment. Paint the entire hoof top to bottom, including the coronet band at the hairline and the bulbs of the heel.

While cleaning feet, take time to inspect the hoof for cracks, punctures, loose nails, or excessive wear on the shoe—all of which mean it's time to call your horseshoer.

If your horse is kept in a soggy environment, watch out for fungal growth (thrush) or rot on the bottom of the foot; oftentimes you'll first detect it by a rank and unusual smell emitting from the sole of the hoof. Consult your veterinarian or horseshoer if you suspect you've found fungus or rot. He or she can advise you on how to treat the hoof.

As long as you've got the hoof lifted, take a moment to inspect your horse's pastern area. Extend your horse's foot at the ankle and examine the back of the pastern and heel area for any scabs or raw skin, which indicate the development of scratches (greasy heel). Rub with your thumbs if necessary to feel for scabs hidden among the hairs. If any irritation is present, clean the area daily with hydrogen peroxide and apply a zinc oxide ointment or bag balm until it clears up. Scratches are usually caused by riding in wet sand or mud or allowing a horse to stand in muck or urine-soaked bedding. This condition can be prevented by cleaning and drying your horse's legs down to the hooves on a regular basis, especially after riding, and by providing clean, dry bedding in your horse's stable area.

Tail and Mane

Tail

Tails are made up of coarse, wiry hairs that tangle easily and stubbornly, so regular combing is necessary to keep them nice looking and manageable. If the tail hairs are fine, a metal comb may be sufficient for grooming. If the tail is thick, ropy, or has been neglected, you will have an easier time with a plastic curry.

Most horses enjoy having their tails combed, as long as they are not being yanked. Stand to the side of your horse's rump, never behind the horse in easy kicking range. Hold a handful of tail hairs in one hand just below the tailbone. Comb out this section, pulling against your hand, *not* the tailbone. Pick up another handful and comb this out the same way, repeating this procedure until the entire tail is tangle free. Always comb out away from your horse so you don't accidentally whack the horse on the hind legs with the comb or curry.

If the tail has been neglected and become a mass of tangled ropes or been matted with cockleburs, manure, or briars, you will be combing all day unless you get help. Don't get frustrated and cut your horse's tail off—there is actually an easy way to tame the worst of tails. First, if the tail is caked with manure or mud, wet it and scrub it clean with a stiff, soapy brush—dish detergent works best to cut through the filth. Next, to make the tangles practically fall out by themselves, apply an equine coat-shine product. Most of these products come in spray containers. Be certain your horse doesn't mind spray before going at its tail, or you may surprise the horse into kicking. Spray the bottle or can from a safe distance to see if your horse reacts. If the horse doesn't seem bothered, move closer and spray toward the ground. If your horse is calm, spray close into the tail but away from the horse, until the hairs are saturated.

If your horse is frightened, spray the liquid on a brush or sponge and apply it in this manner. You can also dilute the solution in water and pour it on the tail. Once the tail is tangle free, use your curry or comb as instructed. The tail should comb out like a dream for weeks after application. This method of detangling may seem rather expensive, but it saves much time and frustration and only needs to be done once if you keep up your grooming practices in the future.

Although some people pull or trim tails to thin and shorten them for fashion purposes, I recommend letting the tail grow to its natural length. Unless you can guarantee a completely fly-free environment, it's only fair to allow a horse to defend itself against flies with the help of a thick, long tail.

Mane

The mane is also coarse and can tangle easily but is much easier to comb out because it is shorter and not quite as thick. If it's really thick and tangled, use a plastic curry and a detangling product. Otherwise, use a metal comb for a more meticulous finished look.

Manes are often trimmed and thinned to a desired length through a process called pulling. This is generally done for aesthetic purposes but can be done to keep a performance rider's hands from becoming entangled. To pull a mane, hold a small section of the longest strands in one hand (no more strands than the thickness of a finger), rat back the surrounding hairs with a comb, then pull out the strands you are left holding. Repeat this procedure with subsequent long strands until the mane has been shortened to the desired length.

Be warned that many horses don't like having their manes pulled and will fight to stop you. If it's important for you to pull the mane of an uncooperative horse, you may need someone to hold it for you, and the horse will probably need to wear a lip chain or twitch to keep it from moving its head or resisting in any other way.

A bridlepath is often cut or shaved in a horse's mane just behind the poll to keep the bridle and halter from tangling in the mane and to make the horse look fashionable. A bridlepath can also work to enhance a horse's sensitivity to the poll pressure of the bridle.

Different lengths of bridlepaths are considered appropriate for different breeds or riding and showing styles. For utility purposes the bridlepath need only be about two inches long, just long enough for the crownpiece of a halter or bridle to lay along. If you keep the mane combed and brushed out of the way while bridling and haltering, there's really no need to cut a bridlepath.

The forelock is your horse's bangs—the part of the mane that covers the poll and the horse's forehead. This area is sensitive on a horse, so be gentle when combing the forelock. You may find your horse loves the gentle combing and will lower its head complacently for you.

It is generally considered unfashionable to cut or pull the forelock; this also takes away the horse's only natural protection against flies on its face or in its eyes. Unless the forelock has become hopelessly matted or infested with lice, let it grow naturally.

Roaching is done to some manes for looks, easy maintenance, or to treat lice infestation. Roaching consists of shaving or clipping the mane short, usually leaving the forelock and hair over the withers intact. At times everything is clipped off, especially if there are lice present since it is easier to treat and rid a horse of lice if there's no mane for the pests to burrow in.

Don't roach your horse's mane to cool it off in hot weather. Your efforts will be counterproductive since the mane actually provides the horse with some shade and helps fend off flies, which are rampant in heat.

Before you decide to roach, be sure this is really what you want to do. A mane takes ages to grow out from a roach job and will stand on end and look thick and frumpy during the growing-out process. Furthermore, roaching may seem low maintenance on a daily basis since there is no mane to comb, but it must be clipped frequently to keep it short enough to look good.

Brushing

A complete body grooming session begins with the rubber curry, which will loosen dried sweat, mud, and caked-on dirt. It will also pull loose or shedded hair to the surface for removal. The stiff body brush is then used to remove all the crud the curry loosened, and the soft brush will polish the coat. Further polishing is done with a rag, rubber mit, or vacuum.

A clean or very smooth thin-coated horse may not need to be curried and could resent the harder force of the curry on its sensitive skin. In this case, the curry, and perhaps the stiff brush, can be bypassed.

Begin currying at the top of your horse's neck, near the ears. Don't reach up suddenly with an outstretched hand; this might frighten the horse and make it flinch away from you. Curry the horse with small, circular motions, pressing the curry against the horse but not jabbing at it. The rubber curry should not hurt the horse, so back off if your horse flinches or tries to move away from the pressure.

Work the curry from neck to rump, always standing at your horse's side. You should remain positioned between the horse's head and the curry to best protect yourself from being kicked.

Be very gentle when currying your horse's flanks, girth, and belly, which are sensitive areas. Rather than currying in a circular motion, follow the pattern of the hair. If the horse gets twitchy while you curry these areas, quit and use a softer brush on them later. Don't use the curry at all on your horse's face or legs, as the hair is thinner there and the skin too sensitive.

Once you've curried your horse, it will probably look like a fluffed up dust ball. You can lay the hair flat and get rid of most of the dust and crud with a stiff body brush. Use this brush on the neck, body, and upper legs, working back and following the pattern of hair growth. Avoid the face and lower legs with the stiff brush.

The soft brush is used to polish the coat and brush the sensitive areas you've been avoiding, such as the face, lower legs, underbelly, and inside haunches. I always start brushing at the head while the brush is its cleanest, then work back, finishing with the lower legs all the way down to the hooves.

A gentle touch while brushing the face will encourage cooperation. Many horses find having their faces brushed a pleasurable experience; others that have been handled roughly become quite head shy when they see the brush coming. Move quietly, follow the hair pattern, avoid bumping the ears or eyes, and avoid brushing dust into your horse's eyes. While you are at the head, take time to feel under the throat, jaw, and chin strap area to check for any scabs or swelling.

Although a soft brush is usually sufficient to make your horse shine, many people like to finish their horses with a rub rag or rubber mit to really make them glow. The rag or mit can be used over all parts of a horse, again following the hair pattern. Stick with hand polishing—avoid using coat-shine products for normal grooming, as they make the coat and anything that touches it slippery to the touch. If hand grooming isn't enough to make your horse absolutely glisten, try vacuuming the horse's coat with a portable handheld vacuum. Be prepared for a horse unfamiliar with this grooming method to offer some resistance.

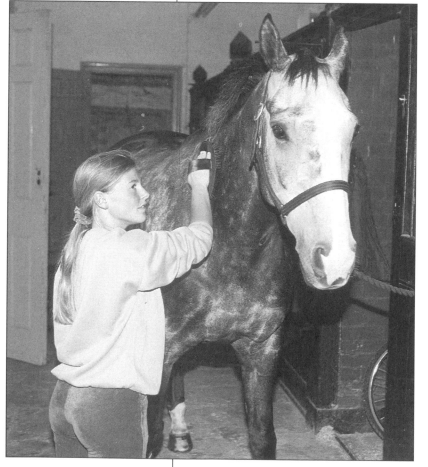

Begin brushing at the head and work back, brushing with the hair pattern.

Remember to use your grooming time to look for any nicks, scrapes, bumps, swelling, or rashes. Don't ignore hidden areas such as the folds under the elbows, the hollow under the jaw, and the genitals.

Pay close attention to the legs as you groom; some leg problems don't show in the form of lameness. A sound leg should be cold to the touch and tight, with the skin stretched over the bones and tendons and no detectable lumps or squishy spots. The more often you inspect your horse's legs, the more familiar you will become with the normal, healthy anatomy, which will enable you to detect a problem early. Consult your vet if anything unusual shows up on your horse's legs in the form of heat, swelling, or lumps.

Bathing

Preparation
As with any other grooming practice, assemble your bathing supplies before you present your horse for its bath. You will need a five-gallon bucket filled with warm, soapy water. You can use a commercial horse shampoo, bubble bath, or mild detergent. The bucket should contain a large, clean sponge. You will also need a sweat scraper to scrape excess water off the horse and enable it to dry quickly. Hang the scraper on a peg within easy reach or place it in your wash bucket.

You can bathe a horse without a hose but will do a more thorough job with one. If possible, connect your hose to hot and cold taps so you can use warm water to spray your horse. This will be greatly appreciated and will give your horse more enticement to cooperate. I recommend using an adjustable spray attachment on your hose so that once you've turned on the spigots you can leave them on without water running everywhere. This also gives you options for the force of spray you will use.

If you lay the hose on the ground, keep it off to the side. A horse will easily puncture a hose by stepping on it and may get tangled in it. The ideal way to hang a hose where it won't be underfoot would be to attach it to a swinging metal arm mounted well above the horse's head. This is similar to what is used at a self-service car wash.

If you plan to blanket your horse after bathing, hang your blanket within easy reach. Use a light sheet or cooler; a heavy blanket will plaster the wet hair and won't allow the horse to dry. Blanketing is advisable if the weather is cool or damp or if the horse is being bathed immediately after heavy exercise; this will prevent its skin temperature from dropping too rapidly.

Ideally, you will bathe your horse on a washrack—an enclosed or semi-enclosed area equipped with running water and a secure means of tying or cross-tying the horse. The surface should be paved or graveled and can be covered with rubber stall mats for better traction. There should be a drainage system to keep water from accumulating on the ground. If you have no such facility, choose an outdoor area on grass, gravel, or pavement at which you can tie your horse securely. Avoid bathing on dirt because you will soon be standing in mud.

Don't use a rubber tie to secure your horse for bathing unless you are in an enclosed or partially enclosed washrack. If your horse has never or only infrequently been bathed, or you are not confident of the strength of your tying anchor or the level of your horse's cooperation, ask someone to hold your horse while you bathe it. Do not try to bathe your horse while you are holding it yourself. You cannot securely control the horse with one hand on the line and your attention on the task at hand. Put a lead shank on the horse around the nose unless the horse proves unmanageable, at which point you may need to resort to a lip chain.

If your horse is held by someone, position it so its rear end is facing a wall or other barricade. If the horse begins to back away it will have nowhere to go. This still gives the horse the option of lunging forward to get away, so make sure your handler is competent.

If the horse starts pushing forward, pull it around to the left until it is facing a barricade. If you are bathing out in the open and the horse tries to get away—either by moving forward or back—keep the horse turning in tight left-hand circles until the horse gives in. If you feel you can't control your horse while bathing in an open area, take the horse into a stall and give it a sponge bath.

Techniques

If you have just come back from a ride and merely want to wash the sweat marks off your horse, you may only need to sponge the sweaty areas with a damp sponge or soapy water. Scrape off any excess water and don't worry about rinsing soap residue. It's relatively harmless and can be brushed off when the hair is dry.

Take time to sponge your horse's lower legs to prevent any clinging dirt or sand from chafing them after it has dried. If the hooves are muddy or dirt caked, it is much easier to wash them now than it is to try to scrape the dried crud off afterward. You are not finished cleaning the legs until you've dried them down to the hooves with a towel; this will greatly help prevent development of nasty and painful scratches (greasy heel).

If you are set for an all-out bath, start by wetting your horse with a hose. If your hose runs only cold water and your horse is uncomfortable with the feel of it, you may be better off skipping this process.

If you use a hose, test your horse's reaction to it first by running it lightly on the ground, then over a front hoof. Wait until your horse accepts the sensation of the water on its hooves before gradually moving the stream up the horse's leg to its shoulder. Do this every time you bathe, no matter how cooperative your horse is, and it will forever remain so.

Always use as gentle a spray as will be effective. Blasting your horse will get it wetter faster, but it may also send the horse charging for the next county.

Spray up your horse's neck to the point where the horse begins to flinch from the water near its head, then reverse and work back along the entire body. Never spray the head or ears, and be very gentle and cautious when spraying the genital areas. If the horse can't abide this, stop and use a sponge in those areas.

To spray between the hind haunches where sweat and mud often accumulate, hold the sprayer under your horse's belly and spray back, standing as far forward as possible. *Don't* stand behind the horse and spray under its tail, and don't ignore this area, as trapped sand or sweat can result in raw, weepy sores.

Once your horse is drenched, take the sponge, squeeze out any excess water, and soap and wipe the horse's face thoroughly. Make sure you include the area behind the ears by lifting or pushing back the halter crownpiece. Wipe the nose out last before you rinse the sponge. It's not necessary to clean the face first, but it seems only decent to use the cleanest possible sponge on the face.

To sponge the rest of the body, saturate the sponge with soapy water and apply liberally to the horse's coat as you move the sponge in a circular motion, working back from the neck. Wash the legs last, as they are usually the dirtiest.

Four or five gallons of water should be sufficient, but if you run out before you finish, make a note to have two buckets ready for the next bath. If you have any leftover wash water, pour it gently over the horse's back as a rinse.

As with brushing, be sure to clean in all the hidden crevices on a horse; trapped dirt and sweat in these areas will eventually cause chafing or raw, weepy sores.

For the most meticulous results, it is best to rinse your horse again with a hose. If you don't have one or have only cold water, you can skip rinsing; it won't harm your horse. Either way, when you are finished bathing and rinsing, use the sweat scraper to remove all excess water from the horse's body. Don't use the scraper on your horse's head or the legs below the knees and hocks, as the scraper is too hard on these sensitive areas. This does not mean you should leave water dripping off the face and legs, however. You should still sponge and towel dry these areas.

After bathing, don't turn your horse loose until the horse is dry, or at least mostly dry. Blanket the horse if necessary and walk it. This will prevent your horse from becoming chilled by standing idle and will speed the drying process by keeping the air circulating around the horse. In addition, it will prevent the horse from lying down and rolling in the dirt too soon, which would mess up your lovely wash job.

As a last note on bathing, don't get carried away with keeping your horse too clean unless you are showing it regularly. Bathing tends to take away some of a horse's natural skin oils, which make the coat glossy and act as a light insulator and protectant from rain. In addition, getting your horse wet affects its basal temperature and makes its system work harder to regain its normal temperature. Therefore, if a horse's health is poor, going from dry to wet to dry again may overtax its system.

Avoid bathing any horse that is ill, weakened by strenuous exercise or malnourishment, or exhibiting signs of a viral infection, such as a snotty nose, cough, or runny eyes. Avoid bathing any horse when the weather is frigid, as the horse will have a much harder time drying out and a much easier time becoming chilled. This is especially true for horses that have grown thick winter coats because the long, dense hair won't dry easily even under ideal conditions.

Grooming for Show

Other optional grooming methods are meant to make a horse look desirable for its class of showing. I will cover these methods briefly, as you will learn them firsthand when you become involved in the circle of your particular showing style. Be aware that show grooming is essentially an aesthetic endeavor and at times is not performed in the best interests of the horse.

Clipping is done with an electric tool made especially for shaving horsehair. Some horses are body clipped (shaved) in the winter in order to get rid of shaggy hair so they will look slick in the show ring. Other horses are clipped in certain areas, such as the bridlepath, inside the ears, the chin hairs, and the long fetlock hairs. Clipping does a smoother job than scissors and is used by many horsepeople whether or not they are showing.

Braiding tails and manes is common for certain styles of English riding and jumping and sometimes for racing. Draft horses are also often braided for performances and parades.

The mane is braided with the three-strand method in fine, tight sections. Each braided section is folded into a loop and secured with tiny rubberbands. The mane may hold only four or five braids near the bridlepath, or the braids can run the entire length of the mane and include the forelock.

The tail is braided only the length of the tailbone, using a French-braid style. The excess tail hairs are usually left free, but may be braided into one long plait, then folded and secured with a large rubber band, tape, or colorful ribbon. This is usually done to keep the tail dry in wet or muddy conditions.

Other mane and tail styles for show purposes include cutting a bridlepath to a certain length, pulling the mane and tail, roaching the mane, cutting the tail to a certain length, or surgically bobbing the tailbone.

Some grooming methods used to make a horse especially flashy in the show ring include painting the hooves black, whitening the socks or stockings and any facial markings with talcum powder or white shoe polish, applying a coat-shine product, rubbing petroleum jelly around the eyes and nose to shine and darken the areas, brushing a checkerboard pattern onto the rump of the horse, and braiding ribbons or flowers into the mane and tail. There are surely more tricks, but again, you will learn them as you become more involved in your particular sport.

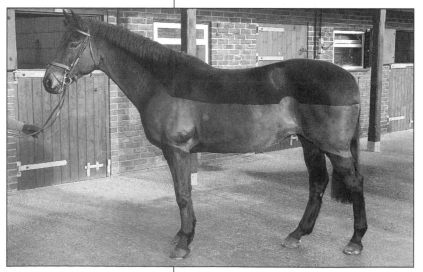

A partial-body clipped horse with a pulled mane and a blunt-trimmed tail. These are mainly aesthetic grooming practices, although they also serve to keep the horse cleaner and neater.

9

The Medical Bag

How to Recognize, Treat, and Prevent Many Horse Ailments

The quality of your horse's health is one of the biggest factors in determining the amount of enjoyment you get from the horse. A healthy horse performs better and more willingly, looks good, and will give you a sense of pride and accomplishment. The healthy horse takes less time and effort to care for than an ill or unsound one and will cost you far less money in the long run.

Prevention

Preventing health problems is always less costly, time- and money-wise, than allowing neglect or abuse to take their toll. Some health problems cannot be prevented no matter how conscientious you are, but an amazing number can. The development of good all-around horsemanship habits is akin to mastering preventive-maintenance habits, and you will never regret the grief you save yourself by investing time, effort, and yes, money in these habits.

Here is a quick reminder of things you can do to keep your horse healthy. Begin, if you haven't already, a relationship with a veterinarian. Set up a checkup schedule, consisting of regular examinations, routine vaccinations, dental care, and a deworming program. Consult your veterinarian as to the best diet you can provide, and ask for advice if the horse appears to fail in health or appearance.

Keep a supply of first-aid materials on hand, as well as a veterinary reference book and emergency veterinary phone numbers. When trail riding, take some emergency supplies along, including a hoof pick and some things for yourself. If you own a cellular phone, take that as well.

Consider the stable a breeding ground for mishaps and illnesses. Use proper fencing, stall, and gate materials and check them regularly for maintenance. Use adequate bedding and ground-cover material, keep it clean, and replace it frequently. Provide fresh, uncontaminated food and water in clean, undamaged containers. Store your horse's food in clean, dry, rodent-proof containers in a secured area out of the horse's reach. Provide areas for shelter and safe exercise. Don't leave trash, tools, equipment, or junk in harm's way. Cover, fill, or fence off any holes or trenches your horse might have access to.

Think of any other horse as potentially harmful to your own. The spread of disease and viruses can be stanched by separation, isolation, and disinfection. Injuries caused by kicking, biting, or excessive play can be avoided by watching herd interaction and separating troublemakers.

Develop your skills as a rider and use them safely and sanely. Avoid high speeds, hard or unstable ground, and busy roadways. Don't play stunt rider or expect your horse to perform acrobatics, and don't jump immovable objects. Check your tack each and every time you use it, and keep a log of your horse's fitness, health, and soundness levels in relation to its performance expectations.

Keep an eye on your horse. Check on it every day, groom it regularly, clean its hooves, and inspect its less conspicuous areas; look for wounds, growths, rashes, tender spots, lumps, and swelling. Get to know your horse's eating, drinking, eliminating, rest, and exercise habits so you will recognize any changes. Observe the condition of the horse's coat, the brightness of its eyes, and the discharge from its nose.

First-Aid Supplies

Every horse owner, no matter how amateur or squeamish, must have some first-aid supplies on hand and an idea of how to use them. A veterinarian is not always available at the drop of a hat, and some wounds or illnesses must be treated immediately.

Medical Supplies

Keep your first-aid supplies stocked and stored neatly in an easily accessible cabinet. I recommend hanging a compartmentalized cabinet with a latching door in your tack room or shedrow to keep these supplies as dirt free and easy to find as possible. You may even want to post an inventory list and your veterinarian's office, home, and emergency phone numbers on the inside of the door. You may be surprised at how panicked and confused you can become when you come upon an emergency medical situation with your horse; this is not the time to find yourself wasting valuable time frantically searching for supplies and phone numbers.

Your supplies should be confined to the basics since you are probably not qualified to treat anything more than a superficial wound or minor lameness.

Wound Treatment Supplies

The initial treatment of a wound, unless it is bleeding profusely, is to clean it. Rubbing alcohol is wonderful for sterilization but not favored by most horses on any open wound or sore. Hydrogen peroxide is my first recommendation, followed by witch hazel, but this also tends to sting and does not encourage cooperation.

When possible, I pour the antiseptic straight onto a wound to clean it, but that's not always the most convenient method. Cotton balls can be used to apply antiseptic cleanser, as can paper towels. For larger wounds, I've found cloth diapers work well for cleaning, as they leave no lint in the wound. To clean minor wounds or dried blood I sometimes use diaper wipes.

You will need at least one wound ointment in your cabinet; the best is an antibiotic ointment available from your veterinarian. Galls, chafing wounds, and sunburns do well with soothing ointments such as zinc oxide, bag balm, or aloe vera gel. I also recommend wound powder to treat and dry weepy surface wounds. A liquid iodine-based wound solution is often convenient to apply, dries quickly, and does not attract dirt as easily as an ointment. I avoid wound sprays since many horses, especially those already traumatized over an injury, protest the application. The sight and sound of the spray can be terrifying to a horse.

Poultice

Some people never use poultice, but I can't do without it. Poultice is a pasty solution smeared on a horse's legs or packed into its hooves. Poultice acts to draw out heat and swelling and will sometimes draw fluids and pus from a wound. Poultice can be purchased at most tack shops or from your veterinarian and comes ready mixed or in powdered form to which you add water. There are various poultices on the market; your veterinarian may even be able to give you a recipe for a home remedy. My recommendation is for a poultice containing kaolin.

Bandaging Supplies

You will need a basic supply of bandages for covering leg and hoof wounds or injuries. You should not bandage leg injuries such as a bowed tendon or swelled ankle without the consent and direction of your veterinarian.

Perforated plastic-encased gauze pads are a must for covering wounds. Sheet cotton should also be used under a leg bandage to keep the wound from sticking to the cloth bandage, but paper towels will work in a pinch. Once in a while you will also need to wrap the leg in cellophane underneath the sheet cotton to create a sweat and reduce swelling.

Wrap a quilted or padded bandage under the final bandage. This pads and protects the leg from the excessive pressure of a stretchy bandage. The quilted bandage should be wide enough to cover the horse's leg from under the knee to below the ankle and long enough to wrap around twice. Your veterinarian can supply these, they are available at some tack shops, you can make your own, or you can use a large cloth diaper or piece of synthetic sheepskin.

The outer bandage consists of a four- to six-inch-wide length of cotton, linen, or stretchy material such as a polo bandage or elastic (trace) bandage. The purpose of this bandage is to hold the sheet cotton and quilted bandage in place. I strongly recommend these bandages not be used without the thicker bandage underneath, unless they are used as support during exercise. Improperly applied stretchy bandages can put enough pressure on the tendons and ligaments of the lower legs to cause them to bow.

Vetwrap is a stretchy, fibrous bandaging material that sticks to itself but not to a horse's hair or skin. It is fairly inexpensive and disposable, and I highly recommend keeping a few rolls on hand. Vetwrap is a quick fix for a bleeding leg wound until the vet arrives, but it must be used with at least sheet cotton underneath to keep the wound from adhering to the bandage and should not be wrapped tight or left on for long periods without a padded underbandage. Vetwrap is also ideal for bandaging abscessed or punctured hooves to keep the affected area clean.

Other Essentials

Rubbing alcohol is a worthy inhabitant in your medicine cabinet. It can be used for cleaning certain wounds, when mixed with warm water it makes an invigorating wash after heavy exercise, and it is an ideal liniment for warm, swollen legs. Alcohol can also be mixed fifty-fifty with glycerin to make a highly effective anti-itch remedy.

Your medicine cabinet hardware should include a rectal thermometer, scissors, razor blades (with one edge taped), a roll of electrician's tape for securing bandages, a pocketknife, a hoof pick, and a stack of clean rags. Keep a few empty plastic containers on hand so you don't have to tote large containers of ointment, liniment, or antiseptics to treat a horse.

Horses aren't the only ones that might need first aid around the barn. You can share your horse's antiseptics, but will want some gauze, surgical tape, and adhesive bandage strips for yourself. I also recommend keeping rubber gloves on hand for use when treating wounds and applying or massaging liniments.

So far I have listed basic but essential first-aid supplies. Over time you will probably add a few more items, perhaps commercial liniment, fly wipe, ophthalmic ointment, cough remedy, or lice powder, but these will most likely be purchased on an as-needed basis.

Wound Treatment

Any wound treatment, whether the wound is fresh or treated daily, must be considered somewhat painful to the horse. Although you can reduce some of the pain and trauma with conscientious handling, you must expect the horse to feel some pain and react accordingly; therefore caution is in order.

All horses are different in their reactions to pain. Some are absolute wimps and will fight or shrink away from any minor treatment. Others will remain amazingly calm and quiet as you scrub at a dirt-encrusted wound. The best policy is to expect the worst from your horse. Confine the horse in a stall or other small, secure enclosure for treatment. Tie the horse in a safe manner and give yourself room to work. Keep all your supplies in a box or bucket out of bumping or stomping distance of the horse. If the horse is too fractious tied up, enlist the help of a handler and put a nose shank or lip chain on the horse. In extreme cases, you might have to resort to a twitch to keep the horse still.

Initial Treatment

Assess your horse's wound immediately. Summon your veterinarian if the wound appears deep or gaping, if bleeding is heavy, pumping, or squirting, or if a cut appears to involve a tendon or ligament. When in doubt, call your veterinarian. Do not apply ointment or other treatment solutions to the wound, as this may interfere with your veterinarian's exam and treatment.

Bleeding Control

Any bleeding should be stanched as quickly as possible by applying a rag or towel and pressure to the wound area. A horse will often not tolerate having something held against a leg wound for any length of time. For your own safety and relief, an emergency bandage can be applied. Wrap sheet cotton around the leg or place some gauze over the wound. Wrap the wounded area of the leg with Vetwrap or an elastic or polo bandage. Your bandage needs to be snug to help stanch the flow of blood, but you must be very careful not to pull on the bandage as you wrap, as you can damage a tendon. Secure the bandage with a strip of electrician's tape wrapped around the upper part of the bandage.

Consider the bandage you use to stop bleeding temporary. Swelling is a natural and rapid reaction at any injury sight; a tight bandage left in place too long will cause excessive swelling and pressure on the tendons. It should remain only until the veterinarian arrives or the bleeding stops. If the bandage becomes saturated, it must be removed and replaced, but you must take care during replacement to keep pressure applied or the bleeding will increase. Whatever the circumstances, I would make one hour the absolute limit for this sort of bandage before it is removed, and if necessary, replaced.

Surface Treatment

When bleeding is controlled, the wound should be thoroughly cleaned. If the wound is in a dirty or muddy area, the entire area should be washed with water and antibacterial soap. The wound should then be cleaned with an antiseptic. If thick or long hair interferes with the wound area, it should be clipped or shaved.

If the wound does not require stitches, you should be able to treat it yourself. If it is clean and fresh, an antibiotic ointment should prove effective in treating and preventing infection. If the wound is weepy or continues to bleed slightly, a wound powder might be in order, but I would switch to an antibiotic ointment as soon as the weeping abates. Wound powders act as surface treatment only, and will not be absorbed by the skin. If this is your treatment of choice, the powder should be reapplied several times daily.

If you are dealing with a puncture wound, you must be sure to clean deep into the wound, and your treatment solution must penetrate to be effective. A squeeze-and-squirt bottle, a large dropper, a hypodermic tube, or a turkey baster can be used to squirt antiseptics and liquid wound solutions into the punctured area. Don't be surprised if your horse resists this treatment. Don't assume lack of bleeding or draining from a puncture wound means it's okay; these wounds close in easily—especially if the area swells—and do not drain well. The fluids and blood will build up to create a painful abscess, so it is essential that you get in there somehow and treat it, then keep it covered to prevent dirt and bacteria from penetrating.

Coverage

All wounds more serious than a superficial scrape should be covered to prevent the invasion of dirt, bacteria, and flies. Unfortunately, there are many areas on a horse that will not hold a bandage—the horse's movements will loosen the bandage or the bandage will not adhere well in the area—so your coverage must be achieved by wound treatments. Wound powder is your best bet for keeping the wound dry and attracting less dirt and debris, but an oil-based ointment will prove more effective in resisting moisture if your horse lives in a wet environment. When possible, I rub a bit of antibiotic ointment into the wound before covering it with powder. You'll create a sticky, pasty mess if you use too much ointment, so be conservative. To deter flies, you can carefully apply fly wipe up to the edges of the wound, but you must avoid getting the repellent into the wound. If flies are a big problem (and they love to feast on a wound), try taping gauze over the wound and applying fly wipe to the outside surface of the gauze. The gauze won't likely stay on for long periods, so be prepared to replace it often.

Bandaging the Wound

When bandaging a leg wound, please do so only on the advice and instruction of your veterinarian. Your vet will supply you with bandages or will tell you what to use. If you are self-treating, you can use the supplies I've previously suggested. Do not self-bandage a wound involving the knee or hock joints without the advice and hands-on instruction of a veterinarian, as these areas are difficult to properly bandage and improper bandaging can do more harm than good.

When bandaging a leg wound, either above or below the knee or hock joint, first apply a wound ointment, thoroughly smearing the wound area. Cover the wound with perforated plastic-encased gauze. Over the gauze, wrap sheet cotton continuously around the area to be bandaged until you have covered it with two layers. If swelling is present or expected, you may need to wrap the area in cellophane to create a sweat, but don't take it upon yourself to do this without the advice of a veterinarian.

Above the Knee or Hock

If the wound is above the knee or hock, you can wrap your stretchy top layer bandage of Vetwrap, elastic, or a polo bandage without a thick underbandage; the padded bandage is not necessary due to the natural padding of the upper leg and would only serve to loosen and cause the stretchy bandage to fall.

The stretchy bandage is long and should be rolled first to make application easier. Start bandaging at the inside of the leg, at least two inches above the wound area. Roll front to back and down, overlapping each layer so one-half inch of the bandage is exposed. When you reach the top of the joint, roll back up the leg until you are again at least two inches above the wound area and have covered the first layer of your bandage. You should not have any or much excess bandage left at the top; if you do, you should unroll and start over.

The leg above the joint is meaty and does not hold a bandage well. For this reason, you must make sure your bandage is very snug. Secure the end with Velcro or safety pins made for horse bandages (they look like heavy-duty diaper pins) and cover this with a doubled strip of electrician's tape. The bandage might still fall, so it must be checked frequently and changed at least once a day.

Below the Knee or Hock

If you are bandaging below the knee or hock, you must use a quilted or padded bandage under the stretch bandage to protect the tendons and ligaments from strain. Wrap this on the outside of the sheet cotton. Watch that the padded bandage is set smooth and flat and that the end does not lie against the flexor tendon. If you find it awkward to try to hold the thick bandage in place while you wrap the outer stretch bandage, you can secure it with some tape, but this tape should not be pulled tighter than necessary.

Wrap the outer bandage as you would for an above-the-joint wound, but always cover the entire area from just below the knee or hock to just below the ankle. When you are fin-

Emergency Wound Treatment

1. Restrict horse's movement.
2. Control blood flow by applied pressure.
3. Inspect wound area. Call veterinarian if:
   - ☐ blood squirts, sprays, or pumps from wound
   - ☐ bleeding does not abate within twenty minutes
   - ☐ wound is deep or gaping
   - ☐ flesh is torn in a flap
   - ☐ wound involves bone, tendon, or ligament
   - ☐ wound extends into surface of hoof

If veterinary assistance is not needed (if wound is superficial, bleeding controlled):

4. Clean wound with antiseptic, clipping or shaving any intruding hairs.
5. Treat wound with antibiotic-based ointment.
6. Cover wound if possible. If not possible, confine horse to clean area.
7. Clean, inspect, and treat wound one to three times daily.

ished, check that the ankle is not exposed at all. Start wrapping at the top, placing the first edge of the bandage on the inside of the leg in the depression between the cannon bone and the flexor tendon. Wrap to the front and around to the back, going down and back up the leg, finishing at the top. The bandage must be placed firmly and snugly in order to stay in place, but again, you absolutely must not apply pressure against the tendons by tugging on the bandage to tighten it.

The Pastern Area

If your horse's wound is below the ankle, your best method of bandaging is with Vetwrap over gauze and sheet cotton. This is a small area with a lot of movement and will simply not hold a cloth bandage very well. This area is also subject to easy chafing and should be rebandaged at least twice daily.

The Hoof and Heel

If your horse has a puncture wound in the hoof or a heel bulb wound, you can bandage the entire hoof and heel area with Vetwrap. If the wound is on the horse's heel, use ointment and gauze under the Vetwrap. If you are dealing with a puncture wound of the sole or frog, clean out and treat the punctured area, pack the sole with poultice or other hoof packing recommended by your vet, then wrap the entire hoof with Vetwrap. A hoof bandage should be replaced twice a day, as it will quickly become soiled and tattered.

Tips for Successful Bandaging

It is vital that your horse stands quietly during bandaging; any shuffling, stomping, or resistance will cause your bandage to be placed improperly. If necessary, have a handler hold up one leg while you are bandaging to prevent the horse's movement. If this is not sufficient to still the horse, have another handler hold the horse under a lip chain or twitch.

Your bandage will not be effective if your horse removes it, and the injury can be worsened by your horse's efforts. You can deter your horse from tearing or chewing its bandage by painting the outside surface with a solution of cayenne pepper and water.

Any leg bandage placed for any reason must be changed daily. A bandage left on more than a day can result in chafing wounds and excessive swelling. If you are bandaging a serious wound, changing the bandage and treating the wound twice a day will greatly enhance healing and help prevent infection. If the bandage does cause chafing in any area, apply copious amounts of petroleum jelly, zinc oxide, or wound ointment to the chafed areas before reapplying the bandage.

The Healing Process

There is a point at which a bandage is no longer useful. Eliminate bandages when the wound shows signs of true healing, is dry to the touch, and is covered with fresh, pink skin. The wound will dry out and begin to scab soon after you discontinue bandaging, but should be left to itself at this point, providing the growth of proud flesh is controlled and the horse does not rub the scab off and redamage the area.

New hair on or bordering a wound sight will often grow in white; many people find this undesirable, especially as it points out the scar on a dark-colored horse. I have had some success preventing the growth of white hairs by rubbing bacon grease or lard on the wound at the first sign of new hair growth. This treatment has its drawback in that the grease tends to attract flies, so fly repellent must be applied to the edges of the wound.

If your horse's wound does not appear to be healing properly or shows any sign of infection, call your veterinarian. He or she can start your horse on internal antibiotics and can advise you as to any changes necessary in your treatment.

Proud Flesh

A unique and undesirable feature of horse wounds is their ability to grow proud flesh. Proud flesh is a fibrous, granular tissue that begins growth inside a wound and continues to grow upward and outward, enlarging the wound and delaying healing. New skin will not cover or prohibit the growth of proud flesh, which will leave an unsightly, raised scar after healing occurs.

Once proud flesh has been allowed to develop, it must be burned off with a caustic solution. If the solution is not allowed to touch surrounding healthy tissues, this causes no pain to the horse. Severe proud flesh or proud flesh that has turned to scar tissue cannot be effectively burned off but must be surgically removed. When considering spending money on treatment, keep in mind that proud flesh is rarely harmful to the horse after healing has occurred; it is simply an ugly blemish.

The growth of proud flesh can be prevented with care and perseverance. Any new proud flesh can be scrubbed off immediately, although the horse won't enjoy this. Caustic solutions can also be applied to new growth to stop the formation, but care must be taken not to touch any surface other than proud flesh, as severe burning will occur. There are some proud flesh treatments available in tack shops and through your vet, and there are also home remedies. Two solutions I've used are copper sulfate powder mixed in cold cream, and salimoniac and vinegar, but you should not use any home remedy without veterinary consultation.

Skin Ailments

There are a variety of skin ailments—some contagious, some caused by environmental conditions, and some from improper care. I will briefly explain the most common ailments and offer advice on what to do about them.

Ringworm

Ringworm is commonly thought of as a parasitic growth under the skin. This is understandable due to the common round shape of the affected area, but ringworm is not a parasite at all; it is an infectious fungal growth which appears as crusty patches of skin, often but not always round in shape.

Ringworm is easily passed from one horse to the next and can be passed on to humans and other animals as well, so any tack or brushes used on an affected horse should be separated and disinfected. Handlers should wash hands after touching a ringworm-infected horse. Stalls, food containers, horse trailers, and hotwalker ties also need to be disinfected. Ringworm has a lengthy incubation period before it appears—as much as one hundred days—so it is often difficult to prevent even with the best of care.

Ringworm is best treated with internal antibiotics and bathing the infected areas with antibiotic wash. Fungicides can be used to control the growth but do not seem to be highly effective in actually killing ringworm. If a fungicide is used, it should be applied twice daily for two to three weeks. Do not discontinue use early even if the ringworm seems to have disappeared.

Girth Disease

Girth disease appears as tiny bumps that turn to crusty scabs. Girth disease is highly contagious among horses sharing the same tack and brushes, stabling facilities, or riders and handlers. It is especially prolific during warm weather and where flies are abundant, as they can pass the infection simply by landing on several different horses. The bumps might start in one tiny, isolated area but can quickly spread over the horse's entire body.

Girth disease is a fungal infection similar to ringworm and sometimes *is* actually ringworm misdiagnosed. It is best prevented by separating and disinfecting an affected horse and everything the horse comes in contact with. An antibiotic wash or one that contains iodine will help kill girth disease. Prompt treatment will help prevent scarring.

Itching Sores

There are three main reasons horses rub or scratch raw spots: insect bites or an infestation of lice or pinworms. Horses also scratch and rub during shedding season but rarely to the extent that an injury occurs.

Any sores caused by scratching will not only be raw and painful, but will continue to itch, thus causing the horse to keep scratching or rubbing the area despite the damage it causes. The best and most immediate treatment I have found is a fifty-fifty solution of rubbing alcohol and glycerin (available from any drugstore). The alcohol-glycerin solution should be applied generously and massaged into any affected area daily or twice daily. The solution works to instantly relieve the itching, and it also is very soothing (the glycerin takes the sting out of the alcohol) and promotes healing.

Lice

Although lice are visible to the eye, many people do not realize a horse is infested until the horse shows up with hairless or raw spots along the mane line or tail base. An adult louse is dark, but the eggs are white and show up easily against dark hairs. Lifting the mane or forelock will usually reveal the presence of lice. Fortunately, lice from horses will not transfer to humans, but they will transfer to other animals, especially cows.

To delouse your horse, you must dust it heavily with lice powder until there is no further evidence of lice. All tack and brushes also need to be dusted, and the horse should be isolated from others until the infestation is controlled. If the affected horse had been turned out in a pasture or other community area, every horse that has shared that space should be dusted and treated as if it too had lice.

Insects

Horses in certain regions are affected by biting insects that cause severe itching. The horse will most commonly scratch itself raw along the croup near the tail and along the mane line.

Horses affected by insects should be kept indoors during the dawn and dusk hours when insects are most likely to bite. When outdoors, the horse should be doused with fly repellent. In a severe case, a horse can be covered with a light sheet and mesh face hood.

Worms

A horse infested with pinworms will rub its tail until it is hairless and bloody. The reason is the adult pinworm lives in the horse's rectum and will occasionally crawl out, causing intense itching and irritation. The best prevention for pinworms is to put your horse on a regular deworming schedule under the supervision of your veterinarian.

Rainscald (Rain Rot)

Rainscald occurs mainly on the backs and croups of horses that are not provided shelter during wet, rainy seasons. Some horses are literally left out in the rain all season until their flesh rots, hence the nickname *rain rot*. Constant exposure of the skin to moisture and rain acts as an irritant that will cause scabbing, matting of the hair, and oftentimes, weepy sores. If the horse is not treated, it may lose all the hair and the top layer of skin in affected areas. The condition may be painful enough to prohibit riding, and it is unsightly. Most often hair growth will resume after healing, but some scarring may occur and the new hair may grow in white or a darker color than the original coat.

Providing adequate shelter is your horse's best protection against rainscald. If your horse must be left to the elements or refuses to use its shelter, an outdoor blanket should be provided. A blanket will provide nothing in the way of protection if it becomes saturated or muddy, however, so you should have several on hand and be willing to change to a clean, dry blanket at least once a day.

There is no cure for rainscald; the skin must be allowed to go through its natural healing process, which will not occur until the horse is removed from its wet environment. To buffet the healing process, clean the affected area daily with a mild antibacterial soap and apply lanolin to keep the skin as supple as possible.

Mud Fever

Mud fever is similar to rainscald, except it occurs on the legs. Again, this condition is caused by excessive exposure to moisture and is aggravated by mud, sand, urine-soaked bedding, or manure. To avoid mud fever, the horse should be provided with clean, dry bedding and a dry place to stand when turned out. After riding on wet or muddy surfaces, the horse's legs should be washed and dried with a towel.

Special attention should be paid to the back of the pastern area, which is slow to dry and easily collects sand and moisture. This area can become inflamed and break open, causing nasty, painful cracked skin, sometimes called scratches or greasy heel. If your horse develops scratches, zinc oxide should be applied heavily to the affected pasterns before riding to prevent moisture from invading. After riding, the area should be cleaned with a mild detergent to remove the ointment, then dried and treated with wound powder. If the scratches crack and bleed, a soothing ointment will be necessary to heal the area, and riding or other hard activity should be avoided until some healing has occurred.

Sunburn

Sunburn is almost exclusively a problem for horses with pink skin and white hair. Horses are fairly resilient to the elements, having a coat that usually adequately protects even pink skin, but sunburn will develop on exposed areas and under thin hair. The back, croup, and muzzle are the most susceptible areas.

Early sunburn appears as inflamed, possibly blistered skin. The skin will then flake and peel, retaining a deep pink color. If left unattended and exposed, the sunburn can become so severe as to cause permanent hair loss and destruction of the top layers of skin.

Sunburn is best dealt with through prevention. Your horse won't do well wearing sunscreen, as it is difficult to apply through the hair. If you suspect sunburn to be a problem, your horse should be kept out of the sun during the hours of most intense sunlight. You can apply sunscreen to fairly hairless areas such as the muzzle, but it needs to be reapplied frequently to be effective.

If sunburn does occur, get your horse out of the sun, stay off its back if this area is affected, and treat the burn with an aloe vera solution. If the burned area must be exposed to the sun, coat it thickly with a zinc oxide ointment to block the sun's rays and prevent further damage.

Tumors

There are three fairly common types of skin tumors that affect horses: melanoma, sarcoma, and warts. These tumors range in severity from merely a blemish to endangering the horse's life.

Melanoma

Melanoma growths can reach ten centimeters in diameter and usually occur on the dark skin of an older gray horse. They are most commonly found under the tail, but they can also appear around the eyes or just about anywhere on a horse's body. Melanoma is not painful for the horse and is most often benign, requiring no treatment, but occasionally melanoma is malignant and requires surgical removal to prevent death.

Sarcoma

Sarcoma or sarcoids are usually found on the head, especially around the ears, and the lower legs of a horse. Sarcoids are viral in origin and tend to grow and spread, gaining entry at any open abrasion or wound. Sarcoids are ugly and painful to the horse, multiply rapidly, and bleed easily when touched or rubbed. Removal is necessary but does not guarantee they won't come back.

Sarcoids can be chemically burned off by painting the tumors with a wart treatment or podophyllin, or they can be surgically removed. They can also be killed by tying a tight string around the base, cutting off the blood supply to the tumor. The most successful actions against sarcoids are cryosurgery (freeze burning) and radiation treatment.

Warts

Warts are a fairly harmless form of tumor. They are usually found on the faces, especially the muzzle areas, of young horses. Warts are viral and are spread only horse to horse. Although unsightly in large numbers, they rarely require treatment and usually disappear within three months.

Abscesses

Skin abscesses are pus-filled ulcers formed under the top layers of skin. Causes vary, but abscesses are commonly due to a foreign body such as a sliver, a puncture wound that cannot drain, or a gall that irritates but doesn't quite break the skin.

An untreated abscess will become quite painful to the horse as the area swells and pus eats the surrounding tissue. An abscess can be encouraged to open and drain by soaking it in warm water and Epsom salts or applying a hot pack or hot cloth to the affected area. Warm poultice application also works well to draw the pus out. If these methods fail to open the abscess, your veterinarian might decide to drain the area with a needle or scalpel. Don't play vet and open the abscess yourself with a knife or other sharp object, as you can promote further infection or accidentally pierce a vein.

Once an abscess is open, it should be treated as a wound. The area should be cleansed with an antiseptic, treated with an antibiotic ointment, and covered if at all possible. If the infection does not subside within twenty-four hours after the area is first drained, your horse may require internal antibiotics.

Galls

Galls are wounds almost exclusively caused by chafing against a piece of tack. Galls most commonly occur at the withers, the girth area, under the chin where the chin strap lays, and on the face from misfitting or rough points of the halter or bridle. Some galls are also caused by constant rubbing in one area, such as on the shoulder or behind the girth by the rider's boots.

Prevention is your best defense against galls. Use clean, properly fitted tack and check it often to see it isn't rubbing the horse. Watch for rusty buckles or chains or rough seams on nylon headgear. Watch that you are not constantly yanking on the reins, causing a chin strap gall, or riding sloppily or lopsided,

A horse kept confined for long periods may injure itself in its frenzy to play hard when given the opportunity.

causing a withers or girth gall. Fat and unfit horses are very susceptible to girth galls, so keep your riding easy and moderate until your horse has achieved some degree of fitness.

When a gall occurs, discontinue riding until the area shows no inflammation and has begun to heal. Treat the gall as you would any wound, using salve such as bag balm or zinc oxide ointment if tack must continue to touch that area; this is often the case if the gall is under the halter area.

Make a thorough examination of your tack to discover why the gall occurred. A gall on the withers is very serious and is often caused by a combination of bad conformation and a poorly fitted saddle or lack of proper padding; in this case you may have to use a different saddle or better pad. If the gall is at the girth area, start using a breast collar if you are not already; this will alleviate the need for an ultratight girth. In addition, switch to a string girth if you're not already using one, and launder it after each use. Thick, fuzzy nylon girths appear kinder and softer but tend to promote galls on susceptible horses because they mat easily, retain more dirt and moisture, and have little if any breathability.

Lameness

Lameness is not an illness or a disease, it is a *sign* of a health or soundness problem. Lameness is characterized by a horse's demonstration of pain, most commonly limping or favoring a limb, nodding its head, changing its gait or stride, or standing in an unnatural position.

Causes and Prevention

Happenstance
Off and on a horse will return from a turn out lame or walk out of a stall lame. The horse may have developed an abscess of the hoof or coronet band or stepped on something sharp and punctured or bruised the sole of the hoof. It may have played hard that day, been kicked or struck while turned out with another horse, or cast itself (jammed against a wall or fence while rolling) and wrenched a joint or cracked a bone. These things are hard, but not impossible, to prevent and are not really considered products of abuse or neglect. Horses with certain con-

formational defects are also more prone to injuries leading to lameness, no matter how conscientious you are about their care and treatment.

Environment

Unfortunately, the majority of lameness problems are the direct result of the treatment a horse receives. If a horse is kept confined for long periods and turned out for short ones, the horse may injure itself in its frenzy to play hard while it has the chance. Tripping over pasture debris or stepping on large rocks or into holes frequently results in lameness. Neglected hoof care often results in cracked hooves or bruising; a muddy, mucky paddock or filthy stall can soften the hooves and allow for the growth of thrush or development of abscesses.

Riding

Riding is obviously a major factor in lameness injuries. Riding on a hard or paved surface will give a horse concussive injuries. Slippery, deep, loose, or muddy surfaces cause tendon and ligament injuries. Riding on rocks can bruise the soles and heels and cause the horse to stumble and fall. Riding fast on any surface is very hard on the joints, bones, and tendons, as are jumping and quick turns, stops, or spins. In addition, a horse that is ridden past its endurance level will become sloppy in its action and be more likely to injure itself.

Tracking the Source of Pain

Lameness is most commonly thought of as a leg or hoof problem, but is not exclusively so. Lameness also involves the stifle joints, shoulders, hips, spine, and skeletal muscles. Lameness can be caused from bone, tendon, ligament, nerve, or muscle injury, and occasionally from injured skin that is irritated with movement. There is even the odd horse that will walk lame during or just after it is cinched tight; this due possibly to pinched skin or pressure on a pinched nerve or bruised rib. These problems are difficult to pinpoint and diagnose, especially for the novice.

Hooves

If your horse comes up lame, either limping, or walking or trotting with a distinct head nod, check the horse's hooves first. Other signs that the lameness may be caused by pain in the hoof are standing with one hoof pointed forward to get the weight off it or leaning back to shift the weight to the heels. Check that the shoe is fitted properly and has not loosened or become twisted. If the horse was recently shod, suspect a nail placed too high. Look for something lodged inside the shoe against the sole; removal of the object may result in instant soundness. Look carefully for a puncture in the sole or frog—you may have to wash the surface, as many punctures do not bleed and will not be easily detected. Last, examine the bulbs of the heels for inflammation and press on them to check for bruising.

Legs

A horse is less likely to limp visibly on a leg injury than a hoof injury, but if the injury is severe enough, it will certainly do so. Other signs of a leg injury are stiff, stilted movement, a wider than normal stance or set down, abnormally high flexion of a knee or hock joint, pointing a front foot while standing, excessive stumbling, and refusal or inability to move or perform as normal.

The leg injury may be glaringly obvious because of intense swelling or heat in the area or because of a source wound such as a kick. Or you may have to search out the affected area by feeling for heat, swelling, or hard pressure, starting at the pastern and working up past the knee or hock. If you're not sure what is and is not normal, compare the suspect leg to other legs, both on that horse and on another horse or two.

Back

A horse can be lame at the area of its back because of spinal or muscular injury. A horse will not appear lame directly because of back pain but will likely try to compensate for back pain and become lame in other areas such as the hips or shoulders.

To test the horse for spinal injury, first stand above the horse and look at the alignment of the spine. The back itself will probably not show misalignment, but the point of the croup will sometimes poke up unnaturally or unevenly, and the neck may show a crook. Next, lay the flat of your hand on the horse's spine at the withers and run it back to the hips, applying firm pressure along the way. A horse with a sore spine will crouch under the pressure.

To test for muscle injury of the back, actually more common than spinal injury, again you will have to use the pressure test. This time, apply pressure with your fingers or knuckles to the *sides* of the spine, working back from withers to hips and again watching for crouching.

Hips

Hips are heavy joints, not easily injured. Unfortunately, when they are injured it is usually a fracture. A horse that is lame due to a hip injury will stand with a dropped hip, often refusing to bear weight on that limb. Even standing straight, the affected hip will commonly be lower than the good hip. During movement, the horse will visibly limp on the affected hind leg; limping on the hindquarters almost always causes limping in front, so be careful to observe the hindquarters separate from the front leg motion.

Shoulders

Shoulder pain is exhibited by limping on the affected side, a shortened stride, and a painful reaction from applied pressure and forced flexion. Since shoulder lameness will be hard to distinguish from a leg or hoof injury, flexion is your best test for determining an injury. Only a veterinarian is qualified to do a flexion test, as an untrained person can increase the injury with mishandling.

Treatment

If you find anything amiss or if your horse is lame and you can't find the source, confine the horse to prevent any further unnecessary movement and consult your veterinarian. As a general rule, if you suspect anything more serious than a stone lodged in the hoof or a high nail, call your veterinarian. Any untreated lameness will be aggravated by lack of treatment or continued use and can regress from a sprain to a bow or a bone bruise to a fracture. In addition, compensating to relieve pain can cause stress or injury to an otherwise unaffected area.

Treatment for hoof, leg, and other lameness-inducing injuries varies widely. Your horse may only need time off from exercise to heal. Your vet may prescribe twice-daily cold-water bathing of the area and an oral anti-inflammatory. You may need to soak out a hoof abscess in Epsom salts. The horse may be confined to the stall and ordered to wear pressure bandages.

Methods to promote and speed the healing process may be enacted. This could be electronic-impulse therapy, which promotes healing by sending electronic impulses to the injured area via a device strapped to the horse. Your horse could have a chemical blister applied to the area or be pin fired. These two controversial methods are used on legs to promote healing of bone by injuring surrounding tissue. For example, when the skin is blistered or burned by hot pins inserted over the injured area, blood rushes to the area and healing is quickened.

If the injury is severe enough, surgery may be required to repair a bone or tendon or to remove bone chips. Only your veterinarian can determine the ideal treatment for your horse, based on the type and extent of the injury. If the injury does indeed require surgery, use a level head when determining the worth of the animal compared to the cost of surgery and the work involved in helping the horse recover.

If home treatment is prescribed, follow your veterinarian's advice religiously. Use the materials, bandages, medication, poultice, and liniments the vet recommends, and stick to the treatment regimen. If you are unsure of your skills in bandaging, practice your techniques on a healthy leg or on another horse.

Bandaging and Using Poultice

As stated in the section on wound treatments, remember never to bandage a knee or hock without explicit instruction from a veterinarian. These areas don't hold loose bandages well, but if the bandage is pulled too tight, it will cause chafing and possibly injure the cap of the hock or point behind the knee.

Many liniments dry quickly and do not require sheet cotton to protect the leg from the bandage or the bandage from the leg. If you use an ointment dressing or bandage over a poultice, you may want to use sheet cotton or paper towels against the leg before applying a bandage. This will save you some laundering time and will prevent the bandage from becoming sticky or stiff. Cellophane wrap can also be used to protect the bandage, but it acts as an air barrier and promotes sweating, so it should only be used on the advice of a veterinarian.

If you are bandaging a lower leg, you will need a padded or quilted underbandage to protect the tendons and ligaments from the tight pressure of the outer bandage. This bandage should be wide enough to cover the leg from below the knee or hock to below the ankle and long enough to wrap around twice. The bandage should be started on the inside of the leg at the depression behind the cannon bone and in front of the flexor tendon. The end of the bandage must not rest on the tendon. The padded bandage should be smooth and straight before applying the outer bandage.

The outer bandage, a lengthy strip of cloth or elastic material of four to six inches in width, should be rolled before application. This bandage should also be started on the inside of the leg and should be rolled front to back and top to bottom, then rolled back to finish at the top. Each layer of bandage should overlap to leave about a half inch of the last layer exposed. The bandage should end on the outside of the leg, and again, should not rest against the flexor tendon.

The padded underbandage will be secured by the outer bandage. The outer bandage must be secured by Velcro or heavy-gauge safety pins made especially for horse bandages. Both the Velcro and the pins should be covered by a double layer of electrician's tape wrapped around the bandage. Cayenne pepper and water can be mixed to a thin paste to paint on the outside of the bandage if you think your horse might chew or tear it. If in doubt, use the pepper; not only will the bandage be ineffective if the horse is not wearing it, but a horse pulling at a bandage can sometimes injure its own tendon.

A good bandage is free of wrinkles or folds and covers the entire ankle. It must be snug enough to stay in place, but if you pull the bandage too tight, you may damage the tendons and ligaments, specifically the flexor tendon that runs down the back of the leg. The best technique is to hold the bandage firmly against the flexor tendon with one hand as you pull the end of the bandage forward, around, and back to the tendon. Lay the bandage against the tendon, then hold it in place again as you add another wrap.

If your horse is uncooperative during the bandaging process, your bandage will come out sloppy and lose much of its effectiveness. You can either have a handler hold the horse under a lip chain or twitch to keep it still or ask the handler to hold up one of the horse's legs while you work to prevent the horse's movement.

Poultice can be used with a bandage, or in place of a bandage in some cases, so it is a good choice for a knee, hock, or hoof injury. Poultice acts to draw heat away from the area of injury and reduce swelling. As heat is drawn out, the poultice paste will dry. Once the poultice has dried and cracked, it should be washed off and replaced.

Medications

Medications are often prescribed for lame or injured horses. These range from antibiotics when infection is suspected or diagnosed, to tranquilizers to discourage the horse from using the injured area more than necessary, to diuretics and anti-inflammatories to reduce swelling, to muscle relaxants and painkillers for relief.

While your horse is on medication of any kind, keep a careful watch for any sign of an allergic or adverse reaction. Watch that the horse continues to eat, that it is not too weak to stand without swaying, that it does not develop diarrhea, constipation, excessive joint swelling, a rash, or hives. Call your vet at the first sign of a problem.

Medicines that reduce pain and relax muscles may give a horse a false sense of well-being. It is vital when using these medications that the horse's movement is confined to prevent it from further stressing the injury until healing has occurred. Give your horse at least two days free of medication before you or your veterinarian make a determination as to the level of soundness the horse has achieved and its ability to use the injured area.

Illness and Disease

Early Diagnosis

Detecting illness or disease in its earliest stages will give your horse the highest chances of success in treatment and recovery. Familiarity with your horse and its habits is a key factor in detection. You must know your horse's normal resting rates for temperature, pulse, and respiration so you will know when they are abnormal. Any changes in the horse's eating habits, consistency of manure, activity level, and coat quality should be noted and investigated. In addition, any cough, nasal or eye discharge, weight loss, unusual sweating, or appearance of anxiety or discomfort should be considered signs of the onset of an illness.

Warning Signs of Illness or Distress

- □ dull eyes
- □ nasal or eye discharge
- □ swelling, lumps, or open sore under jaw
- □ swelling at throat
- □ lethargy
- □ refusal to eat
- □ refusal or inability to perform at normal level
- □ frequent or lengthy lying down
- □ repeated rolling on the ground
- □ diarrhea
- □ difficulty passing or inability to pass manure or urine
- □ trembling
- □ sweating at rest
- □ anxiety
- □ turning head back or biting at belly

Checking for Fever

Almost every illness is accompanied by an elevated body temperature. The basal temperature of a horse is one hundred degrees Fahrenheit or thirty-eight degrees Celsius. A temperature check is best taken with a rectal thermometer. To get the truest reading, the horse should be quiet and rested and should not be exposed to high temperatures or direct sunlight.

There is some danger of being kicked while taking a horse's temperature. To avoid this, stand well to the horse's side when inserting the thermometer. Many horses will clamp their tails if you try to lift them; you can usually convince the horse to cooperate and lift its tail for you by lightly scratching or tickling the base of the tail. Never leave the thermometer unattended—you must stay and hold it until a reading can be made. There is a chance the thermometer will

Vital Signs of the Horse

Basal Temperature: 100 degrees Fahrenheit
(38 degrees Centigrade)

DANGER ZONE: 103 degrees or higher

(Check rectally with a thermometer.)

Resting Pulse Rate: forty beats per minute

DANGER ZONE: sixty or more beats per minute
while at rest

(Check with finger pressure inside lower jaw, behind pastern, or inside elbow, or check by listening to chest.)

Resting Respiration Rate: eight to sixteen breaths
per minute

DANGER ZONE: twenty breaths or more per
minute *while at rest*

(Check by watching expansion and contraction of barrel or by listening at nostrils.)

break if the horse is extremely uncooperative; to avoid this have someone hold up a front leg to prevent the horse's movement.

Taking the Pulse

Pulse rate can also help you detect an illness, especially an acute bout of colic. A normal resting pulse rate for a horse is forty, and this number should not vary much. A resting pulse rate higher than sixty should be considered a danger sign. Finding a pulse on a horse is not easy. There is an artery just inside the lower jaw that is fairly accessible and one inside the upper foreleg in front of the horse's elbow. The pastern also has a light arterial pulse. If you cannot locate a pulse, try pressing your ear against the chest in the area of the heart.

Measuring Respiration

Respiratory rate should also be measured. A normal resting respiratory rate for an adult horse is about twelve breaths per minute, but eight to sixteen breaths is considered normal. You can usually measure this by simply watching the horse breathe.

Prevention

Vaccination

Veterinary technology has improved by leaps and bounds in the last century. We now have many vaccines available for common and contagious horse diseases. They are not outrageously expensive and don't have to be administered frequently; in my opinion only a fool would neglect to vaccinate a horse. Your first responsibility as a horse owner should be to start an immunization schedule. If you have any doubts about when or if your horse was vaccinated before you took over stewardship, assume it was not and treat it accordingly.

Hygiene

Some illnesses and diseases cannot be vaccinated against or cured with antibiotics. At other times, a horse will lose its immunity to a viral disease before it is revaccinated or will be exposed to a virus before it receives the vaccine. In these cases it is best to try to prevent illness through hygiene.

Horses that are stabled or pastured together and share the same tack and equipment are most susceptible to viruses, but any horse can come down with a viral illness. It will be picked up at horse shows, in vans and trailers, on trail rides at common tying and watering areas, and from the hands or clothing of a person who has handled another horse. It is also possible for flies and rodents to spread a virus.

Any stall, trailer, or van that has been recently used by another horse should be wiped or sprayed with a disinfectant. A horse should have its own feed containers and water buckets whenever possible. Shared tack should be cleaned and disinfected if there is any sign of a virus in the barn, and bits should be dipped in disinfected water after each use. Rodents and flies should be kept to a minimum; this can be done by keeping the stable area clean, storing feed in tightly secured containers, and using fly repellent.

If a virus appears, the affected horse should be isolated as completely as possible. Its tack and brushes should be separated and disinfected, then kept only for that horse. Anyone touching the horse or its stall, gate, or equipment should wash hands before handling another horse.

Digestive System Protection

Stomach-related illnesses can often be prevented. Any change in a horse's diet should be done gradually with daily monitoring of the horse's manure and urine output. This is especially important when changing a horse from dry hay to rich grass or increasing the horse's grain ration. Vitamins should be measured carefully according to package instructions or a veterinarian's advice. Food supplies should be checked for any sign of dust or mold and should be stored in clean, dry, tightly-secured containers. Toxic plants should be removed—not just poisoned—from the horse's grazing area, and the use of weedkillers should be avoided in grazing areas. Horses sometimes get bellyaches when fed too soon or watered too much after exercise; this can be prevented by giving the horse small amounts of water at intervals and waiting until the horse is completely cooled before feeding.

In addition to what you feed your horse and when, how you feed it can also make your horse ill. Feeding on the ground can cause the horse to ingest sand, dirt, pebbles, sticks, mud, and parasites, all of which can cause digestive disorder. Allowing the horse to bolt its food may cause intestinal obstruction due to large, unchewed particles; this can be prevented by adding large stones to the feed tub to make the horse work for its food. Hay dropped in dirt or mud often loses leaves, the most nutritious part of the stalk. A horse can't easily retrieve the leaves without eating a lot of mud or dirt, so you will find yourself feeding expensive, low-nutrition stems.

Poor teeth cannot properly chew food, which leads to constipation and intestinal obstruction. Parasites interrupt the digestive system and rob the horse of important nutrients. Regular veterinary care that includes dental care and a deworming routine will prevent these problems.

Bad water can make a horse ill. Even if your water source is pure, failure to clean your containers will result in contaminated water, especially if there is a lot of algae growth or rust present. A horse will not drink warm, rancid, or frozen water, leading to dehydration and constipation.

Equine Infectious Anemia

Equine infectious anemia (EIA) is an infectious virus that cannot be vaccinated against and cannot be treated. A horse may be affected by symptoms of the disease or simply act as a carrier. Since EIA is deadly, there have been laws enacted to prevent spread of the disease, with very successful results. Horses crossing state or national borders are required to test negative for the disease, as are horses entering racetrack and horse show facilities. A Coggins test must be performed by a veterinarian and proof of negative results must be documented. Any horse found to test positive for EIA, whether it appears in perfect health or not, should be destroyed.

Equine Rhino-pneumonitis (Herpes) and Influenza

Both the highly infectious equine rhinopneumonitis (herpes or rhino) and equine influenza viruses display similar symptoms. Influenza can lead to pneumonia or death in the horse and is almost totally preventable through vaccination. Rhinopneumonitis can be immunized against but is still rampant in stable areas, especially among young horses, due to the fact that so many horses do not receive the vaccine, receive it after exposure, or lose their immunity before being given a booster vaccine. Its effects may be so mild as to go unnoticed or so severe as to cause paralysis or abortion in a mare in foal.

Prevention can be achieved through immunization and by following a strict program of hygiene, including regularly disinfecting any shared tack, food and water containers, trailers, vans, and common areas.

Rhinopneumonitis and influenza are similar in appearance to the common cold. Symptoms may include nasal discharge, coughing, sneezing, lethargy, loss of appetite, and fever. Any infected horse should be isolated and rested until all symptoms are gone and the horse appears "bright." The horse should not be subjected to stress or extreme climate conditions. Return to exercise should be gradual and measured by the horse's ability to perform.

Antibiotics are minimally effective as a treatment for either virus. Anti-inflammatories may reduce fever, but can also mask symptoms. Cough remedies may hinder release of excess mucus and cause it to build up in the lungs, so they should be used conservatively and only on the advice of a veterinarian. To encourage the discharge of mucus, try feeding the horse low to the ground and walk the horse to promote coughing.

Pneumonia and Pleurisy

Pneumonia has a variety of causes; it is characterized by infection and buildup of fluid in the lungs. Foals, aged horses, and horses weakened by conditions such as influenza, malnutrition, or exhaustion are especially susceptible to pneumonia.

Pneumonia shares many of the symptoms of influenza or rhino. The horse will have a fever, snotty nose, cough, and dull coat and will be lethargic and off its feed. In addition, affected horses will be unwilling to move much or lie down and will exhibit labored breathing. There will be an audible wet sound in the lungs.

Pleurisy is a form of pneumonia involving the pleural sac surrounding the lungs. It is characterized by excessive fluid buildup in the pleural sacs and formation of adhesions on the lungs.

Veterinary treatment is a must for pneumonia and pleurisy, as there is a high fatality rate for these infections. The horse should be kept confined in a temperate climate, treated with antibiotics, and its fever should be controlled by blanketing or other methods. Treatment for pleurisy may include draining the fluid from the chest cavity. The horse will require a long rest period after recovery to prevent recurrence. Horses suffering from pleurisy rarely recover to full usefulness.

Strangles

Strangles is another highly infectious disease. It will first be noticed by excessive amounts of thick, pussy discharge from the horse's nostrils. The lymph glands under the horse's jaw will swell and abscess, breaking open to drain thick pus. The neck and throat area will also swell. The horse will have a fever and loss of appetite, partly due to the fact that swallowing is painful. If prompt treatment is not received, strangles can spread to other parts of the horse's body or settle in its lungs.

Strangles has become rare in the United States in recent years due to development of a vaccine. This disease, therefore, should never appear in your barn. If it does, however, you must isolate the horse and seek veterinary attention. Antibiotics will be used, as well as stall rest, fever reduction, and treatment of abscesses. Strict hygiene while handling the horse must be used to prevent the spread of this disease.

Colic

Colic is not a disease; it is simply a catchall name for intestinal disturbances. Colic can range from discomfort due to excessive gas to a painful intestinal blockage caused by undigested food, to agony and probable death caused by a twisted intestine.

It is impossible to home diagnose the type colic your horse suffers. Severity of pain is a good indicator, but every horse has a different reaction to pain and cannot "tell" you how much pain it is in. Seek veterinary advice at the first sign of any colic and insist on a visit if you are at all concerned.

A colicky horse is always in some kind of pain. The horse may lie down and rise frequently, kick or bite at its belly, or pace. There may be frequent attempts to urinate, groaning, or frantic rolling. The horse's area may be devoid of recent manure piles, as the horse is unable to pass any, but often the horse can still pass some manure, at least for a while. A horse in severe pain will sweat, either all over the body or at the neck and belly. Its temperature will usually rise and its respiration and pulse rate will be high.

Leave all treatment for your veterinarian. Do not try to oil or drench the horse yourself, as you can harm more than help. Confine the horse and try to keep it as quiet as possible—oftentimes a soothing voice and gentle, steady patting will offer the horse some comfort in its pain. Do not force the horse to walk or stay on its feet—rolling and lying down will not cause the horse to twist its intestines, as thought in the past.

Most cases of colic need never occur. They are often caused by the food the horse eats and its eating habits. As previously stated, any dietary changes must be made gradually to ensure that digestive intestinal bacteria have a chance to adjust and do their job. Rich green grass should not be given as all-you-can-eat fare, as it can lead to bloating and painful gas. Teeth should be attended to regularly to ensure the horse chews its food properly, and measures should be taken to prevent a horse from bolting its food. An ample supply of fresh water will encourage the horse to drink, providing moisture that will help keep digestion flowing. Horses with chronic constipation are in danger of impaction; they can be helped by adding bran to their diets. Straw is difficult to digest and can cause an impaction. Any horse suspected of eating its straw bedding should be switched to shavings or some other inedible bedding material. Finally, worms and parasites are major factors in colic. Worms entering the digestive tract will damage or block the intestines. A regular deworming program along with good pasture management to reduce parasites will greatly enhance the chances that your horse never suffers from colic.

Tetanus

You should never need to witness the devastating effects of the tetanus disease, as vaccinations are readily available. Your horse should receive its first vaccination at three months of age and be given a booster vaccine every year of its life.

Tetanus affects the nervous system of the horse. It is a poisonous organism that lives in dirt and manure and enters the system via any open wound or abrasion. As the toxins take over, the horse will develop muscle spasms leading to contractions, stiffness, and convulsions. Death is likely.

If you are not sure whether your horse has been immunized against tetanus, and it receives a wound, your vet can administer an antitoxin that will provide immunity for about two weeks.

If your horse does come down with tetanus, there is little you can do for it. Provide a safe, heavily bedded area to protect it from injury during convulsions. Call your veterinarian and be prepared to euthanize to save the horse from unnecessary suffering.

Laminitis (Founder)

Laminitis is a painful condition that involves inflammation of the laminae, or pedal bone, in the hoof. Horses with untreated or chronic laminitis develop rotated pedal bones, which causes the hoof to grow in an unnatural upward position until the toe curves up off the ground. The crest of the neck is also affected and may become enlarged to the extent that it becomes permanently curved.

Laminitis is most commonly caused from overeating lush, green grass or rich grains. Toxins from excess carbohydrates cut off blood supply to certain areas, particularly the hooves, causing degeneration of the affected tissues. Laminitis can also be caused by excessive ingestion of water after heavy exercise, galloping on hard surfaces, and is occasionally an aftereffect of a bout of colic or a high fever.

A horse with laminitis will attempt to keep weight off its hooves. It will resist movement and stand leaning back on its heels. It will walk mincingly with tiny steps and will lie down as often as possible to get off its feet. The hooves may be warm, there is usually a very hard pulse in the pastern area, and the sole of the hoof often appears to bulge out.

Early treatment is vital for any chance of recovery from laminitis. Call your veterinarian immediately if laminitis is suspected. Get your horse away from rich food and restrict its diet. If you've just discovered your horse has gotten into the food store and eaten a dangerous amount of grain, try feeding a thin bran mash to promote diarrhea and restrict further eating for twenty-four hours, then halve the horse's diet for another few days.

If the horse is in such pain as to sweat or breathe rapidly, you may need an injectable pain reliever. Otherwise, your vet will most likely prescribe oral pain medication. Hosing or icing the hooves may also relieve pain. Walking the horse may improve circulation to the feet to reduce the condition, but if the horse is unable or unwilling to walk, it would be cruel to force it.

Once the pedal bone has rotated or dropped, laminitis is considered chronic. In this case, the best you can do for your horse is to provide anti inflammatories to ease discomfort and try corrective shoeing methods, which will change the hoof shape to reduce rotation of the pedal bone and give the horse a more comfortable stance, and will also help protect the sole from dropping farther.

Navicular Disease

Navicular disease is a source of chronic lameness in some horses. The disease affects the navicular bone of the interior hoof; it is degenerated by blood clots blocking the flow of blood to the bone. Deterioration of the navicular bone causes acute pain when the horse is exercised but is also a hindrance while the horse is at rest. The horse is often lame on both front hooves, rarely the hind, but may come up lame on just one foot. A navicular horse may be lame all the time or on intermittent days.

Only a veterinarian can properly diagnose a horse for navicular disease. Once a diagnosis is determined, you will have your work cut out for you. The lameness is chronic and relatively untreatable, although blood-thinning drugs sometimes loosen or eliminate the blood clots and restore blood flow to the area. This will not be effective if the navicular bone has undergone severe degeneration.

Corrective shoeing is often used to shift the horse's weight to a more comfortable position on the hooves. Painkillers and anti-inflammatories can be used to mask the pain but aggravate the problem by encouraging the horse to do more than it ought. Many navicular horses are heel nerved; that is, the nerves supplying the area are cut so the horse no longer feels the pain and can continue to be useful in some way.

Worms and Parasites

I've already mentioned worms several times within this text because worms are such a problem for horses and are so unnecessary.

Origination

There are a variety of worms and parasites that are attracted to the horse's digestive system. Some are a problem only in certain geographical areas, but most affect horses in any region. They most commonly enter the horse's system as larvae clinging to grass the horse eats, although they can also be picked up in dirt when the horse is fed on the ground, or in infested hay. The botfly, not a worm at all, lays eggs on the horse's legs or other areas. The horse licks the eggs, which then enter the body and develop into larvae inside the stomach.

Effects

Worms and parasites wreak havoc on a horse's system. They often feed off the horse's stomach contents, denying the horse essential nutrients. Worms that enter the intestinal tract can damage intestinal walls and cause blockages, resulting in colic. Other worms migrate through the liver and lungs, causing tissue damage and flu-like symptoms. Large red worms migrate through intestinal arteries, causing damage and health-threatening blood clots. Bot larvae perforate the walls of the stomach and pinworms cause intense rectal itching, leading to raw, bleeding areas around the tail.

Signs of Infestation

A horse with worms may display the symptoms of a common cold or flu, or may colic frequently or severely. The horse may also have a dull coat and eye, lethargy, a thin frame with bloated belly, and tail hairs rubbed out at the base. Your horse can also be clinically tested for the presence of worms by an examination of its manure droppings.

Treatment and Prevention

A regular deworming program is a good defense against parasites and worms and the best treatment for a horse already infested. Your veterinarian will advise you what treatment to use and how often. There are over-the-counter deworming medications you can self-administer, but do this on the advice of your vet. If your vet thinks it best to alternate home treatment with veterinary treatment, do so.

The larvae the horse ingests is laid from worms that have exited the horse via its manure. Regular removal of manure from grazing and feeding areas will greatly reduce the number of eggs. By regular, I do not mean once a year or so—you must remove the manure at least once a week, every other day being ideal. If this seems outrageous to you, and you can't picture yourself walking around a pasture picking up horse doo, join the crowd. Most people won't perform this chore, at least not often enough to be effective, and this is precisely why worms and parasites are so rampant.

Do not feed hay that was cut from a grazing area, as it will likely be infested with eggs. Feed your horse grain and hay off the ground in clean containers. If you hang a hay net, place a feeder, rubber mat, or small sheet of plywood underneath so the horse doesn't have to pick dropped hay out of the dirt.

Bot eggs are light yellow and easily detectable on most horses. They adhere to hairs and cannot be easily rubbed, picked, or brushed off. Cut them off with a razor blade at the first sign. The longer they are left on the horse, the more chance they have of entering the horse's system.

Azoturia (Tying Up)

Azoturia is akin to a massive charley-horse type cramping of the horse's hindquarters and sometimes its shoulders. Azoturia is caused by excess lactic acid in the muscle. Inability to release this acid leads to muscle damage and muscular cramping. In severe cases the kidneys are affected and blood will be seen in the urine of a horse shortly after the hindquarters have "tied up."

Horses that are fed a high-grain diet are most susceptible to azoturia, as their bodies are sometimes unable to process the excess lactose. They may show no sign of azoturia if regularly exercised, but may tie up during exercise after having taken a few days off. Lack of selenium in the horse's diet is also thought to be a factor, and some horses just seem more sensitive to the effects of excess lactic acid than others.

To avoid azoturia, horses missing regular exercise for even a few days should have their grain rations reduced. Vitamin supplements containing selenium can be added to the horse's diet. Ample water and electrolytes should be provided to help flush the kidneys of toxins. Sudden, stressful exercise should also be avoided, particularly if the horse is not accustomed to this and is unfit or of a nervous temperament.

A horse suffering from azoturia will be in a considerable amount of pain. Its gaits will become short and stilted, especially in the hindquarters, and the horse may be unwilling to move. In extreme cases, the horse will sweat and develop tremors.

Exercise should be halted immediately at the first sign of tying up. The horse should not be forced to move more than is necessary, and you should not attempt to walk the horse out of the cramp. Blanketing will help loosen the muscles by warming them, and liniment may also relieve some muscle tightness. Although you should certainly consult with your veterinarian, most horses will come out of azoturia before a veterinarian has a chance to arrive. If the vet does get there, and the horse is still in pain, muscle relaxants may be administered to relieve the cramping.

Care of Teeth

Although horses do not commonly suffer from cavities, they do have particular dental problems that require attention.

Sharp Edges

One of the most common dental problems is sharp edges of the molars. The grinding surface of the molars, top to bottom, is not even; eventually sharp edges develop where no grinding has occurred. These edges will cut the tongue and inside of the cheek and can make chewing painful. A bit will press the cheek and tongue against the sharp molar edges to aggravate the condition.

Your veterinarian can smooth the sharp edges by rasping (floating) the teeth. This should be done at least once a year, more often if you notice a problem. Your horse may be spitting unchewed food, may bleed from the mouth area, or may fight and flinch under pressure of the bit.

Dental Caps

Young horses are often affected by dental caps. Dental caps occur when permanent molars grow over and attach to temporary "baby" molars. The baby molar doesn't release and will interfere with the horse's ability to eat and chew. A horse with caps will eat slowly, drool excessively, and spit clumps of unchewed food.

Your veterinarian can pull the caps. Since they are no longer attached by the root, pulling is easy and relatively painless, although some bleeding might occur.

Extranumerary Teeth

On rare occasions, a horse will grow its permanent incisors behind or beside temporary incisors that are unwilling to fall out. This again makes eating difficult and often leads to inflammation and infection. The temporary teeth must be extracted to correct the problem.

Wolf Teeth

Some young horses grow wolf teeth, small premolars embedded in the gums. Wolf teeth tend to be loose and can interfere with bit action, causing pain and poor bit response. If your horse is showing any sort of negative reaction to bit pressure, the vet should check for wolf teeth along with sharp-edged molars. Extraction will be necessary but is simple and relatively painless since the wolf tooth is not rooted.

Infection

Occasionally a horse will suffer an infection in the gums or the root of a tooth. The infection has little chance of draining and will often abscess. The abscess is usually discovered when the horse's jaw or side of the face swells.

Consult your veterinarian if an abscess is suspected. Treatment may involve extracting an infected tooth or draining the abscess from the outside surface.

Eye Problems

Consult with your veterinarian at the first sign of an eye problem. Short of an emergency, do not treat or medicate a horse's eye without explicit instruction from your veterinarian, as you are likely to further injure the eye with improper treatment.

There are several signs of an eye problem. Watch for clouding, spotting, or a shadow on the lens. Look for discharge of any sort. Note if the eyelid is swollen or if the horse blinks frequently or is unwilling to open an eye.

If your horse has suffered a serious eye injury, you may not be able to wait for your veterinarian to begin aid. If the eye is bleeding, clean the area with warm, sterile water and hold a wet, lint-free towel or rag firmly over the eye. Do not use a paper product or cotton, which will leave material in the eye. If the eyeball is displaced from the socket, do not touch the area, but hold the horse's head as still as possible, with a lip twitch if necessary.

If you can see a foreign object in the eye, try holding the horse's eyelid open with your fingers and blowing the object out with a quick hard puff of air. This maneuver takes some skill and is not always appreciated by the horse, so don't keep trying if it doesn't work on the first or second attempt. Never try to work the object out with your fingers or any other instrument. Often the object will wash out on its own with the horse's tears; if this doesn't happen in a reasonable amount of time, your veterinarian can provide treatment.

Care of the Penis and Sheath

The penis of the male horse is encased in a sheath, or prepuce, unless extended for urination or during sexual arousal. The penis and sheath are susceptible to infection because the moist, dark orifice of the sheath is an ideal breeding area for bacteria. If infection occurs, the sheath will commonly ooze pus and fluid. The penis will not fully retract and will show signs of inflammation. The penis will look waxy or scaly and may have weepy sores or pus in the folds. Call your veterinarian at the first sign of infection.

Avoiding infection is far easier than treating it. Cleaning the sheath and penis at least twice a year should ensure your horse's health in this area. This is something you can do yourself, although you may ask your veterinarian or some other gullible-but-skilled person to perform the task for you.

It is best to have someone hold the horse for you while cleaning the area, and I recommend using a lip chain or nose shank to keep the horse still, as some horses vehemently resist treatment. Kicking is a possibility, so always stand close to the side of the horse, forward of the flank. If the horse kicks forward at you, shove your weight into its side to push it off balance and deflect the kick.

Use warm water and antibacterial soap. I recommend wearing rubber gloves, but this is a personal preference because I'm (quite) a bit squeamish. Reach into the sheath and pull the penis down and out by the head, extending it as far as possible. Clean the entire penis, including the opening at the tip, with a rag and warm, soapy water. Pull the penis forward and clean inside the sheath as far as you can reach with the water only. Be prepared for your horse's protest. Rinse and dry the entire area before you are finished to ensure you do not leave any remaining soap that can cause irritation.

∩ ∩

I've mentioned the importance of carefully handling an injured or ill horse. I cannot overemphasize this point. The personality of a horse can change radically when it is suffering pain. A reliable, gentle animal can react violently and in an alien manner to your attempts at aid. This is not always the case, though; some horses will seek out human attention in the hope of finding relief from their suffering.

Prepare yourself for a variety of reactions. Always confine the horse and use methods of restraint when administering treatment. Enlist the help of a skilled handler whenever one is available. Don't put yourself in a position in which you can be struck, kicked, or crushed, or from which you cannot escape.

Consider the emotional well-being of the horse. Reducing stress and anxiety in a suffering horse can encourage cooperation and promote recovery. When treating or handling the horse, move quietly and easily and use soft words and pats for reassurance. Avoid screaming, shouting, running, or panicky movements.

Create a peaceful environment for recovery. Keep noise levels low and separate the horse from high-activity areas. Don't hover around the horse's area or allow curious onlookers to hang around unnecessarily. If observation and regular checks are necessary, try to set up a method in which you can watch the horse without its knowledge. This may mean putting the horse in a windowed stall or observing it from an adjoining stall. If your horse must be made aware of your presence on continual checks, keep your visits as comforting and stress free as possible.

10

Before You Step Up

Planning and Preparing to Ride

Education

Horseback riding is undoubtedly a skill best developed with hands-on experience. Sitting astride is not, however, the only way to learn to ride, and for greatest gains should not be the exclusive teaching medium. You can do nothing but benefit if you are willing to take time before ever setting foot in a stirrup to learn some of the techniques and concepts practiced by successful riders.

Read, read, read. Of course you must make study of this book a priority, but you should also read up on riding techniques written by different types of instructors. Pick up both English and Western riding magazines and pay close attention to any troubleshooting or advice articles.

In addition to reading, you can learn by listening. Some of the most valuable knowledge is crammed between the ears of skilled riders who wouldn't dream of taking time to write anything down. Join a riding club, haunt show grounds and riding or training stables. Eavesdrop and ask questions. Never be timid about asking simple questions. Veteran and highly skilled riders sometimes forget how much there is to learn and assume you know more than you do, so they neglect to explain things clearly.

Observation is a powerful educational tool. Watch your instructor give riding lessons before you sign up. Go to horse shows, gymkhana events, and 4-H

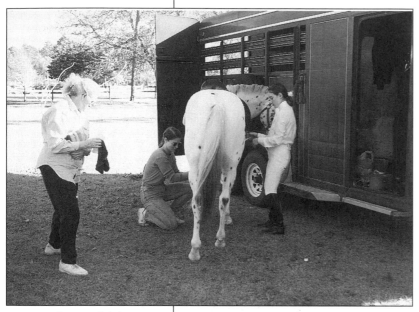

No matter how much help is available, the rider should be present and active in setting the tack.

competitions. Watch instructional videotapes and videos of Olympic horse events. Pay close attention to the methods riders use to maneuver and correct their mounts, and watch the ways various riders sit at different gaits and in different saddles. Don't assume every rider you observe is an expert; watch carefully to discern which riders are effective and which are not.

Your education must not revolve exclusively around the actual experience of riding. I don't believe anyone should be permitted to ride without first learning to properly tack and untack a horse. It's foolish to rely on someone else to saddle your horse for you. Not only do you need this knowledge, but you need to be present and active in the tacking process in order to check over your tack and make sure it is in good working condition and has been set on the horse properly. Nobody else will be as concerned as you are about your safety and well-being.

Choosing a Mount

Before proceeding, I think it's time to speak of the choice you have made, or will make, in picking out your mount. I believe the ultimate preparation for riding includes choosing an appropriate mount and getting to know that horse as well as you can before you begin.

You can learn to ride just about any horse, but a good choice when you are starting out can make all the difference in building confidence and enjoying the experience, which is ultimately what this horse stuff is all about. If you've purchased a horse, I hope you have carefully followed the instructions from Chapter 4 and have chosen a sound, well-mannered, decently trained animal. I cannot assume, though, that every reader has by this time taken possession of a rideable horse. Whether you own a horse or plan to borrow or rent one, you still need to ensure this is the right mount for your needs, so I will list some guidelines.

Physically, the horse you choose to ride should be healthy and give no indication of lameness. If you are planning to ride on any paved, rocky, or graveled surface, your mount should be shod. Your mount should be at a level of fitness appropriate for your intended riding, or you should be willing to take time to get it fit by riding slow and easy for some time.

There should be no sores, rashes, or raw spots on any area of the horse the tack will touch or that will interfere with the horse's movement. Pain or irritation caused by tack can make an otherwise docile and obedient mount behave poorly or dangerously under saddle.

Your mount also must be mature enough to ride, both physically and mentally. Horses are broke to ride as young as eighteen months. Unfortunately, many eighteen-month-olds (think of them as yearlings) are not actually mature enough to be ridden and can develop physical and mental problems if pushed too soon into riding. As a rule, never ride a horse younger than two years. Even this will prove too young for many animals.

Consider the size of your potential mount in relation to your own size. A horse that is absurdly large will be difficult to properly tack and impossible to mount without help. In some cases, a horse that is too large will be hard for a small rider to control. On the other hand, an unusually small mount will be awkward to ride, will tire more easily, suffer more back strain, and perhaps make you look silly.

Take into consideration the temperament of your mount. Although you may have dreamed of galloping bareback on a sandy beach astride the Fiery Black Stallion, this might not be the type horse that will bring you long hours of relaxation and enjoyment. As a beginner, you will do best to seek out a horse that is gentle and trustworthy by nature, not easily flustered, excited, or agitated, and one with a good background of training and experience in the type riding in which you want to participate.

Don't stress yourself searching for the absolute perfect mount—perhaps there is no such thing. Every horse will have its own little quirks. What matters is that *you* see the horse as perfect for your needs, with your eyes wide open. You will learn to tolerate, get along with, and even enjoy any minor faults your horse might display if it is generally an all-around nice horse to ride.

The Riding Facility

I believe it is vital to preplan each ride. You should know where you are going and how long you will be riding. There should be someone around to help in case of an emergency. Short of this, you must inform a responsible party of your riding schedule, even if you ride in the same area at the same time every day.

There are a variety of riding facilities you might choose, and I suspect you will try out many different types. All are appealing in some way; all can be hazardous at some time. There is the insular arena that can become a bit boring after time; the trail, which can be enormously pleasurable or could test your endurance and survival skills to the limits; the ever-convenient pasture or alluring open field that might contain hidden hazards; the fun and enticing exercise track in which strict rules might be enforced; the romantic beach that could be a dream or an obstacle course; lakes and rivers that might appear much safer than they really are; and of course, commonly used roadways, which can prove an adventure in risk taking.

The Arena

The safest area to ride in is an enclosed arena. Your horse is contained if it gets loose somehow, you cannot be lost or caught out in bad weather, you will not encounter traffic or other hazards that might frighten your horse or endanger you, the surface is (usually) ideal for safety purposes, and horses tend to mind their manners because of the limited freedom they are allowed.

The arena should have a high board fence or walls the horse can't jump or you can't be thrown over. The fence or walls should be smooth and free of any projections you could catch your leg or foot against. Ideally, the corners should be rounded.

The surface of the arena should be cushioned by shavings, peat, sand, or hog fuel, and should be kept leveled and lightly dampened to keep the dust down and the traction good.

An outdoor arena

The arena should be large enough to canter or lope a horse—at least sixty feet in diameter. If it's too small, don't try to canter or lope, as your horse could slip on the tight turns and fall.

The Trail

The trail can be a wonderful place to ride and very enjoyable for both horse and rider because of the changing scenery and sense of adventure. Trail riding is perhaps the most widely shared interest for all types of riders. A good trail is a great schooling ground for a green horse and is greatly appreciated by show and performance animals that spend most of their time practicing fixed patterns inside an arena.

The trail

If you've planned a long trail ride, you will be wise to research the area you've chosen. Note the terrain, weather patterns, any obstacles such as a narrow bridge or deep river that must be crossed, and the distance you plan to cover. You need to predetermine suitable resting areas and an adequate source of food and drink for both you and your horse. You must also be prepared for any possible weather conditions you might be caught in and pack along extra clothing, drinking water, or gear accordingly.

If your ride will take you away from a populated area, you need to inform someone where you will be and how long you plan to be out, as well as pack a first-aid kit, emergency food supply, hoof pick, knife, and wool blanket. If you've got a cellular phone, pack that as well. These provisions apply whether you are riding in a group or solo.

The easiest trail to ride is a wide dirt path, level or of gentle slopes and cleared of all obstacles and debris. Avoid steep trails, which tire your horse, cause saddle sores, and may cause the horse to lose its footing.

Avoid narrow trails with steep sides at which a horse could fall if it left the trail; rough, rocky trails that might cause your horse to stumble or go lame; trails with obstacles such as large logs, tightly spaced trees, and low-hanging branches; trails littered with garbage such as broken glass or pieces of metal that could be stepped on; and trails with heavy non-horse traffic such as logging trucks or tractors, bicycles, strollers, or motorcycles.

The Pasture or Open Field

A pasture or paddock can be a good riding area, but it can also be quite hazardous. Never ride in a pasture fenced with barbed wire or poorly marked wire of any kind. If your horse gets loose or runs off, it could run through the fence before it realizes what it's done. You should also avoid open fields bordered by paved roads, whether or not the road is highly trafficked. If you lose control of your horse and it gallops onto a paved surface, it will be surprised by the slick surface and will likely slide and fall.

Stay out of or stay at a walk in fields with deep grass; you won't be able to see hidden rocks, gopher holes, or other obstacles on the ground that could trip your horse or cause it to snap a leg. Ride slowly in fields with humps or steep hills, and don't get in a hurry on slick, wet grass, snow, or mud.

Never ride in a pasture where horses or other livestock are turned out unless you are purposefully riding herd. Loose animals will likely approach and harass you and your horse, possibly causing a fray.

The Exercise Track

Some boarding stables cater to racehorses and riding horses and will have a track on-site. If you board at a stable shared with racehorse trainers, avoid using the track during normal training hours. Otherwise, this can be a good place to ride. The surface of an exercise track is usually ideal and is often enclosed or semi-enclosed with decent fencing or rails. Riding on a track does not instantly transform you into a jockey or your mount into a racing machine, however, so don't get carried away out there.

The Beach

If a sandy saltwater beach is available, this could be a dream ride, as the surface near the water is ideal and you can often ride for long, uninterrupted stretches. There are, however, some precautions and rules that apply for beach riding.

Keep your horse out of the deep, dry sand or drifts of an upper beach. It is as difficult for them to move through as it is for you, and can cause early exhaustion and excessive strain on tendons and ligaments. Stay out of surf higher than the horse's knees because it's easy for the horse to lose its balance. Watch closely for rocks, driftwood, or other debris in the surf that could trip your horse. Heed any posted ordinances and stay away from shellfish beds and sunbathers. Avoid traffic such as four-wheelers, dune buggies, mopeds, bikes, and pedestrians.

The Lake- and Riverfront

If you are at a lake or river, follow the same safety rules as you would for beach riding. If you are thinking about riding your horse into the water, consider the unknown surface the horse must traverse. It may be deep mud, which will cause your horse to flounder, or there could be hidden rocks, logs, or broken glass that may injure the horse. The current of a river could cause a horse to lose its balance or be pulled downstream. Besides that, riding or swimming your horse through deep water can ruin your tack and you can easily fall off, leaving you at the mercy of your horse's flailing legs.

The Road

A road may be the only convenient place to ride in your neighborhood, or it may be necessary to take the road to get to a better riding area. Either way, use extreme caution when riding on a road.

Stay as far to the shoulder as possible and face traffic. Avoid roads without shoulders or with blind turns. Don't ride a horse on a roadway if it is prone to spook, afraid of traffic, or nervous and prancy. Never ride faster than a walk, as your horse can develop stress injuries from the hard surface and easily slip and fall on the slick pavement (all pavement is slick to a horse's hard hooves, especially if shod).

Keep a watchful eye out for anything that could unexpectedly frighten your horse, such as barking dogs, heavy trucks or equipment, bicycles, strollers, or motorcycles. Don't allow curious children to run up to your horse, and turn your horse's rear end toward any approaching dog to frighten the dog and ward it off.

When crossing a bridge, dismount and lead your horse across; this could save you from being thrown over the side of the bridge. Bridges often have less shoulder than a roadway, so wait until the bridge is clear of traffic before entering. Once you're on the bridge, use hand signals to slow any approaching traffic.

Don't expect drivers to respect your space. Some drivers are exceedingly cautious when approaching a rider; others will actually tease and torment you and your horse by swerving toward you, speeding up, or honking. Expect the worst from all and act accordingly. If there is a driveway you can duck into as a car passes, take it, but don't leap onto someone's manicured lawn or flower bed. If you cannot get far off the road, stop your horse and turn it toward the oncoming vehicle. This will let the horse see what's coming and will give you a chance to look the driver in the eye, which will often earn you some respect, if not courtesy.

The Surfaces

The leg of the horse is built long and of rather fine bones so the horse can run fast for long distances. This makeup, however, makes the leg rather spindly in proportion to the horse's massive body (compare the density of your legs to the thickness of your trunk, then look at a horse's build). The bones of a horse's legs are practically fragile, too easily damaged from stress or impact concussion. The joints are also fine, with very little cushion to absorb the impact of the horse's weight at fast speeds, tight turns, and hard stops. The tendons and ligaments of the horse's leg are tightly strung and can be pulled or strained fairly easily if a horse overextends a joint. An improper surface or a decent surface ridden at an improper speed are two of the most significant factors in determining whether a horse stays sound or becomes lame.

The hooves of the horse must also be considered. The hooves are small with a hard, smooth surface that is susceptible to slipping on hard or slimy surfaces. Although a shoe will protect the hoof from bruising or puncture, it does not benefit the horse greatly in traction unless it has stickers (metal tabs or cleats) or is made of rubber. In addition, the horseshoe does not normally cover the sole of the horse's hoof, so bruising or puncturing can still occur if the surface is especially rocky or strewn with debris such as broken bottles, tin cans, building materials, or nails.

Surfaces that warrant extreme caution for impact injury include pavement, hard-packed dirt (graveled or bare), and frozen ground. These surfaces will also cause your horse to slip and fall. When forced to ride on these surfaces, you must keep your horse at a walk.

Other unsteady surfaces that may cause your horse to fall are ice patches and packed snow, mud, wet clay or grass, plywood flooring, or old wooden bridges or walkways, which can be polished smooth from traffic or slickened by rain, ice, or moss growth. If you must ride on any of these surfaces, *stay at a walk!*

Rocky or steep surfaces can cause your horse to lose its footing and fall. This is especially a danger if you are riding through a rock-strewn riverbed or lake, as you won't be able to see the slick rocks under the surface. A deep, loose surface such as dry sand is also difficult; this is commonly where tendons and ligaments are injured, as a horse will overextend its joints trying to get good footing.

The manner in which you ride your horse has much to do with its ability to deal with a poor surface. I've already stressed the importance of staying at a walk on bad or questionable surfaces, but even a decent surface can give way or cause impact injury to your horse's legs if you ride too fast, stop too hard, or turn too tight.

Tacking

Tacking is the act of dressing your horse for a ride. It consists of saddling and bridling a horse and attaching any other equipment necessary for riding.

The sequence of tacking is not too important, but if you ride without a halter underneath the bridle, wait to bridle until last. I do this even when the horse will keep its halter on because it gives the horse less chance to chew on the reins or bump the bit on a wall or fence, which may hurt or frighten the horse.

Saddling

Your horse should be tied securely with a halter and tie line before tacking. Don't bridle the horse first and use your reins to tie it and don't let the horse wander loose while saddling. A wandering horse can knock the saddle off before it is secured and frighten itself, become entangled in the straps, or stomp on and damage the saddle. A loose horse also has more chance to bite or kick you while you're tightening the girth or cinch, or could just leave if it's not in the mood for a ride.

Always brush your horse before saddling, not just to pretty up the horse but to lay the hair smooth and remove any clumps of dirt or manure or stiffened patches of salty, dried sweat that might irritate the horse under the tack. Too often welts and galls are the result of tack rubbing on a poorly groomed animal.

The tack should be laid out and accessible, but not on the ground where it can pick up dirt or bedding and be stepped on. If you must lay the tack on the ground, spread a rug or towel down first and keep it out of the horse's reach. Separate the pad from the saddle and lay it on top, since this will be put on before the saddle. If you use a breast collar, it should be completely detached from the saddle to prevent tangling or hitting the horse with stray straps while setting the saddle.

Always begin saddling from the left, setting all your equipment on the horse from this side. You will have to move to the right side to adjust straps and check that everything looks smooth and straight, but the major adjustments are done on the left.

Lay the towel or saddle blanket on the horse's back first. If you keep your saddle towels or blankets folded neatly after washing them, they will have a natural crease down the middle to line up with the horse's spine so you can set it straight. The towel should always

A properly placed saddle neither touches the horse's elbow at girth, nor exposes the withers.

extend up the neck so it can be folded back over the pad, but a blanket can lay flat if you choose.

With the pad or blanket covering the withers and extending a couple inches up the neck, place the saddle on the pad with about a hand's width of pad extending in front of the saddle. Pull the whole thing back in one piece until the front of the withers barely shows. Pulling the whole rig back a few inches will help smooth the hairs to their natural and most comfortable position for the horse. Pulling free the mane hairs over your horse's withers will also reduce discomfort.

To properly place the saddle, don't do like the cowboys on the screen and toss the saddle single-handedly over the horse's back. Most horses will vehemently protest this treatment. Tossing a saddle can cause your horse to shy out from under the flying saddle and can bruise its back or send straps and stirrups flying and hitting things such as the horse or you. Again, your horse may not stand quietly while being smacked in the head by a stirrup.

If you are using an English saddle with a thin stirrup leather, pull the right stirrup iron to the top of the inside stirrup leather. Thread the end of the stirrup leather through the iron to hold the iron in place at the top. Your English saddle should be stored this way to reduce wear on the leather, so you shouldn't even need to think about it while tacking.

If you have a Western saddle, lay the right stirrup and stirrup leather over the saddle. *Don't* hang the stirrup over the saddle horn because often as not it will come unhooked and bash you in the head.

Lay all the right-hand straps of your saddle over the top of the saddle, including the girth or cinch if it is attached. Pick up the saddle with both hands, your left hand under the pommel, your right hand under the cantle. Lift the saddle so it clears the horse's back and set it straight down on the pad. Don't drop it or plop it. If you are too short to properly set the saddle, get help or stand on a bucket or bale.

Once the saddle is set and pulled back into position—the pad almost entirely covering the withers and the front of the pommel at the midpoint or just back of the midpoint of the withers—you can begin girthing or cinching the horse.

Cross to the right side of the horse. When crossing sides, don't pass under the horse's neck or in front of its head. Instead, stand facing the rear of the horse at the flank and place your near hand on the horse's rump. Pass around the back of the horse, keeping close to the hind legs and pivoting your hand in the same place while your arm swings over the top of the rump. This will prevent surprising the horse as you pass behind it through its blind spot and help stop or blunt any kick.

On the right side, check that the underskirt of the saddle is lying flat, not folded under. Lower all straps and lay them straight. If the girth or cinch is not attached, buckle or tie it on now. An English-style girth should be attached by both buckles midway up the billet straps. If the girth has elastic on only one end, buckle the end with no elastic. If you are using a Western cinch, buckle it midway up the latigo strap or tie it on.

To tie the cinch to the latigo, pull the latigo through the cinch ring inside to out and up through the latigo ring outside to in. Do this twice. When you have passed through the latigo ring the second time, take the end of the latigo strap, cross it over the front of the latigo attached to the cinch, and bring the strap back under the latigo ring, threading it out the ring through the middle and under the strap you just crossed over. Tighten the knot and run the excess latigo strap, if it hangs lower than the horse's belly, through a slot provided at the front of the saddle or through the backcinch slot or ring.

While still working on the right side of the horse, buckle the breast collar to a ring provided at the front of the saddle near the pommel. If your saddle has no such rings, you can attach the breast collar to the latigo rings or billet straps, although this may set it too low on your horse's shoulders. Only attach the collar to the right side—don't finish buckling it onto the girth and left side until the saddle is secured by the girth or cinch; if the saddle falls off before it is secured by the girth or cinch, the breast collar will prevent it from falling free and may cause a wreck.

Once all straps are attached and straight on the right side, cross back to the left. Now lay the left stirrup over the saddle or pull the stirrup high in its leather to raise it out of your way. Again, make sure you don't hook your Western stirrup over the saddle horn because it can fall and conk you on the head.

As a final check on the position of the saddle, pull the girth or cinch up against your horse's belly as if you were going to attach it. The girth should not touch the horse's elbow, nor should it be farther back from the elbow than about three inches. Your girth should lay at the flat, firm area under the horse's barrel in front of where the belly begins to round out.

If the breast collar you use is meant to be looped around the girth or cinch at the bottom of the Y, run the girth through the loop before beginning to girth up. Many Western breast collars snap to a ring attached to the cinch. In this case, it should be attached last.

To secure the English saddle, pull up on the girth billet with your right hand and pull down on a billet strap with your left. This will hold the saddle in place and bring the girth to the billet. Buckle the girth snugly on to the billets, without using any force to tighten it. Your buckle should reach less than halfway up the billet, but you should not have had to struggle to get it on to the bottom notches. If you cannot reach the billets with your girth or if you can buckle the girth without strain near the top of the billet, you need to readjust the girth higher or lower on the right side.

After the girth is attached, tighten the girth one notch at a time. Untie the horse and walk it in a circle before pulling the girth to its tightest position. This helps the horse adjust to the squeeze and prevents pinching by loosening the skin under the girth. If your horse is especially twitchy about a tight girth, you can also lift the front legs (one at a time) and pull them forward to stretch and loosen the skin under the girth, but walking the horse will usually do the same thing and is less bother.

To secure the Western saddle, run the latigo strap through the cinch ring and pull the cinch up so it loosely touches the horse's girth area. Run the latigo through the latigo ring, down through the cinch ring again, and up through the latigo ring again, just like you would have done on the right side when attaching the cinch. When the latigo has passed through both rings twice, pull down on the end of the latigo near the latigo ring while simultaneously pulling up on the same strap at the bottom near the cinch ring. This double-pull method helps tighten the cinch with less effort while holding the saddle in place.

When the saddle is snug, walk your horse for a moment, then continue tightening it. When it is as tight as you feel you can get it (you shouldn't be turnip-faced), buckle the cinch on to one of the latigo notches on the saddle or tie it on as instructed to do on the right side of the saddle—by taking the end of the latigo, crossing over the front of the latigo ring, running the end of the strap under the latigo ring outside to in, then out the middle of the ring, and under the strap laying horizontal across the front. You might want to use this tie for extra security even if you've buckled on the cinch.

As with the right side, any leftover low-hanging latigo strap should be hung out of the way on a ring or through a slot. If there is a backcinch attached, buckle it on now, leaving enough slack to enable you to place your hand between the backcinch and the belly.

To finish attaching the breast collar, buckle the left side to the ring near the pommel, the latigo ring, or the billet strap. The breast collar should be tight enough to keep it from sagging but not so tight as to impede shoulder movement or cause chafing. Some English collars have strips of elastic near the ends where the straps attach to the sides of the saddle; these are meant to be worn a bit tighter since the elastic stretches with the horse's shoulder movement.

Always check the position of the breast collar strap that attaches to the girth. Make sure it is centered; if it gets pulled off to the side, it can rub under the horse's elbow and cause an ugly, hard-to-heal gall.

Never hop on a just-saddled horse. Horses hold their breaths, push out their rib cages, and brace themselves against the cinch- or girth-tightening process, so no matter how tight you think you've gotten your girth, it may be loose five minutes later when the horse has relaxed. Even if your horse doesn't blow out, it may be uncomfortable with the newly tightened girth or cinch and may buck or lunge if you step up and move out too quickly.

To prevent being caught riding with a loose girth or having a sensitive-skinned horse buck, lunge, or rear underneath you, walk your horse around for a minute or two, then recheck and retighten your cinch if necessary. Don't be surprised if you have to do this several times. If you have an English girth, you may be able to do your final tightening after you've mounted by lifting the flap under your leg and pulling up the billets. You will have a good deal of leverage in this position. This also allows your mount to walk around as you tighten the girth, which is more comfortable for most horses.

Bridling

Your horse should remain tied during the bridling process. If you plan to ride with a halter under the bridle, leave the horse as is. If you will be riding without the halter, unfasten the halter, drop the nosepiece off the horse, and refasten the halter so it's hanging around the neck just behind the ears. If you're worried this tie won't hold your horse, do your bridling in an enclosed area such as a stall.

Before bridling, check over your bridle, making sure all straps are untwisted and attached securely. Unbuckle the throatlatch so it hangs free and loosen or unbuckle the noseband if there is one attached. Let the headstall out a few notches and drop the browband down a bit on the headstall to give yourself plenty of room to pull the headstall over the horse's ears.

Many people lay the reins over the horse's neck before bridling. I prefer to drape them over my arm and wait until I am ready to move the horse to pull them over the horse's head. This way if the horse gets loose before I've finished bridling, the bridle won't be hanging around its neck to be dragged or stepped on.

There are two common ways to bridle a horse. One method is to hold the bit in the left hand and the crownpiece of the headstall in the right hand. Standing just behind the head and facing forward, place your right arm over the horse's head so the wrist rests over the poll and the hand holds the crownpiece in front and between the horse's ears. Push the bit up into the mouth while simultaneously pulling the crownpiece behind the ears.

I prefer the second method. Rather than hold the crownpiece over the ears, I gather in my right hand both sides of the headstall just below the browband. While standing in the same position as before—just behind the horse's head and facing forward—I wrap my right arm around the horse's nose and press the wrist of my right hand, holding the headstall against the bridge of the horse's nose while pushing the bit into the mouth with my left hand. As the bit is raised in the mouth, I raise my right hand to pull up the headstall and take up the slack.

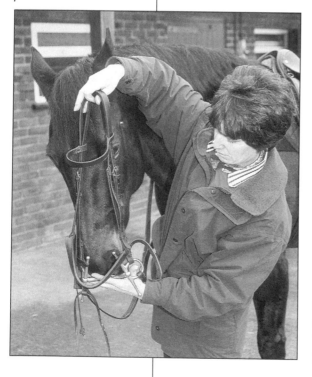

One method of bridling. The bit is pushed through the teeth as the headstall is pulled over the ears.

When the bit is in place, I release it and use both hands to pull the headstall over the horse's ears.

I prefer the latter method because the horse has a harder time lifting its nose to avoid the bit. It's easy to actually push the horse's nose down into the bit. It's also an easier way to bridle horses that are sensitive around the ears since you don't have your wrist and hand hanging between its ears.

If you come across an exceptionally ear-shy horse, it may not allow you to pull the headstall over its ears without a fight. This is a bad time to get in a struggle with your horse since any pain or punishment you inflict will be associated with the horse's original fear of having its ears touched. I've found it much easier to remove the browband from the bridle, unbuckle the headstall, and strap it on like a halter, pulling it gently up the horse's neck. Over time, especially if you devote some time daily to petting the horse gently around its face, upper neck, and eventually its ears, most horses will come to accept that nothing bad is going to happen and will allow you to bridle them normally. If not, you may have to resort to holding your horse's head still with the help of a lip chain or twitch.

As far as putting the bit in the horse's mouth, it's not always as easy as just pushing it in. If you push a bit against a horse's front teeth, the horse won't usually yield to the pressure and open its mouth. More likely, it will clench its teeth or throw its head up.

To bit even the most stubborn horse, hold the bit in your left hand so the bar lays across the flats of your fingers. Curl your fingers lightly against the bar and push it toward the teeth. At the same time, push your thumb into the corner of the left side of the horse's mouth. Apply pressure with your thumb down and back against the horse's gum until it gives in and opens up. It usually takes very little pressure; most horses will open their mouths automatically as soon as you insert your thumb.

The instant your horse opens its mouth, push the bit through the teeth and use your right hand on the headstall to pull the bit into place. Keep the slack out of the headstall until it is over the ears to ensure the bit does not accidentally drop out of the horse's mouth.

Once the bit is in place and the headstall set behind the horse's ears, you can make your adjustments. Tighten the headstall until there is only room for a flat hand or two fingers placed sideways under the headstall along the cheek. The bit should be high in the corners of the horse's mouth, with a couple of creases formed there. When your headstall is adjusted, double-check to make sure your horse's tongue is under the bit. You may have to stick your fingers in the back of the horse's mouth to find out, but the horse won't bite if you stay back near the corners of the mouth and don't dawdle.

By holding the headstall against the bridge of the nose, you force the horse's nose downward and into the bit during bridling.

Push the browband up so it almost touches your horse's ears. You can lay the horse's forelock under the browband and down the center of the forehead or pull it free of the browband, but don't leave the forelock tangled in the browband or crownpiece where it might irritate the horse.

Buckle the throatlatch so you can just put a fist between the throatlatch and the horse's windpipe. This will give the horse room to breathe, yet still be tight enough to be effective in holding the headstall on the horse if it is pulled.

If you use a shank bit, your chin strap should lay above the chin just below the jaw in the crevice formed there. It should be adjusted so you can lay your fingers underneath it without pressure against your fingers. Too tight and the chin strap will antagonize the horse and make it overreact to rein pressure. Too loose and it will be ineffective in stopping or slowing the horse. The chin strap used with a ring or D snaffle can be somewhat looser since it is not actually used to stop or slow the horse, but is just there to keep the bit centered when one rein is pulled.

To properly set a noseband, adjust it lengthwise, if possible, until it rests an inch below the point of the horse's

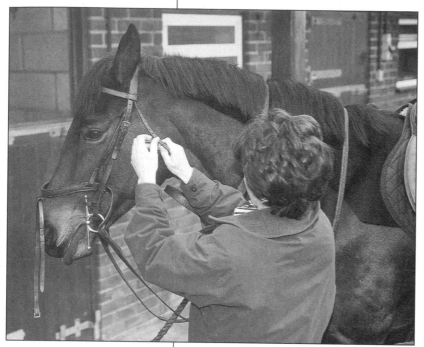

The throatlatch and noseband are buckled after the headstall is placed.

cheekbone. Around the nose, the fit should be tight, with only a finger's worth of slack underneath. The reason for the snug fit, which is also the reason a noseband is used, is to keep the horse's mouth closed while riding. If you feel this is unnecessary or it bothers your horse enough to make it toss its head when ridden, you can remove the noseband. If it is sewn on to the headstall, just buckle it loosely.

The hackamore is placed just like a bridle but is easier to do because you don't have to place the bit. The hackamore nosepiece should lay on the bridge of the horse's nose midway between the nostrils and the point of the cheekbones. The chin strap on a hackamore lays higher than that of a bit; it should be positioned just below the midway point between the chin and the cheekbone area, perhaps two inches above the chin.

∩ ∩

Once your horse is tacked, it is always wise to lead it with the halter and lead line. If the halter is worn under the bridle, pull the reins over the horse's head and attach them loosely to the saddle by hooking them over the saddle horn or tying them to an available ring. If the reins are thick and short, you may have to use another thin length of rope to tie on the reins. If the reins are extra long, they can be hooked behind the cantle.

If you ride without a halter, you can still lead with a halter by placing the halter over the headstall. Take care not to catch the shanks of the bit or hackamore on the halter as you are pulling it on.

If you choose to lead your horse by the reins, take them off the horse's neck. You will have no lead line if they are laid over the horse's neck. If a horse pulls back and you try to stop it, you will actually be pulling the horse away from you by tightening the rein on the off side.

Hold both reins in your right hand and the slack in your left, exactly as you would a lead line. Never jerk on the reins while you are leading the horse, as the pressure you exert on the bit and chin strap is extreme and can cause the horse to rear.

Never lead a horse by the chin strap. This is like having no lead line at all. In addition, it will break easily if it's made of leather or chain with leather ends, and again, pressure here is hard on the horse's mouth.

There are more tack accessories available than those I've mentioned, such as martingales, blinkers, and boots. I am not covering these here because I don't believe they should be used on a whim, but I will mention some in Chapter 12. If you feel you need additional equipment for enhanced control or performance, your instructor or trainer should advise what you need and how to use it.

The Rider

All riders should be outfitted with boots, gloves, properly fitted helmet, and long sleeves.

Last, you should prepare yourself. You may choose to do yourself up smart and outfit yourself in full English garb: breeches, jacket, high leather boots, etc.; or Western attire: chaps, cowboy boots, big belt buckle, and the like. Most of this apparel is functional for riding, but it can add up to a lot of money. You can get by with less.

There are certain items you absolutely must wear to ensure your comfort and safety. Long pants are an absolute requirement—you need only ride in shorts once to realize how much bare legs chafe against a saddle, especially if you are riding properly with a good knee grip. Riding bareback is not much better on bare legs, especially after your horse begins to sweat.

I also highly recommend wearing long sleeves for riding, even in warm weather. This may sound unnecessary, but the sleeves offer a bit of protection for your arms in case of a fall. A friend of mine questioned this advice with the argument that some days are just too hot to wear long sleeves. I find it contradictory to say it is too hot for a rider to be comfortable in long sleeves but okay to expect a horse to wear a saddle, carry a rider, and perform.

This next bit of advice I'd like you to consider a rule, not a recommendation. When riding, anyplace on any horse at any time, you must wear a helmet suitable for the purpose, and your helmet must be strapped on with a fitted chin strap. This applies to everybody, even Western riders that prefer to wear a hat. Hats are fashion accessories—*not* protective devices. Everybody that rides falls off at some time and head injuries are a genuine, horrific possibility if you ride unprotected.

An additional way of protecting yourself is to wear a safety vest. A safety vest is padded to protect ribs, collarbones, and tailbones, probably the bones most commonly fractured during a fall, especially if you are stepped on.

I also recommend boots. Boots made for riding will set your foot in the stirrup more securely and will minimize the chance that your foot might be caught in the stirrup during a fall. They may also protect your toes a bit if you're stepped on. Choose boots with a low heel, thin rubber soles, and narrow toes for best fit, grip, and protection in the stirrup. Heavy work boots are too wide and thick soled and may get caught in the stirrup. There are also riding shoes available styled like athletic shoes or hiking boots, but if you have exceptionally large feet, the toes of these shoes may be too wide—and dangerous—for your stirrups.

Consider the weather before dressing to ride. In cold weather, feet and hands tend to get chilled easily because they are held out in the open or set idly in icy metal stirrups, so plan on gloves and wool socks. The gloves should be riding gloves or other formfitting sports gloves with palm and finger gripping surfaces such as brushed suede.

Any jacket you wear should be loose enough around the shoulders to allow free movement in any direction and should not be so long that you wind up sitting on the tails. Some long jackets made for riding are split in the back to prevent this. Take care never to allow a jacket to slip over your saddle horn when riding or you could find yourself hung up during a fall.

Chaps are often used by riders, both English and Western. Chaps were originally designed to protect the legs of cowboys as they rode through brush, but are useful in several other ways. First, chaps can keep your legs warm and fairly dry in inclement weather. Second, the leather or suede chaps are made of has a stickiness that helps a rider keep a firm, secure seat in the saddle. And chaps are usually attractive, so most riders are happy to wear them.

When preparing yourself to ride, you must consider more than what you wear. It is also vital that you take into account the state of your health. If you are not well, you may easily become weak or dizzy while out on your ride, nauseated from the motion, or you could lose your equilibrium, diminishing your balance. In addition, exposing yourself to the elements may lower your body's defense system if it is already weakened.

You also need to be honest with yourself about any joint or back problems you have, or have had. Riding will most likely aggravate these conditions. Consult your doctor before stepping up.

Avoid riding when you are pregnant. The possibility that riding may damage your fetus or cause miscarriage is small but not unheard of, and of course, falling will greatly increase the risk. It's simply not worth it.

Never ride while under the influence of drugs or alcohol or when you are emotionally upset or physically exhausted. Even if you don't hurt yourself in this manner, you will likely ride poorly enough to abuse or injure your horse and could make yourself a liability to others as well.

11
Command from Above

Control and Balance
Riding Techniques

*I*f you have taken the time to get to know your horse on the ground, you are apt to have a better experience when you begin riding. Time spent with your horse on the ground allows you to become familiar with your horse's general temperament, habits, mannerisms, and quirks and should help you develop better communication skills. In addition, your confidence in riding will be strengthened by the confidence you've built while handling your horse around the barn.

You need to spend quality time with your horse; true familiarity cannot be achieved simply by planting yourself on a bucket outside the stall or spending hours hanging out at the paddock rail. To really get to know your horse, you must groom it regularly and extensively, handle it on the lead line in and around the stable area, and practice your tacking techniques, using your chosen mount as a guinea pig. Make yourself available to hold your horse for the farrier and the veterinarian, be there at least once daily to feed it, and reserve some time to simply pet and talk to your mount. Your efforts should prove to be time well spent as you and your horse develop lifelong trust in one another.

This time may also be a factor in changing your mind about the entire horse experience or at least about this particular horse. You can learn enough about your horse's temperament to guess before you ever step up if this horse is going to fight or be frightened, easygoing or bullheaded. You will also discover enough about your own reactions to be able to decide whether you are truly ready or willing to go on with the adventure and begin riding.

The following riding instructions are designed to teach you to ride safely and effectively and to keep your horse under control without resorting to abusive measures. There are various instructors that teach different styles aiming for a show ring or performance ideal. Although my instructions will inevitably help you look good in the saddle and improve your horse's performance, my concern is not that you win a ribbon, but that you stay in the saddle, stay healthy, and have a good time.

Mounting

Your horse is now tacked and waiting for you to mount. Before you even think about putting a foot in the stirrup, you must check your girth one last time. Nothing will dump you off a horse faster than a loose girth or cinch. If the saddle feels loose—if you can get a hand under the girth or cinch or you can pull the saddle side to side—tighten the girth or cinch again and walk the horse for a few minutes. Check once more and repeat tightening and walking if necessary.

Never mount a horse with a newly tightened cinch without walking it first. The horse could feel pinched and may buck, lunge forward, or freeze up when you put weight in the stirrup; even the most docile animal can react violently to a pinched girth. In addition, a horse can continue holding its breath and pushing out its rib cage much easier while standing still than when forced to move. Failure to walk the horse may result in the saddle loosening again soon after you've mounted and started off.

Your horse must be standing still in order for you to mount. If your horse is moving around, shuffling, attempting to evade you, or impatient to start off, you could find yourself hopping along on the ground with a foot caught in the stirrup. This is not a desirable position since you could so easily fall and be dragged.

The simplest way to keep the horse still while you mount is to have someone hold it. I've found, though, that people tend not to be hanging around when you need them, therefore it is best to teach your horse to stand quietly without outside help.

Take your horse to a corner area if one is available. Stand your horse so it's facing a wall or fence and its right side is close against another barrier. This will limit the animal's movements somewhat, although it can still move back or toward you.

If no corners are convenient, simply face your horse at a wall or fence. Don't aim your horse toward the exit or path you plan to take to begin your ride; it unnecessarily tempts the horse to move forward and get going, whether you're ready or not.

After a horse has proven it will stand still for mounting while its path is blocked, you can try standing the horse in an open area, but avoid your direction of exit. If the horse moves at all in any direction when you begin to mount, stop your action, pull gently on the reins (too much pressure will encourage the horse to back) and tell the horse firmly "No!" or "Whoa!" Repeat this until your horse gives in and stands still. If your horse refuses to stand still, or becomes frustrated or more fidgety over your efforts, take it back to the wall or inside a high-ceilinged stall and practice there. Whatever you do, don't get on until that horse is standing still or you will have reinforced a very bad habit.

Before you mount, the reins should be laid over your horse's neck. If someone is holding your horse for you, he or she should do so with a lead line or by holding on to the left rein *only* just below the bit. If you allow your helper to grasp both reins, you will have given up your control of the reins and the horse.

Take both reins in your left hand above the horse's neck. Hold the reins in the crotch of your thumb and forefinger and place your left hand on the crest of the horse's neck, about a foot in front of the pommel. There should be little slack in the reins, but you should not pull them tight because this signals the horse to move backward to escape the pressure of the bit or hackamore.

Stand at the girth area, facing slightly forward toward your mount's shoulder. Don't face the side or rear of the horse; you'll end up poking it in the side with your toe when you mount, which is generally not appreciated and could

Pull yourself up with your left hand holding the rein and crest of the horse's neck or mane and your right hand on the pommel of the saddle. Make sure to swing your leg clear of your mount's rump.

be read as a signal to move forward or sideways. Use your right hand to hold and position the stirrup for your foot. The stirrup should be pulled out slightly from the horse's side and turned so that when you put your foot in it your toe will be facing forward rather than jabbing into the horse's side. If you believe your horse to be the least bit skittish, rub its shoulder and girth area with your hand or the stirrup before mounting. This will almost always eliminate flinching when the horse first feels your foot against its side.

Place your left toe in the stirrup. If you can't reach the stirrup, you can drop it to a comfortable length for mounting and readjust it afterward. If the stirrup isn't easily adjustable you can stand on a bale of hay or straw or some other very stable mounting block. Avoid the use of a bucket, which can too easily be overturned.

When your foot is set, with only the ball of your foot touching the bottom of the stirrup, let go of the stirrup with your right hand and grab the pommel or the saddle horn, keeping your left hand on the horse's neck. Pull yourself up by the crest of your horse's neck and the pommel or horn, swinging your right leg high so as not to boot your horse on the rump, which would not please your horse much and might result in a negative response.

It is very common to see a person mount a horse with the left hand on the saddle horn or pommel and the right hand on the cantle. Don't do this. Mounting in this manner puts all your weight against the saddle and can cause it to roll, even if it's fairly tight and especially if your horse has flat withers. Pulling on the saddle this way also puts a great deal of pressure against the horse's withers and spine, which can pull the horse off balance and injure its back. By using a horse's neck as one of your handholds while mounting, half your weight is redistributed away from the saddle and spine to the neck, which is strong and far more flexible than the spine or withers.

If you feel insecure with your hold on the horse's neck, you can gather up a handful of mane and use this to pull yourself up on the horse. Horses are fairly insensitive and surprisingly tolerant about having their manes pulled, as long as you grab a sizable clump of hair.

If your horse begins to move forward once you've begun to mount, balance yourself with your right hand still firm on the pommel or horn and pull the horse to a stop with the reins in your left hand, giving a verbal command of "No!" or "Whoa!" If possible, do this without raising your hand off the neck, or at least without lifting it high.

If your horse sidesteps away from you as you step up, step back down and move the horse against a barrier on its right side to prevent that movement. If it backs up, move it so there is a barrier behind to stop it.

Say you're halfway up and kind of stuck—perhaps your horse is tall and you can't easily step down without leaving your foot caught in the stirrup. If your horse refuses to stand still and you have no way to block its movement, you can control your horse until you're safely mounted by turning it in a tight circle.

To turn your horse while mounting, take a shorter hold on the reins nearer to its ears, with the left rein tight and the right rein slack. Slide your left hand down the neck toward the withers, keeping it on the horse's neck or as low as possible. This puts pressure on the left rein only and will pull the head around to the left and force the horse to turn sharply into you if it decides to move. If the horse is resistant about flexing its neck toward you, jiggle your left hand to create intermittent pressure, which is harder for your horse to ignore. As your horse turns tightly into you, use the centrifugal force created to swing your right leg over and find your seat.

Once your right leg is over the horse and you are sitting in the saddle, find the right stirrup and put your toe in only as far as the ball of the foot. You may have to reach down with your right hand and hold the stirrup in position; this is better than poking around with your foot and inadvertently signaling the horse to move before you're ready.

Don't neglect to use your voice commands to let your horse know what you want from it. If you consistently say the word "No!" or "Whoa!" in a firm voice the moment your mount starts to shuffle, and follow this with a rein signal to stop, your horse will soon associate the two signals and should quickly learn to respond to your voice without you ever touching the reins.

Dismounting

Once you've gotten on a horse, it's really handy to know how to get off the right way. Dismounting is too often taken for granted and done improperly, but if you get off a horse the wrong way, you are putting yourself at risk of injury.

There are several foolish methods of dismount I must strongly recommend you never use. Probably the most common mistake is to step off a horse using the left stirrup as a stair on the way down. This is actually very dangerous because if your horse moves or bolts, your foot will be hopelessly caught in the stirrup. It's very difficult at this point to get back on and likely you will fall and be dragged.

Another unfavorable method of dismount is to lift your right leg and swing it over the horse's neck, sliding off the side of the horse on your rear end. A horse can be easily startled by a leg crossing overhead and may jump or raise its head suddenly in defense of an expected blow. If it does either of these things,

Both feet must be removed from the stirrups before dismounting. As in mounting, hold the crest of the neck or mane and the pommel, then swing your right leg over until you are resting your pelvis against the saddle.

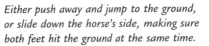

Either push away and jump to the ground, or slide down the horse's side, making sure both feet hit the ground at the same time.

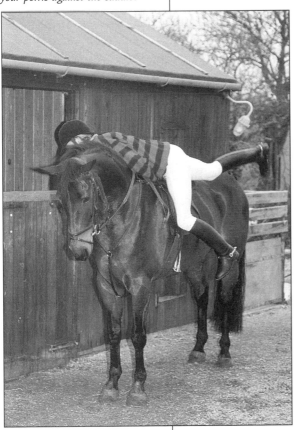

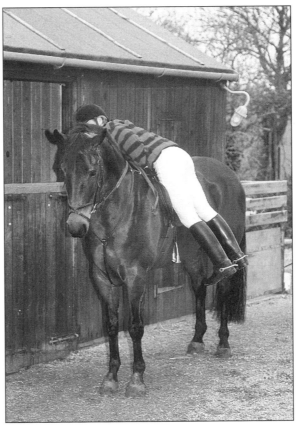

you are in a position in which you will be knocked or thrown off balance and will most certainly fall.

One of the stupidest ways to get off a horse is to slide off the horse's rump down its tail. Yes, I really have seen people do this. Your horse may be the type that will tolerate this kind of behavior, then again it may not. There's only one way to find out, and I would not take the risk.

Climbing from a horse to a fence rail, platform, or another horse is also hazardous. When you reach out and shift your weight toward another object, your horse will instinctively want to move away from the uneven pressure on its side and may leave you hanging in midair.

You might also think twice before bailing off a moving horse, even when it is only walking. There is simply too great a risk that you might stumble and fall or turn your horse loose. Your impatience will also reinforce impatience in your horse. If you can't wait to dismount until your horse is fully stopped, your horse will see no reason in the future to stand quietly while you mount and dismount.

To safely dismount, stop your horse and settle it to make sure it's not going to move again, then remove both feet from the stirrups. Hold the reins in your left hand just as you did when mounting. Grasp the crest of the neck or a hunk of mane and the pommel or horn on the saddle, again, the same as you did while mounting. Lean forward and swing your right leg clear over the horse's rump and slide down the side of the horse on your belly. With this method of dismount, you won't pull the saddle over, nor will you be attached to the horse in any manner that will leave you caught if the horse moves. In addition, both your feet will hit the ground at the same time, reducing the risk of stumbling or falling and giving your ankles and knees a break.

Setting Stirrups and Reins

Stirrups

After you've mastered mounting and dismounting, get back on your horse and check the level of your stirrups for proper length. A stirrup too long will reduce your lower body leverage and make it impossible to use the stirrups for balance. Stirrups set too short will cause you to push down too hard on the stirrups, which will force them back behind you. This in turn tends to push your toes down and in farther than is safe. Short stirrups also reduce your ability to grip with your knees, cause you to bounce more when trotting and cantering, and set you harder on your tailbone, which can make both you and the horse very sore.

At the proper stirrup level, you should be able to stand in the stirrups with your heels down and a fist's worth of space between your crotch and the saddle. While sitting, your legs should be slightly bent at the knee at an angle that puts your knee in a vertical line with your toe.

Take time to readjust your stirrups until they feel right, even if you must get off several times to do so. This is a good opportunity to practice mounting and dismounting and will ensure you have a more comfortable and controlled ride.

Reins

If you are using split reins, do yourself a favor and tie them together so they can't be dropped to the ground while you're riding. If you have a single continuous rein that is exceedingly long, it should also be tied off at a proper length.

Using reins of the proper length is important so you can control your horse with one hand if necessary, or if you are using both hands, to keep you from pitching forward if your mount props or stops suddenly. The reins between your hands will slam up against the horse's neck when you're thrown forward and stop you from falling farther than the reins allow. This has saved me from falling off or smacking my nose against a horse's neck countless times.

To find the right rein length while mounted, pull the reins up so your hand is about a foot above the pommel of the saddle and there is little slack. Tie your knot at the point on the reins where your hand rests. You should have optimal control from this length, but you can test this by lightly pulling back on the reins until your horse lifts its head and begins to respond to the pressure. If your hand is within a few inches of your torso or raised to your face or your ear, the reins are too long.

Some horses lower their heads and stretch their necks out when walking, so a rein that seemed the proper length at a standstill may turn out to be too short. Check your rein length again while riding at a walk. If your arm is extended over your horse's neck to reach the end of your reins, adjust them to a longer length. This will prevent you from leaning too far forward or riding too heavy on your horse's mouth and will also save your arms from becoming unnecessarily fatigued.

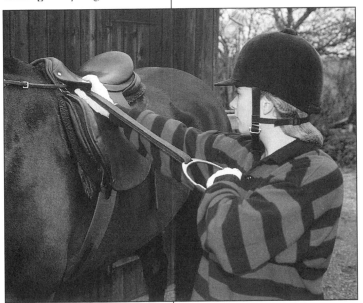

Checking stirrup length

If you choose to ride with long or split reins, you must learn to take a cross. Taking a cross is a method of adjusting your reins to whatever length you need. Since you can adjust your cross as many times as is necessary without untying a knot, there are some advantages of taking a cross over tying your reins at a set length, but I still believe it's easier and safer for a beginning rider to use a preset rein length.

To take a cross, simply cross your reins above the pommel to form an X or a figure eight. Hold both ends of the reins at the cross with no more than six inches between your hands. To lengthen the cross, let your hands slide apart until the reins slacken, then bring your hands back together. To shorten the cross, walk your hands up the reins, crossing hands as you go until you reach a desired length.

Achieving Good Posture

Good posture in the saddle will enable you to send the clearest messages to your horse. It will also tremendously increase your balance and decrease body and back soreness (for both you and your horse). If you practice good posture from the beginning, you will forever after feel uncomfortable and awkward when slouching, slumping sideways, dangling your legs, or arching your back. I have talked to many, many riders that practice good posture and find one thing in common with all of them: an absence of back pain and disorders and a low level of fatigue. I believe this is because of the good spinal and abdominal muscle support developed by hours of riding with proper posture.

Body Position

Set yourself in the saddle with your back straight and your shoulders squared but relaxed—not thrust back. Be mindful of your lower back, as it is a common mistake to sit in the deep seat of a saddle with hips thrust forward and lower back arched. This position will force you to bounce and can cause back strain. Your upper arms should be held close to your body so they don't flap at the canter, which tends to frighten a horse. Your legs should be positioned so your heels are in a straight line with your buttocks. Your knees and thighs should be pressed into the saddle and your lower legs held just off the horse's sides. Your heels should be lower than the bottom of the stirrup and your toes pointed out just slightly.

Always keep some pressure on the bottoms of the stirrups to keep leg movement to a minimum and foot position set. This will also help prevent losing a stirrup. Make it a habit to touch the bottom of the stirrup with only the ball of your foot. You cannot support your weight for long with your toe, and placing your arch on the stirrup bottom will increase the risk that your foot might be caught in the stirrup if you fall. I have, when desperate to break the shoved-in-foot syndrome, removed the boots from certain of my riding students. Riding barefoot makes a person far more aware of what part of the foot is set in the stirrup, and most people find it is actually painful to set the stirrup against the arch of a bare foot.

I find many riders are lazy or unmindful about keeping a firm grip on the saddle with their knees and thighs. Failure to do this will cause you to bounce harder and lose your balance far more often than is necessary.

Correct posture for all riding styles

Consistent gripping develops thigh muscles that will quickly make this an unconscious habit. To teach my floppy-kneed students to keep a firm grip on the saddle, I have them practice riding with a twenty-dollar bill tucked under each thigh just above the knee. The secret to success is to insist on large bills that come from the rider's own pocket.

Hand Position

The beginner should hold the reins in both hands at all possible times to ensure balanced control over the horse's head. The reins should be held evenly just above the pommel or horn, raised no higher than six or eight inches. They should not be pulled tight, nor should they hang slack. Bring up the slack until you feel some contact with your horse's mouth. By this I mean you should feel a bit of resistance at the end of the reins but not enough that your horse shows a response such as backing or tossing its head. Your hands can be held in a thumbs-up or thumbs-in position—both are effective. Some riding styles dictate the thumbs-up position; I personally prefer the thumbs-in method because I get better response from a horse with lighter pressure.

Off and on you will hear mention of a rider's hands. A rider will be said to have good hands, light hands, heavy hands, etc. I truly believe the hands make the rider. The lighter the hands, the better the rider, the more responsive the mount.

A good rider does not use the reins for balance. Balance is achieved through good posture and leg grip. The rider's hands are ideally used only to communicate with the horse.

The arms of a rider with light hands stay close to his or her sides. Pulling back on the reins, unless a horse is running off, is done with a flick of the wrists or a squeeze of the fingers, rather than the bend of an elbow. Only when a horse proves unresponsive should a rider resort to an arm pull for stopping, slowing, or turning.

The reins should be held inside the fingers, not gripped in a fist. This affords the rider better manipulation with the hands, rather than resorting to using the arms to move the horse around. Even when a rein is pulled by the extension of an arm or elbow flexion for stopping, turning, or backing, the final signal should be given through the hands, with a light flick of the wrists.

Thumbs-up hand position on reins

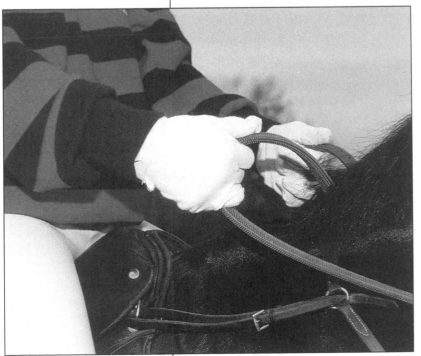

Light hands will pay off by teaching your horse to respond to subtle signals and teaching you to read your horse's responses. Heavy hands create a dull-mouthed horse at best and often a horse that fights excessive rein pressure through head tossing, grabbing the bit, or rearing.

Focus

Stargazing is a term used to describe a horse that travels with its head raised or constantly tossing. Not only is the horse difficult to control and irritating to ride, the horse literally cannot see where it is going and is bound to stumble, run into and over things, or become startled when it discovers something it should have spotted earlier.

This undesirable trait is not unique to horses; I have witnessed too many stargazing riders. You don't necessarily need to be looking at the sky to be a stargazer; if your focus is somewhere off in the distance you might as well be studying the stars.

I no more advocate staring at the ground than staring off in the distance. Your focus should shift constantly from your horse to your environment. You must always look ahead and to the side in order to spot and avoid potential spooks and obstacles before your horse does. At the same time, it is vital to check the ground directly in front of you to avoid sharp rocks, pits, humps, or other ground hazards. You must also learn to constantly read your horse's body language. The ears and head position are a good first indicator of your horse's intent. A suddenly raised head may signal alarm. Pinning its ears or shaking its head side to side may warn you of an upcoming attempt to buck.

Using Basic Signals

A key step to successful riding is to learn to give your mount signals it can understand and willingly obey. A horse has the capability of learning simple voice or word commands and instinctively picks up your intent through the tone of voice you use. It is very possible to calm a terrorized or skittish horse with a soothing tone or singsong voice. You can often stop a horse midstep of bucking by barking at it with a harsh, clipped "No!"

Your body movements, from a sharp kick to your horse's ribs to simply shifting your weight in the saddle, will be learned and read as signals. A sloppy, bouncy, leg-swinging, arm-flapping rider will invariably confuse and frighten a horse that has been conditioned to read and respond to light body signals.

Various devices are used to control a horse and signal it to perform or stop performing. The bridle is the most common and frequently used device to signal a horse. Whips and spurs are used as often to almost imperceptibly signal a horse as they are to harshly discipline one.

When sending a command message to a horse to perform in any way, always use the lightest signal first, either alone or combined with another subtle signal.

Only when a message is ignored should you increase your tone of voice or use of force. This will ensure your horse does not feel punished before it has done anything wrong. If your mount responds to your first and lightest signal, a reward is in order, which will encourage further quick and eager responses. By a reward, I do not mean you should hop off and feed your horse a carrot. Simply easing your heels from its sides or allowing some slack in the reins rewards the horse and lets it know it correctly did what you wanted. With horses in training, I use many vocal rewards; an enthusiastic "Good Boy!" or "That's it!" will be heard, understood, and appreciated.

Getting Started and Stopped

Your go signal to your mount is generally given with voice and body commands but involves the reins as well. To signal your horse to move forward from a standstill, you will simultaneously send three signals: (1) Give a go voice command by chirping, clucking, or making a kissing sound. Don't "Yee-Ha!" your horse unless you're ready for an explosive response, although many lazy horses would simply ignore this. (2) Lift your reins a bit and push them forward slightly over your horse's neck. (3) Squeeze in with your knees and press your calves into the sides of the horse, just behind the girth. Don't push back with your heels too far or lean over the horse's neck to give it rein, as these actions will force your upper body forward and off balance.

If your mount did not respond to your first signals to move forward, do all three again with increased emphasis. Make your voice command sound more

Even, relaxed (not slack) hold on the reins will keep your horse walking in a straight line.

anxious, higher toned. Raise the reins higher and make a flipping motion with your wrists as if to throw the reins at the horse's ears. Increase the pressure of your calves and grind your heels against your horse's sides.

If your horse did not respond to any of the previous signals, it is either unbroke, scared frozen, or more likely, spoiled and dulled by a rider that did not enforce his or her commands. At this point, you must exert some authority. Give your mount a good, sharp kick with both heels. At the same time, slap your thigh so the horse can see your hand raised and hear a sharp noise.

Before I go any further, I feel it is important that I remind you about establishing dominance over your horse. Once your horse accepts your dominance, a lot of future confrontations and power struggles can be avoided.

To enforce your dominance, you cannot act timidly or treat your horse as if it were a fragile doll. The moment a horse ignores a command you're sure it understood, get after it immediately with a sharper command. Never use the same soft command twice. This advice stands for any phase of handling or riding. Remember you are not giving requests, you are giving commands.

Once your horse is walking forward, keep it in a straight line by holding the reins evenly. Keep a bit of slack in the reins as long as the horse remains at a walk and you want the horse to continue moving forward, but don't let the reins droop or dangle to the point that you would be unable to pull back and stop the horse if it surged forward suddenly.

If your mount veers or tries to turn, correct it by pulling lightly in the direction you prefer with the inside rein and pushing it with pressure from your outside leg.

Practice slowing and stopping your horse by pulling straight back toward your rib cage with the lightest effective pressure until you get a feel for the degree of pull it takes to stop your horse from a walk. If your reins are held at the proper length, you should be able to do this by simply bending in your wrists. Always release the pressure as soon as your horse stops or you will force it into backing up, tossing its head, or rearing. Release of pressure also acts as a reward.

In addition to pulling on the reins, you can signal your horse to stop by settling your weight a bit back in the saddle, removing your calves from the horse's sides, and using the verbal command "Whoa." Use a soft tone of voice; it's not necessary to speak harshly unless your horse ignores you or resists the stop.

If your mount stops unrequested, first make sure you didn't inadvertently pull back on the reins, then keep it moving forward by pressing or tapping with your heels.

Don't let yourself get into a pulling match with an eager horse that constantly tugs at the bit and tries to break into a faster gait. Jiggle your wrists so the horse can't lean into the bit and pull against something steady. At the same time, you can tell the horse "Easy" in a low, lazy tone. This ought to get the horse off the bit. If it doesn't, you're either being too meek or you may need to use a more severe bit or a tighter chin strap on the horse.

Turning

There are two methods used to turn a horse by the bridle: plow-reining and neck-reining. Plow-reining simply means that if you want to make a turn, you pull back and out with the inside rein, which will bring the horse's head and body around and *pull* it into a turn.

To neck-rein, you will *push* the horse into the turn by laying the rein against the horse's neck on the opposite side of the direction you want to turn. Allowing itself to be pulled into a turn by plow-reining is a more natural reaction for a horse than neck-reining. Many horses are never properly trained to neck-rein and won't instinctively respond to this signal.

For the smoothest turn, use both hand and leg signals. This rider is pulling his mount's head into the turn with the right rein while lightly pushing its rear end out with his right calf. His left hand is pressing the outside rein against his mount's neck while his left toe lightly pushes the horse in front of the girth.

As a beginner riding with both hands on the reins, it's best to use both methods of reining simultaneously on all horses. This will ensure a response and help you keep your reins balanced. In addition, this method of reining will help teach or remind your mount to neck-rein, which should be considered worthwhile training for any horse as it encourages a horse to turn without pressure from the bit.

Although a horse will often turn by rein signals alone, you should make a habit of using leg signals to ensure the horse turns its body, not just its head, and to create a more responsive animal that is less reliant on rein yanking. Once a horse learns to respond to your leg signals, you may not even need the reins to turn the horse. Voice commands are generally not used to turn, although if your horse misinterprets your signal to turn as a signal to stop, you may need to verbally encourage it to keep moving forward.

Your horse should always be moving forward when you signal it to turn, even if you only step it out one pace. If the horse is standing still when you signal it to turn, it will be forced to pivot and may wrench an ankle or trip.

When you are ready to turn, pull your inside rein back and out. Your outside hand should follow parallel to your inside hand, which will automatically press the outside rein against the horse's neck.

At the same time you are reining, press the horse's side with your inside heel just behind the girth and press your outside foot against the lower part of your horse's shoulder, just in front of the girth. When you push back with your inside heel, you are pushing the horse's rear end away from the direction you want to turn. When you push forward with your outside foot, you are pushing the horse's front end into the turn. This creates a smooth, easily rounded turn, rather than a stilted L-type turn.

Practice turning in both directions, giving your horse enough space while making its turns so it is not forced to spin or pivot. Try turning just with the reins, then just with your leg pressure. You will probably get stronger results with the rein pressure. If you get no response to the leg pressure, you can increase the pressure while at the same time moving your inside heel back and your outside toe forward. Your horse will need much practice if it has not been turned with leg signals before, so don't resort to kicking the horse until you are positive the horse understands your signals and has chosen to ignore them.

Backing

There are times when you may need to back your horse. If your horse has not been trained to back properly, as too many horses are not, you may not have much luck with any signal.

Assuming here that your mount is trained to back, signal it to move back from a standstill by pulling the reins toward your pelvis in a give-and-take motion with both hands. At the same time, sit deep against the cantle of the saddle and squeeze lightly with your knees. Some people also use a firm verbal command of (surprise) "Back." Always keep your hands low when backing to avoid causing the horse to toss its head, and always start from a standstill—commanding a horse to back while it's moving forward is similar to throwing a car into reverse before stopping.

Your horse ideally should tuck its head to back, but don't be surprised if your horse offers some resistance to the extra rein pressure by raising its head. If it moves sideways while backing, straighten your horse by pulling in on the rein on the side it is wandering toward.

Be aware that a horse can't see straight back behind itself, so it is often cautious and not terribly thrilled to be going in that direction. You can increase your horse's confidence by not allowing it to back into holes, objects, or uneven ground surfaces, letting the horse move as slowly as it wishes, and not being excessive in your demands.

Whips and Spurs

At times you can enhance the effectiveness of some of your signals with an unresponsive horse by carrying a whip or wearing spurs. There are those in the horse industry that believe all riders should wear spurs and carry whips at all times, the belief being that it's better to have them and not need them than to need them and not have them. I see the merit in this but still lean toward discouraging the use of whips and spurs, especially by novice riders. The idea that a rider will carry or wear such devices but not actually use them is not very realistic, and I hate to see a rider become dependent on whips and spurs when most horses respond surprisingly well without them. Spurs, especially, can be abused by a novice. If an unbalanced rider allows his or her heels to bang against a horse's sides, or squeezes heels in panic, a horse will be spurred cruelly and unnecessarily. I have also seen horses that are regularly ridden with spurs eventually become numb and absolutely unresponsive from the constant jabbing and prodding; I once even saw a horse with callused-over scars at the spurring area of its sides.

If you decide you must use spurs, choose a blunt-edged pair. Blunt-edged spurs are easier to use properly than rowels and are severe enough to get most horses going.

When riding, use the spurs only to press into the horse's sides—just as you would if you had no spurs. Avoid constant tapping or jabbing, which will only serve to irritate, sour, and numb your mount, and avoid out-and-out kicking. The unexpected pain can cause quite a reaction underneath you.

Using a whip means taking one of your hands off the reins, which might cause you to lose balance or lose control of your mount. My advice is to avoid

Correct whip-in-hand position is handle up, tip down.

carrying one unless your horse is very stubborn and unresponsive, or you need to correct a bad habit.

If you decide you need a whip, carry it with the tip up in your back pocket or under your belt behind you. This keeps it out of your way and out of the horse's line of vision until you need to use it. If you prefer to hold the whip in your hand, you must learn to grip it handle up between your thumb and palm and controlled with your pinkie and third finger. Your index and second finger will grip and control the rein. This is not easy and should be practiced on the ground.

When using a whip for light signals, always keep the handle up. Turn the tip up only if you feel you must use the whip with your arm raised to slash the horse (you should rarely, if ever, need to do this). If you carry your whip in your hand, you can use it to tap your horse's shoulder without losing your hold on the reins. This tapping can be used to move a horse forward, but is most clearly interpreted by a horse as a signal to turn, as a horse will instinctively move sideways to avoid the whip.

A more effective signal to get a horse to go or increase its speed is to tap it on the rump with the whip. To do this, you must first get centered rein control in one hand. Then take your whip, handle up again, and reach back, without turning your body, to tap your horse on the side of the rump. Keeping your balance and hitting your target are both very important when using the whip. You must expect a sudden reaction from your horse anytime you touch it with a whip. If you've lost your balance and your horse surges forward, you could find yourself rolling off its rump. If you miss your mark and accidentally whack your mount on the flank, you could cause it to buck or scurry sideways. My best advice would be for you to practice your whipping technique on the ground, sitting in a saddle or on a barrel or some such thing.

Once in a while a whip can be used to signal an unwilling horse to turn. I've already mentioned tapping a horse on the shoulder to get it to move away from the whip into a turn. The other method, best used for tight turns, is to tap the horse low on the rump or just behind your leg on the same side that you want it to turn. In other words, if you want to turn left, tap the horse on the left side behind your leg. This will push the horse's rear end out while simultaneously urging it to move forward, thus automatically forcing it into a turn.

∩ ∩

All the above-mentioned techniques for signaling a horse should be practiced at a walk in a safely enclosed area until you feel you've mastered them. Don't consider yourself successful until you get reasonably immediate responses from your mount without a struggle. If you cannot control your horse at a walk, you will certainly get yourself into trouble at a faster pace.

Finding Balance

By learning how to signal a horse at the walk, you have begun to build a foundation that will help support you while you work on your balance at faster paces. It is exceedingly difficult to concentrate on developing your balance if you haven't yet learned to control the speed and direction of your mount. At the same time, you can't control a horse very well by sending garbled signals as you are bouncing and sliding all over the saddle or sitting in the dirt. For this reason, it is imperative that you learn to balance yourself right away and *practice, practice, practice* until you get a sense of equilibrium in the saddle.

Picture yourself as a tripod, balanced on three legs. As a rider, your three points of balance will be the balls of your feet and your rear end. Push your feet slightly forward and press down on the balls of your feet. Notice how this action pressed your seat down in the saddle. At the point in which you feel equal pressure at your seat and both feet, you have reached a

Pressure against the seat of the saddle and the stirrups, combined with good rein contact and a firm knee and thigh grip, will greatly enhance balance.

point of balance. This is generally the balance you will use at the walk and canter and sometimes the trot.

This three-point position of balance sometimes pushes your feet forward farther than would be considered acceptable in the show ring, but is very effective in keeping a beginner's seat planted in the saddle. Using your feet and seat for balance does not excuse you from gripping with your knees and thighs for balance; however, these two methods complement each other. Pressure on your feet and seat will prevent bouncing; a good upper leg grip will prevent pitching forward or sliding side to side.

Walking

While riding at a walk, practice your points of balance. The (light) pressure you exert should be against the stirrups and seat of the saddle. Your knees and thighs should grip the saddle firmly, but your lower legs should be relaxed—not squeezing against the horse, which would push your feet back too far and send inadvertent signals to the horse to increase its pace.

Don't let your hips swing side to side with the motion of your horse, and don't let your upper body sway or bob up and down. Rather, let your pelvis rock forward and back with the saddle while keeping your back erect. Tuck your "tail" a bit to prevent arching your lower back.

When turning your horse at a walk, increase the pressure a little on your outside stirrup while decreasing the pressure on the inside stirrup. Keep your seat squared in the saddle and don't lean with your upper body.

If your horse changes directions suddenly without a signal from you, you will feel your upper body thrust in the opposite direction. Straighten quickly, bracing your hands against the pommel or the horse's neck if necessary. Again, use more pressure on the outside stirrup and press against the horse's side with your inside leg. This will not only help you stay on, it will signal the horse to stop moving in that direction.

Stop your horse as soon as you feel you've regained your balance. Reduce the slack in the reins and keep better contact with the horse's mouth to prevent any further unexpected movements.

When stopping a horse, even at a walk, your body will naturally lean forward unless you prevent the motion. Take a deeper seat by pressing your feet down harder and relaxing your lower back. Lean back slightly while pulling back on the reins. Keep your lower legs just off the horse's sides so it's clear to the horse you no longer want it to move forward.

If your horse stops abruptly or without first receiving your signal, you won't be prepared and you will feel yourself thrust forward. Stop yourself by bracing both hands, or the end of the reins between your hands, against the pommel or the horse's neck. Get your weight back immediately and squeeze the horse with both legs to signal it to continue forward.

If your horse surges forward unexpectedly you will, predictably, be thrust back. If you've neglected to keep a good grip with your knees and thighs, your feet may come up and forward at the same time. If this happens, get your feet back and under you, and if necessary, pull your upper body forward by grabbing the pommel or horn of the saddle. *Do not ever* use the reins to pull yourself forward or balance yourself.

All the techniques mentioned so far should be mastered at a walk before increasing your horse's speed. Before you go on, you would do well to humble yourself with a simple exercise that will not only show you how well you've picked up on balance, but should work to increase your balance tremendously.

You will need a handler to carry out this exercise. Ask a handler to lead your horse at a walk in various directions without warning you of his or her intentions. Your handler should start the horse from a stop, stop the horse, make circles, figure eights, and squared turns. While all this is going on, you are going

When posting, the rider catches herself with her knees on one stride then drops to the saddle on the next.

to be mounted, eyes closed and arms raised to the sides. Off and on, lower your arms and cross them in front of you, then raise them to the sides again. If you feel you are going to fall, tell your handler to stop immediately, but don't open your eyes during the exercise, not even for a second. Don't be disappointed if it takes several sessions of this exercise before you get your bearings and achieve some sort of equilibrium, and don't be shocked if you feel a bit queasy, as motion sickness can occur even at a walk if your eyes are shut.

Trotting

The trotting gait of a horse is one in which the horse places two feet on the ground while two feet are raised, with the opposing front and hind leg raised while the opposite legs are on the ground. This gait is jarring and nearly impossible to manage without some degree of bouncing.

Western riders avoid bouncing to a good extent by trotting their mounts at a very slow pace, almost a walk. They call this pace a jog. The Western rider can remain seated fairly comfortably in the saddle this way, but his or her upper body still bobs more than you would normally see at a walk or canter.

When jogging a horse sitting down, your balance is centered in your seat. Your lower legs will be relaxed and there is very little pressure on the bottom of the stirrups. As always, maintain a good thigh and knee grip.

At a faster-paced trot, Western riders often keep themselves from bouncing by standing in the stirrups. Balance is maintained by the weight set in the stirrups, a good knee grip, and by leaning forward and holding oneself up by gripping the mane, neck, pommel, or horn.

Standing can be a precarious position. Besides the fact that you only have one hand to steer if you use the other to grip for balance, you are also more likely to be tossed around by any unexpected movement. If this happens, it's best to sit right down until you've regained your balance, stopping your horse if necessary.

The English rider posts to avoid being bounced around at the trot. Posting looks like an exaggerated bounce but is actually a controlled and very comfortable method of riding a trot that eliminates jarring. Posting can be done at any pace of the trot.

To post, let your horse start off trotting a step or two while you remain seated in the saddle. When the motion of the horse bounces you up and forward, catch yourself by squeezing with your thighs and knees, then immediately drop back into the saddle. Continue to catch yourself on the upward bounce and drop back into the saddle to the rhythm of the horse's trot. If your horse changes its rhythm, sit out a couple of steps, then resume posting to the new rhythm.

The secret to posting well is to avoid standing in the stirrups when catching yourself. There should, in fact, be only enough pressure on the stirrups to prevent you from losing one—your knees will catch and lift you. This will give you minimum rise out of the saddle, which is the ideal. While posting, balance is controlled mainly by a good knee grip, but you can also lean forward and rest your hands or the reins between your hands against the crest of the horse's neck just forward of the pommel. This again gives three points of balance: the knees as two points and the third point fluctuating between the weight set in the seat of the saddle and the weight moved forward over your horse's shoulders.

If your horse moves unexpectedly in any direction while you are posting, do as you would have done in any other walking or trotting situation. Sit down, recenter your upper body, and get your feet out in front a bit, pressing down on the off-side stirrup. Stop the horse if necessary and correct your handhold on the reins by reducing slack until you can feel the horse's mouth and the horse can feel your hands.

Cantering (Loping)

The balance you will use at the canter, lope, or gallop is much like you used to ride at the walk, but with the extra momentum and bounce of these gaits, it will take more practice and concentration to achieve.

The canter is a four-beat gait, starting on a hind foot and ending on a front lead—a front foot that extends farther and hits the ground a little harder. As soon as a horse lands on its front lead, it uses this leg to propel its rear end off the ground into another stride. The force of this push thrusts the rider up and forward. When the horse's rear end lands, the rider is slammed back into the saddle. This action creates a bounce if a rider sits loose and allows it. With practice, you will be able to remain steadily seated while cantering, loping, or galloping.

The centered seat. The rider's weight is centered over the horse's girth.

The forward seat. The bulk of the rider's weight is shifted over the horse's shoulders.

The Centered Seat

To balance yourself in a centered position while cantering, move your feet slightly forward and press your bottom deep into the seat of the saddle. Keep a firm grip with your knees and thighs and some pressure on the stirrups. Relax your pelvis and let it rock forward and back with the motion of the saddle. Your upper body should be erect, your upper arms close to your sides, and your hands low. There should be minimal movement of your upper body and absolutely no head bobbing; all your motion and shock absorption should be contained in your pelvic area and knees.

As long as you can reach your reins at the pommel, it's not necessary to lean forward. In fact, if you find it necessary to lean forward to reach your reins, you need to readjust their length because leaning forward will displace your deep seat and make it impossible not to bounce. In addition, leaning forward may cause your feet to be pushed too far back, which will reduce your balance, force your toes farther into the stirrups than is safe, and may cause you to accidentally squeeze your horse with your heels, inadvertently signaling it to pick up the pace.

The Forward Seat

Some people deliberately gallop a horse while leaning forward or standing in the stirrups; this is a completely different style of riding at the canter and might be a good choice if you have a horse that has a rough, rocky gait that is difficult to sit. It is also wise to shift to the forward position when you increase your horse's speed from a light canter to a brisk gallop. For one thing, this often gives you and your mount a heightened sense of control, as you will naturally ride a little closer and heavier on the horse's mouth. This also makes up for the increased bounce generated by the faster pace. By leaning forward or standing and shifting weight to the horse's neck and shoulders rather than the seat of the saddle, bouncing can be eliminated altogether. The knees and stirrups are used to support the rider's weight; the knees especially are important as they also act as shock absorbers. The rider must keep both knees flexible to allow them to bend and straighten (not lock) with the rise and fall of each stride.

To gallop standing up or leaning forward, the bulk of your weight should be transferred from the center of the horse and the seat of the saddle to the shoulders of the horse and the area your knees will press into.

If you are riding in a Western saddle, do not use the saddle horn to balance yourself when leaning forward or standing. Your hand will be off the rein and held too close to your body to be very effective in maintaining your balance.

Keep both hands on the reins with only a short section of rein between your hands—no more than six inches. If your reins are long, tie them shorter or cross them. Allow the horse very little slack—not just to keep it from running off, as some may think to try once you've quickened the pace, but to give it something to balance itself against since your forward weight does offset the horse's natural balance. You must be very careful here not to take up so much slack that you are yanking on your mount's mouth, and don't dare rely on the reins to hold yourself forward or balance yourself.

Lay your hands so the rein between them acts as a bar with which you will press against the crest of the horse's neck. This prevents you from falling forward if the horse stops suddenly. Feel free to take a handful of mane, right at the roots, to help keep your hands in one place and balance yourself, but be aware that when you do this you may give up some control of the reins.

When your hands are positioned and you feel you have a good hold on the reins and adequate contact with your horse's mouth, stand up and grip with your knees. Your seat may remain touching the saddle, but no weight will be pressed down against it. Keep pressure in the stirrups to help keep your feet forward, but don't use your stirrups to stand—your weight should be pressed mainly upon your knees. This position may be difficult for you to master and may feel awkward, and at first you may not have the leg strength to hold yourself up with your thigh muscles. If you are having difficulty, practice at a walk until you've built some strength and coordination and use your centered seat to canter in the meantime.

To steer the horse while galloping with your weight forward, turn your inside wrist in the direction you want the horse to turn and press the horse's side just behind the girth with your inside calf. If this does not generate a response, slide your inside hand back toward the pommel of the saddle. Try not to lift your hand off the horse's neck. If you cannot steer or maintain a straight course in this manner, sit down, slow and get control of your horse, and practice some relatively small circles and figure eights at the canter with a centered seat until you feel your horse will respond to a lighter rein signal. Then and only then should you resume your attempt at riding in the forward position.

Turn your horse only in gradual, easy circles while galloping or cantering in the forward position. If you want to turn the horse tighter at this speed (which you shouldn't unless you fully trust your balance and control over the horse), you must sit back in the saddle and recenter your weight, perhaps moving your feet forward a bit. This not only helps you balance yourself, it also helps balance your horse. A horse is much more likely to stumble in a tight turn if all your weight is centered over its front legs.

As with the slower gaits, if your horse makes a sudden unrequested move in any direction, your balance will be thrown off. You must recover by recentering yourself. Brace yourself with your hands on the neck or pommel and force your bottom back in the saddle by getting your feet forward and pushing back. Grip hard with your thighs and knees, but resist the urge to shove your feet back and squeeze the horse with your lower legs to stay on. You will only throw your weight unfavorably forward and will lose your lowest points of balance. And of course, your mount will interpret this hard, sudden squeeze as a request to move faster or jump harder, which will only serve to make staying on that much more difficult.

Regaining your balance becomes, predictably, more difficult as the speed of your horse is increased; this is why I must stress that you practice your balancing techniques at a slow pace before you go racing wildly off into the sunset.

Fine-Tuning

Once you have developed a sense of equilibrium while riding at all gaits and have mastered control over your horse, you can work on a few techniques that will make your horse look better, enhance its balance, and encourage it to become more responsive to lighter commands.

Collection

Your horse may naturally collect itself while under saddle or it may already be trained to do so when cued. Even a horse that has not been previously schooled to collect itself should respond relatively quickly when given the proper encouragement.

Collection is a manner of posturing in which a horse readies itself to receive commands. A collected horse will appear outwardly alert and rather tightly strung. The neck should be raised, but arched or bowed, and the chin should be tucked so the horse's head is at a vertical or near-vertical angle. This appearance should be consistent whether the horse is standing or cantering. A collected horse is more likely to respond instantly to a cue and will be athletically more prepared for better maneuverability. Collection also enhances a horse's natural balance.

The premise behind collection is that the horse's energy is contained so it is ready for whatever physical endeavor you ask it to perform. If you have a highly responsive or well-trained mount, it may naturally collect itself without any cues from you. A lazy or poorly trained animal will not, however, collect itself without your instruction.

To signal your horse to collect itself, squeeze in with your knees and calves as if you want the horse to move forward. Simultaneously, lower your hands to the level of the pommel and pull back lightly and intermittently with your wrists. This action will prevent the horse from increasing its pace while pushing it forward into the bit, ideally bringing the horse's chin in toward its chest, thus the vertical head position.

You must be cautious when collecting your horse not to overcue it, as this may cause confusion and resistance. It is probably best to work on your cues at a walk and slow trot. A standing horse may rear in confusion, and a cantering horse could react by tossing its head or hopping up and down.

It's not necessary to continually cue your horse to collect itself, and in fact, this would soon irritate and frustrate your mount as you would not allow it a chance to relax. Collection is best used to prepare a horse to change gaits, to force it to stand at attention, and to control the horse's action at a canter. A collected horse at a canter will be more upright and balanced, with a more even, higher step on all fours, rather than a ground-sweeping, long-strided ker-plunk and dramatic head drop at the end of each stride.

Changing Leads

You should understand by now that a horse's four-beat cantering gait ends with emphasis on one of the front legs. That leg, called the lead, extends farther and hits the ground harder than the opposing leg. A horse takes its leads with both a front and hind leg, but the front is emphasized most. A stride may go like this: right hind hits the ground first followed by left hind (the lead), then the right front hits the ground followed by the left (the lead). End of stride. The horse uses its front lead leg for propulsion into the next stride.

The collected trot. The horse's head is near vertical; its gait is tight and balanced.

The uncollected trot. The horse's nose is extended; its gait is long and loose.

A horse is naturally supposed to take whichever lead is to the inside of a turn. This is because the brunt of the horse's weight will land on the lead leg, and it can therefore lean into and balance itself better in a turn. Surprisingly, many horses will not take the correct lead without cues or will switch leads in front but not in back, or vice versa. This is called cross-firing or cross-leading and is dreadfully uncomfortable to ride, unattractive to watch, and frequently causes stumbling.

To cue a horse to take a particular lead, perhaps the simplest method is to move from a trot to a canter while making a turn, nudging it with an outside heel behind the girth. This should encourage the horse to pick the inside lead without any other cue.

If you are cantering and find you must change your horse's lead, you can do one of two things. First, you can slow the horse to a trot, then immediately move it back into the canter, exactly as explained above. The second method is to remain at a canter while giving the horse a cue to change leads—a lead change at a canter is termed a flying lead change. To make a flying lead change, you must offset your mount's balance somewhat. To do this, take enough slack out of your outside rein to pull your horse's head to the outside and make it think you want it to turn in that direction. Before your horse has a chance to respond and make a turn, let loose the outside rein to abruptly release the horse's head while at the same time giving it a quick nudge with your outside leg behind the girth. This will push your horse's weight unexpectedly to the inside, forcing it into the correct inside lead.

This horse is on its left lead. The left front leg is the last to land in a stride and is used to propel the hindquarters into the next stride.

For some horses, changing leads is an athletic challenge, especially flying lead changes. The importance of proper leads may be negligible for pleasure or trail riding, but it is essential for any performance or show animal to enhance its balance (and please the judge). If your horse is awkward or uncomfortable about lead changes, give it a lot of practice by doing figure eights and small circles at the canter. I find it best not to bully a horse or continually antagonize it into changing leads because it is often not aware of what you are trying to achieve—it is more likely concentrating on direction and speed. You will get better, more natural results if you simply slow the horse to a trot and start over, or if you can gradually decrease the size of your circles and figure eights until your horse discovers for itself the benefits of taking the correct lead.

Maximizing Your Horse's Balance

As previously mentioned, your own balance in the saddle can enhance or interfere with your horse's balance; it is often necessary to redistribute your weight to aid your horse in certain situations.

When making a turn, set your weight back in the saddle and lean out slightly so that when the horse bends into the turn, your trunk remains upright. Lean a bit of weight on the outside stirrup and decrease the pressure on the inside stirrup. Stay off the horse's shoulders during a turn; your horse needs weight over its hindquarters to give it a push and will overbalance and tend to stumble if your weight is too far forward.

When stopping a horse, always press your weight back against the cantle of the saddle to put weight over the horse's hindquarters. This will encourage the horse to stop by tucking and dropping its hindquarters, rather than jamming on the brakes with the front legs, and is essential if you are making a stop from a gait faster than a walk.

When riding up an incline, push your weight forward over your horse's shoulders to give it better footing with its front legs. Don't just lean forward, get your rear up and out of the saddle by standing in the stirrups. If you're climbing a very steep hill, hold yourself forward by grabbing a handful of mane. If the mane is roached or there is insufficient mane to hold, grab the horn or pommel. This is one of the only times it is acceptable to hang on to the horn for support.

When descending a hill, lean back in the saddle until you are sitting upright and level. This puts your weight back over the horse's rear end to help the hind legs dig in and find footing and takes your weight off the front end, which could trip the horse or push it forward too fast.

Avoid climbing or descending at any rate faster than a walk. Trotting or galloping uphill is taxing for a horse and can tear a muscle or ligament. Going fast downhill is a sure way to lose control of the horse since the horse has trouble controlling its own speed once it gets rolling. In addition, it is very easy for a horse to lose its footing trotting or galloping down a hill and it could easily fall.

The rider helps his hunter-jumper rise over the obstacle by shifting his weight forward.

Bareback Riding

Riding bareback is more difficult than riding with a saddle because the only way you can hold yourself on is by gripping with your legs and holding a handful of mane. This is a wonderful way to improve your natural balance, however, since you're forced to rely on yourself to stay centered rather than stirrups, horns, knee pads, cantles, and the like. I recommend all beginners spend some time riding bareback, so long as you have a predictable, well-mannered mount and a safe riding area.

Mounting

The easiest way to mount a bareback horse is to ask someone to boost you up. Stand with one hand on the mane and one hand on the center of the horse's back. Lift your left leg, bent at the knee, and have your helper boost you by pushing up on your shin as you jump. Don't expect your helper to actually lift you; you must do most of the work by jumping and pulling yourself up with your arms.

If you're alone and reasonably athletic, you can jump on without help by holding on as just instructed. Jump up so you land with your belly on the horse's back, then pull yourself into a sitting position. You can also swing up by holding the mane with both hands, facing the rear of the horse, and swinging up so you are vaulted onto the horse's back. Neither of these mounting methods may be appreciated by your horse, especially if you attempt a vault but only make it halfway up. If you're not certain of your horse's willingness to stand cooperatively, or your athletic ability, take precautions by mounting in an enclosed area.

The methods just mentioned will be impossible for some not-so-athletic riders, especially if the horse is tall or uncooperative about standing still. You can still get on alone, however, if you use a mounting block or bale of hay or straw as a stepping stool. Make sure you put the horse in an area where it can't move away from you if you mount this way, ideally in a stall if the ceiling and doorway are high enough that you won't bump your head.

Balance

A sense of balance is vital for keeping yourself centered on the horse's back. You will need to practice at slow paces and make gradual, easy turns before you achieve equilibrium. If you get in a hurry, I can guarantee you will take a tumble.

You'll probably find that the forward motion of a bareback ride is not too much more difficult than riding in a saddle if you've already developed a good knee and thigh grip. The hardest thing to overcome is the side-to-side sliding, especially on a turn. You can give yourself a better grip for this by wearing chaps or riding on a bareback pad—a stirrupless pad held in place by a girth strap. The bareback pad is also wonderful for keeping your pants clean and protecting your rump from a hard spine. Be aware, though, that the bareback pad is not meant to be used with stirrups—they should be removed and the straps cut to prevent them being reattached. Stirrups are deadly on a bareback pad, as the pad will naturally slip to the side or under a horse's belly if uneven weight is set in a stirrup. You should also avoid riding on a loose pad or saddle blanket. If it slides, you'll go with it.

Sit back and keep your knees slightly forward. Squeeze the horse's sides with your knees and thighs to hold yourself on. Don't grip with your lower legs unless you need to signal your horse. Rock your pelvis with the motion of the horse's back and use your hips to keep pushing yourself to the center when you begin to slide sideways.

A common problem with bareback riding is that riders tend to use the reins to balance themselves. This is unfair and abusive toward the horse that is having its mouth yanked and is reprimanded for responding to inadvertent signals to stop and turn.

If your balance is wobbly, grab a hunk of mane and leave the reins for steering and stopping. If your horse has no mane, tie a piece of rope or pull an uninflated inner tube from a bicycle tire around the horse's neck and use this as a handhold. Don't become dependent on a handhold, however; think of it only as an emergency aid for those shaky moments. Riding constantly with a handhold will force you to lean forward, which actually decreases your balance. It also takes up one of your hands, which would be more useful holding a rein. You will be much better off in the long run to slow the horse until you find a pace you're comfortable enough with that you don't feel the need to hang on. Believe it or not, if you are patient and persistent, you will eventually be able to gallop bareback with nothing more than your knees to hold you in place.

12

The Imperfect Mount

*What to do When
the Ride's not so Smooth*

Behavior problems of the horse that may occur during riding include head-tossing, prancing, refusing commands, spooking and propping, running off, bucking, and rearing.

Some undesirable behaviors are annoying, others are extremely dangerous and cannot be tolerated. Often they are caused by human error and could be prevented with a bit of knowledge and effort on the rider's part. Whatever the circumstances, ignoring a problem under saddle or convincing yourself that your horse's poor behavior is cute or inevitable due to its high-strung nature will only serve to reinforce bad habits and create an animal that is disrespectful, unpleasant to ride, and a potential hazard to you or its next unsuspecting rider.

Head-Tossing and Stargazing

Repeated head-tossing while under saddle may indicate your horse has a nervous or excitable temperament. This condition may be chronic or caused by stressful circumstances such as a first parade venture, a ride in unfamiliar territory, or jitters in expectation of a speed performance such as barrel racing. Head-tossing can also signal a problem with your bridle, your horse's mouth or teeth, or the way you handle the reins.

On occasion, a horse will learn to toss its head in order to flip up the shanks of the bit. This causes the rider to lose rein control and gives a clever horse a chance to run off or otherwise disobey.

Stargazing is almost identical to head-tossing and usually shares the same causes. A stargazer generally travels with its nose in the air and its eyes to the sky. It can do this without tossing its head up and down, but generally a stargazer is also a head-tosser. A stargazer cannot see the ground on which it is traveling and is prone to stumbling or running into things. In addition, it is extremely difficult to get rein control over a horse with its nose pointed so high, so it is imperative the horse be corrected.

First, examine your horse's mouth for any possible problems by pushing your fingers into the corners or grasping its tongue to force its mouth open. Check that the tongue is under the bit and the bit is high in the corners and not bumping against a tooth. Look for loose teeth, intrusive wolf teeth, sores at the corners of the mouth, or bleeding gums.

Check the bridle for any possible irritants. Make sure the headstall is not too tight, the browband is not in the horse's eyes or pressed against an ear, and there are no loose straps that might slap your horse in the face or eyes when the horse is moving. Check that there are no rough or sharp edges under the fastenings that might chafe your horse's face.

Feel around the bars, joints, and corners of the bit for any sharp edges or crusty buildup. If you are using a noseband, loosen it a notch or two to see if that helps. If you are using a hackamore, check under the nosepiece and around the jaw for any sores or swelling. Last, check that your chin strap is not pinching, chafing, or cutting the horse's jaw or chin area.

If all looks well and your horse consistently tosses its head with different bridles, bits, or hackamore nosepieces, you might assume your horse is a nervous or excitable type and is fidgeting with its head, or that it has developed the habit in defense of a rider with heavy hands or in memory of a time when its mouth was sored by a poor rider or tack. In this case, this habit is as hard to cure as nail biting.

As a means of prevention for a nervous horse, you might have luck by offering your horse more chances to exercise. Try turning it out more often in a large space. If that's not possible, you can ride it more often and for longer, slower sessions or you can walk it or lunge it before riding.

Watch the way you are handling the reins. Lighten up on your hold and lower your hands as far as possible to see if this eases your horse's head-tossing. Unfortunately, many horses will not respond favorably to light hands if they've already become accustomed to having their mouths yanked. If you lighten up, the horse will either assume you are giving it permission to take off or will ignore your efforts to be kind and will continue head-tossing. This does not mean you should give up, however. Try riding in a small, confined area, always keeping your hands light and low, to see if your horse can eventually catch on to the fact that you are not going to abuse its mouth.

If simply lightening your hands does not help, it may be time for some mild discipline. Correct your horse by keeping light intermittent pressure on the reins, jiggling the reins when the horse tosses its head. Don't be surprised if your horse reacts by shaking its head more; just keep jiggling. Don't lose your temper and resort to jerking on the reins. This will not stop the horse from head-tossing and could cause it to throw its head back in your face or rear.

Another method that works occasionally is to ride with a companion or talk soothingly or sing to your horse. If a horse's nervous head-tossing stems from being separated from its buddies or lacking confidence while alone on a ride, a buddy or reassurance from you that it is not alone can be quite effective. Remember that horses are herd animals by nature and tend to be uncomfortable when isolated.

The last method I would try is restraint. You can deter head-tossing with devices such as a tie down or running martingale, and you will probably find this a must with a stargazer.

The tie down is a noseband on its own headstall strap. Another strap is attached underneath the noseband and runs between the horse's front legs to attach to the girth or cinch. It can also be attached to the center chest ring of a breast collar instead of the cinch, but is not as effective this way.

The tie down prevents a horse from lifting its head higher than the strap will allow and reprimands the horse by bumping its nose but will not stop side-to-side head-tossing. If you use a tie down, adjust the length of the strap so your horse can raise its chin to a level even with its withers. Don't get overenthusiastic and tie the horse's head too low; it will fight the excessive restraint and possibly rear.

The running martingale consists of a strap that runs from the girth through the horse's front legs, then splits into two straps, with a ring attached to the end of each strap. The straps are held in position by a collar strap around the horse's neck and chest. The reins are threaded through the rings, which work to keep the reins low and thus to keep the horse from raising its head.

The martingale works well to keep a horse's head down and enhance proper head set while riding, but a horse can still toss its head while wearing one if it really wants to.

There are a few other restraint devices that can be used to prevent head-tossing, such as draw reins or a tie-down strap attached to the horse's chin strap, but most are not intended for use by novice riders. If you feel you need to use restraint more severe than a tie down, I strongly suggest you do so only under the advice and supervision of an instructor or trainer.

Prancing

Prancing is rather pretty to watch and brings to mind a happy, spirited horse. You'll find, though, that it gets tiresome real fast if you are riding a prancer that won't quit. Prancing is a high-stepped trot or canter at a pace as slow as a walk and often entails side-to-side motion. The gait is uncomfortable and hard to sit without bouncing. It's also hard on the horse's shoes and often a horse will knock itself on the ankles with its hooves, resulting in bruises or cuts.

Prancing is a sign that your horse is nervous, excited, or anxious to get somewhere. You can't really get after a horse for prancing by yelling at it, hitting it, or jerking the reins because this will only upset an animal that is already on edge and could promote some far more serious leaping around.

The best way to prevent prancing is to take the excitement out of the ride. Go on longer, slower rides until your horse becomes bored. Give the horse more out-of-saddle chances to wear itself down, such as running around in a big, open pasture. Avoid unfamiliar riding areas or places teeming with activity.

For a quick, temporary fix while riding, every time your horse prances move it up into a brisk trot. Keep it trotting until the horse seems more settled, then slow down to a walk. If the horse resumes prancing, you resume trotting.

To correct the horse and break the habit for good, bring the horse to a complete stop every time it starts

One method of discouraging prancing is to move your mount into a trot the moment it begins to prance.

prancing. Talk to it soothingly and pat its neck. Don't move forward again until the horse stands completely still on a slack rein, even if this means waiting through long periods of fidgeting. Stop again every single time the horse starts prancing. This can be a very tedious exercise since you may have to stop the horse a hundred times, but it could be the only way you will convince your horse that prancing is not allowed—ever.

An occasional horse is so hyper it will not be able to stop fidgeting no matter how many times you try to make it stand quietly. If you press your point with such a horse, it will resort to rearing or running backward. If you are so unlucky as to end up with a horse like this, try walking the horse in tiny circles (small enough that the horse can't prance) rather than stopping it, at least until your horse is worn down enough to obey your command to stop.

If your horse has previously been involved with extremely stressful activities such as barrel racing or roping where explosive starts and quick stops are expected, or walking parades where the horse is subjected to overwhelming commotion, you probably will need tranquilizers to control the horse's prancing when exposed to similar situations. In this case, you can either accept and put up with your horse's behavior or avoid those situations entirely.

Refusing Commands

There are several reasons a horse may refuse a command, the simplest being that it didn't understand the command or never felt your signal. A horse may refuse to obey you to test your dominance or to enforce its dominance if it has gotten away with refusing in the past. The refusal may also come about because the horse is too frightened to obey or is not physically capable of fulfilling the command.

The first thing you need to do when a horse fails to respond to a command is to consider whether the horse actually received your command. Are you so afraid of hurting your horse that it's unaware of your leg pressure when you signal it to move forward? Did your horse refuse to stop because its chin strap was loose and it didn't feel much pull on the reins? Do you bounce and bobble so much the horse can't tell when you've sent a signal? If you are not delivering your signals properly, you need more practice at a slow pace in a small enclosure until you feel your mount is responding directly to your intended signals.

If you are certain your horse received and ignored your command, decide if there are any outside factors that might have caused the horse to refuse. Some horses will resist stepping forward onto an unfamiliar surface or into water. Some are unwilling to leave their companions. Others are afraid to venture into unfamiliar territory. In fact, most outside factors are based on fear: fear of falling, fear of isolation, fear of being injured or trapped, and fear of the unknown.

You must decide how important it is for your horse to cooperate in a fearful situation. If you've asked the horse to cross a rickety wooden bridge over a churning river and your horse said "Nuh-uh," it was probably justified. On the other hand, if the only way out of a barn is under a low doorway and the horse doesn't care to duck its head, it really must learn to go through.

Be firm, calm, and unrelenting when urging a horse through or by something it's afraid of. Speak to the horse. Keep good contact on the reins and use leg pressure to prevent the horse from turning, backing, or sidestepping away. Your horse may dance, shuffle, or try to wheel back. Keep pressing it forward with your legs and hands and use a very gruff, firm tone of voice.

If the horse is determined in its refusal and you feel you are reaching a stalemate, get help. Have someone follow the horse at a safe distance, off to the side so as to be in the horse's line of vision. Your follower should urge your horse to move forward by waving his or her arms or a long whip and yelling in a threatening manner. The behavior of your helper may frighten your horse more than the original object of its fear and convince it to obey.

If no help is available, get off the horse and try leading it by the obstacle. This sometimes works instantly, as a frightened horse is a much better follower than leader. But don't get in front of your horse and try to drag it. You will end up in a pulling match or get trampled if the horse leaps forward. Stay beside your horse and lead it as you would any other time. If it continues to refuse, use a long whip or the end of your lead or reins to smack the horse on the side of the rump.

The key to success is your own determination and perseverance. If you give in and allow your horse to refuse to cross or pass something it is wary of, you will have a far more difficult time convincing your horse to obey the next time it encounters something it doesn't like.

Measure your achievements in baby steps. If your horse takes one tentative step in the right direction, slow, soothe, and reassure the horse with encouraging words and pats before asking for the next step.

When urging a horse past something frightening, don't be lax about your posture and grip in the saddle or careless about where you are standing or how you are holding on to the horse. Some horses will refuse repeatedly, and then surprise you by abruptly changing their minds and leaping forward or jumping the object of fear in order to get by it as quickly as possible. If you are caught off guard while riding, you could easily be thrown. If you are leading the horse you may fall, be trampled or dragged, or turn the horse loose.

If your horse is not reacting out of fright but refuses simply to test your dominance, do as you would to get the horse past something scary, only this time don't be quite so nice.

The moment your horse refuses out of stubbornness, yell fiercely at it and kick it hard with your heels or grind your spurs into its sides. Use both hands on the reins and leg pressure to prevent the horse from turning away from the direction you've chosen. Most horses will be convinced quickly that you are the boss and must be obeyed, if you believe it yourself.

If your horse did not respond to your verbal ferocity and kick, use a short whip such as a riding crop to bat the horse across the rump as soon as it refuses, making sure you still have a good hold on the reins with one hand. Never give the horse time to think about obeying. There is nothing to think about. Never use the whip to tap or tickle a refusing horse; you'll get no respect that way and the horse will soon ignore it.

If you use the whip properly, you will only have to hit the horse once. If you want to continue to carry the whip as a reminder, keep it out of sight until it's needed, such as in your back pocket or under your thigh, then wave it out in the horse's line of vision as soon as the horse hesitates to obey. Quite often a view of the whip is as effective for a horse as feeling the sting. Only hit your horse with the whip if it actually refuses. The moment the horse moves forward for you, stop your whip action, and do not resume unless the horse actively refuses again.

An additional reason your horse might refuse to obey is that you've asked too much of it. A horse has an incredible endurance level, but if you push it past exhaustion, it will eventually refuse to go further. Shame on you if you ever let your horse get even near being this tired.

If your horse is ill or malnourished it may not be able to perform at the level of a normal horse. Don't expect it to.

If you expect your horse to go over unreasonable or unsafe terrain, such as a riverbed with a strong current and slippery rocks, a large log or high-jump obstacle, ice, deep mud, slick clay, or a steep hill with poor footing, the horse may justifiably refuse and save both of you some grief. Unfortunately, many horses won't refuse but will trust the rider's judgment and end up injured or injuring you. If that happens, you may never see that level of trust again, even when you deserve it.

Propping and Spooking

Propping is what a horse does when it abruptly stops or ducks to the side, usually at a gait faster than a walk. Most often a horse props because it spooked from something unexpected or has encountered an obstacle it feels unable to handle. Less commonly, a horse will make a habit of propping after learning it is an effective way to remove a rider.

Spooking is any reaction a horse makes in response to something that has frightened it, whether this is something it has seen or heard. A horse may spook simply by slowing and raising its head to look at or listen for whatever frightened it, or it may prop, rear, run backward, wheel away, or stop and refuse to go past or toward the scary thing.

The best way to stop a horse from spooking and propping is to anticipate the action and take preventive measures. This entails identifying anything in your riding area that could frighten your horse. Every horse is different, so pay special attention to what your horse is timid about.

If you are on a trail or in an unfamiliar area, look ahead to try to identify anything scary before your horse does. Bright objects, litter, anything that flutters in the wind, cycles, or dogs are all possible spooks. Even a person can scare a horse if he or she is standing out of good visual range and hard to identify, makes an unexpected move, or is wearing bright or flappy clothing.

Just as important as looking for spooks, watch your horse to see what it's looking at and gauge its reactions. A suddenly raised head and tensed body is often your first clue the horse is going to spook.

If you ride in an arena or other area used regularly, watch out for any changes that weren't present the last time you rode. If a tractor is parked beside the arena for the first time, it's likely to spook the horse. If a gate is newly painted white after always looking dull and weathered, this could be cause for your horse's alarm. Even fresh puddles of water after a rainstorm may spook your horse.

When you see something you think might frighten your horse, slow down to a walk. Take the slack out of the reins to prevent the horse from turning away. This also gives more contact between your hands and your horse's mouth, which is reassuring to the horse. Set yourself deep in the saddle and prepare to give the horse leg signals to keep it moving forward and straight.

You should not allow your horse to stop and ponder the spooky, as it will often scare itself more this way. Neither should you rush the horse past the object of fear. Keep your own composure and urge the horse on, correcting it if it slows or tries to turn away.

Do not whip, spur, or otherwise hurt a horse to get it past something spooky. The horse is already afraid and thinks something is going to hurt it. By physically reprimanding the horse, you will have created an association between the frightening object and pain. You have confirmed to the horse that its spooky *really* is bad and should be avoided at all costs in the future. Next time you try to go by the scary thing, the horse will not only spook again but will react more emphatically. You should resort to a whip only if you come to a stalemate with a horse in trying to force it to pass or approach something scary. In this case, you can use your whip to tap your horse's shoulder as you urge it forward with firm leg signals. Shoulder tapping does not cause the horse pain but is still irritating enough to convince a horse to move forward rather than turn back.

A normal horse will only spook on occasion. If your horse spooks constantly, it will get very tiresome to ride and may hurt you at some time. You can condition your horse to minimize spooking by subjecting it to many frightening objects in a controlled environment. Set up an arena or small, safely fenced paddock with different objects, starting with one or two the first day and increasing the variety every day. Set a bicycle or park a vehicle against an outside post. Scatter white PVC pipes, construction cones, beach balls, and balloons on the ground. Hang sheets or a stable blanket over a rail. Have an observer sit on a rail, climb up and jump off the rail, or walk around with an open umbrella, and let a dog wander loose.

Depending upon how spooky your horse is, you can ride the horse through your obstacle course the first day, or you can start conservatively and turn the horse loose for a while to discover things for itself. Whatever you do, stay slow and reassure the horse constantly, but insist, once you are riding, that your horse follow through on the course you've chosen, even if you need to get off and lead it.

Sometimes while out riding, a horse will see something scary that you just can't see or would never dream could frighten your horse. The horse will prop and you will be unprepared and be pitched forward or off the side.

Propping is one of the easiest ways to fall off a horse because the movement is so sudden and forceful. You will feel like a crash-test dummy if you are not prepared and holding on properly. The best way to prepare yourself is to ride at all times like your horse may prop at any moment. This does not mean tensing up and gripping two handfuls of mane. This just means being mindful of maintaining good posture and points of balance, as well as keeping both hands on the reins and good contact with the horse's mouth. It means riding in control.

If you get lazy or overconfident and let your reins hang slack or your feet dangle in the stirrups, you will have no defense when the horse takes a dive to the side or slams on the breaks. In addition, you must watch your speed. The faster you ride, the more chance you have of falling off. You must gauge the familiarity of the area when gauging your speed. An acceptably brisk canter in an arena or on a frequently used trail may be treacherous on an unknown trail with blind turns.

The methods of maintaining balance have already been discussed, but here's a reminder. When a horse props or makes an unexpected move, get your feet in front of you and push yourself back into the seat of the saddle. Grip hard with your knees and thighs. Get your body centered and erect as soon as possible, pushing off the neck with your hands if necessary. Increase the pressure in the stirrup on the opposite side of the direction the horse is going, and decrease the pressure on the inside stirrup while squeezing the horse with your inside leg to discourage further movement in that direction. Use your reins to prevent further sideways movement and bring the horse to a halt. If you are shaken, take a deep breath and wait or walk your horse until your confidence returns. If it doesn't return, terminate the ride.

If the horse propped because it was truly frightened, there is not much you can do in the way of punishing the horse, as it was acting instinctively, if foolishly. You should try to get it over its fright, though, so urge the horse at a walk past, around, or through the spooky. Stay calm and reassure the horse with your voice and hand-mouth contact. Don't let the horse stop or turn away if you can possibly avoid it.

If your horse propped because it was hoping you'd fall off, this is another situation entirely. If you survived the prop and you're still on, get after your horse immediately. Stop the horse, yell at it, turn it in a tight circle, and at the same time smack it on the rump as hard as you can. Turning the horse will keep it from jumping forward when you hit it.

After you've reprimanded your horse, stop and calm it. Punishing a horse must always be immediate and short, whether or not your temper has been abated.

If you were too busy righting yourself in the saddle, you couldn't get the horse stopped, or you fell off, forget reprimanding the horse. Although the horse certainly deserves punishment, it will be too late to have any worthwhile effect and will only serve to confuse the horse.

Wait until you resume riding, then stay at a slow enough pace that you are sure you can maintain control and keep your seat if the horse props, even if this means staying at a walk. The moment the horse makes a move to prop, reprimand it, making sure you use an absolutely deadly tone of voice. Be conservative in increasing your speeds so you never feel you could lose control and fall if your horse attempts to prop. You will be much more successful in breaking the habit if you can stop the prop before it is carried out because every time the horse gets away with propping, the habit is reinforced.

Running Off

For a rider whose horse has never run off this may sound like an exhilarating experience, but anyone that's been aboard a runaway horse understands it is absolutely, heart-stoppingly, terrifying.

When a horse truly runs off, its only goal is to go as fast as it can for as long as it can. It will run blindly at, into, and through just about anything. A horse should never be allowed a chance to run off.

One of the most likely times a horse will run off is if a rider allows the horse to race at full speed. The horse may become excited and refuse to slow down when the rider signals it to do so. The easiest way to prevent this is to never ride a horse at an all-out gallop or any pace faster than you are absolutely certain you can slow it from.

Your tack is your key to preventing a potential run. Your bridle must be fitted properly, especially in regard to the chin strap and bit. Your headstall and reins should be checked before bridling to make sure there are no wear spots or bent buckles that might give or break.

Your saddle can also be a factor in controlling a run. You will need leverage to stop the horse; this leverage is derived from pushing forward in the stirrups with your lower body while pulling back on the reins with your upper body, standing up if necessary. If your stirrups are too long, they will be ineffective; when you pull hard, your upper body will be forced forward and your legs forced behind you.

If your saddle is loose or ill fitted, it will ride up the horse's neck when you push forward with your lower body. Your leverage is lost when your saddle is pushed too far forward because the saddle will feel unstable and your legs will end up too far back to be any use.

As mentioned earlier, riding at a pace slow enough to control your horse is essential. You must also keep the horse from leaning into or grabbing the bit. To do this, keep intermittent pressure on the reins, jiggling them constantly with your wrists. Don't jerk, just jiggle, and use the lightest effective pressure at all times. If you're too rough on the reins, your horse will eventually become numb to your signals and ignore you altogether, or it may fight the pressure by rearing or tossing its head.

If you find you must jerk on the reins or lean constantly against them to keep your horse under control, it is time to increase the severity of your bit or chin strap and do some work with your horse in a controlled environment.

If you are using a ring snaffle, switch to one with shanks and an effective chin strap. If you ride with a curb bit, get a higher port curb or tighten the chin strap. If you are using a hackamore, tighten the curb chain or switch to a stiffer nosepiece. If your horse roots down into the hackamore to avoid rein pressure, you may have to switch to a bit. If your horse throws its head up to grab the bit and take off, use a tie down or running martingale on the horse.

If you move up to a stronger bit or other equipment, ride in an enclosed area no larger than an arena until you are confident you've gained some control. Don't rely solely on your equipment, though; wear your horse down enough that it isn't constantly trying to take off before you venture into freer spaces. Don't practice riding your potential runaway in a wide-open pasture or field, especially one with wire fences. A horse has ample room to run off in a field and could unthinkingly charge through the fence.

Despite all your precautions, there is still the possibility your horse could run off with you at some time. Perhaps you will break or drop a rein; maybe your horse will be stung by a bee and you'll be caught off guard. Whatever the reason, it's vital that you know how best to react. I have heard of some people who believe in bailing off when all control is lost, thinking they at least know where they will end up. I can't do this and can't recommend it. There may be some circumstances in which this is your best choice, such as if your mount is headed pell-mell for a trafficked roadway, but there is an enormous risk of serious injury in bailing off a fast-moving horse.

Your first priority is to try to regain control. Stand up in the stirrups, take as short a hold on the reins as you can muster, lean back, and yank on the reins. Don't just pull, as you will give the horse something to brace against. Yank in quick, hard, seesawing jerks by pulling on one rein, then the other. Yank for your life and don't worry about hurting your horse's mouth. Keep your horse in a straight line or steer it toward the safest course possible, avoiding any sharp turns or declines. If there is a detectable hill, steer the horse *up* the incline; this will naturally reduce the horse's momentum.

If you've gotten no response in your attempt to pull the horse to a stop, and you feel you are completely out of control, don't tire yourself out pulling futilely. Instead, keep steering the horse on a safe path until it wears down and slows itself. If there is no safe path, your mount is totally out of control, and you feel you are in danger of the horse falling or hitting something, understand that *no matter what you do* you are at risk of injury, *but you must do something*. This is the point when some choose to bail off, and this may be your choice. It's not mine.

What has worked for me in the past is to point the horse at a blockade and let it run straight toward it so the horse can see it will hit if it continues running. A good blockade would be the solid wall of a barn or a tall, stout wooden fence. Most horses will react by trying to veer off. You must continue to force the horse straight. No horse will deliberately hit a solid barricade, so by giving the horse no alternative, you may force it to decide to stop. Unfortunately, many horses will wait until the last moment and prop, either slamming on the brakes or diving sideways, so you must be as braced and ready for this as possible— you *can* stay on if you prepare for the slam. You will need to bury both hands firmly in the mane, while at the same time you maintain a hard, tight grip on the reins. Set yourself deep and far back in the saddle and jam your feet hard against the stirrups, pushing them forward and out so you can stop a thrust or slam in either direction. *Do not* think you can hang on by wrapping your legs around the horse—you must have your feet out in order to brace yourself.

The moment your horse breaks its stride is the moment you have your best chance to regain control of your horse by yanking it to a complete stop; this means taking your hands off the mane. If you doubt your ability to stay on without a manehold, wait until your horse has stopped at the blockade or veered off, then use one rein to force the horse into the tightest spin possible until you can convince it that it's not going forward.

A common mistake made with a runaway horse is to try to steer the horse one direction when the horse is determinedly headed another. What this does is bend the horse's neck and head to the side while its body continues forward. This blinds the horse and puts it off balance, making the possibility the horse will fall or hit something much more likely. Make sure that whatever direction you steer your horse while it is running off, you turn gradually enough that the horse's head is pointed forward and its body follows.

I know the subject of horses running off is alarming, but please be aware that most horses will not run off, or will quickly respond when signaled to stop. It is very rare to be caught in an out-of-control situation, and you can almost always avoid it.

Provide your horse with enough exercise, both under saddle and turned out, so it doesn't feel the need to race out of control. Use the proper tack and equipment and check your tack before every ride for signs that something might break or that straps are loose or improperly fastened. Ride at a controlled pace, in a safe area, on a horse you know well.

Bucking

If you think now that nothing could be worse than running off, you've forgotten about bucking. Bucking can range from joyful little skips to the all-out twisting, diving, head-between-the-legs stuff you see in a rodeo.

If you have been careful about choosing your horse, there should be minimal bucking. If your horse bucks all-out bronc style under saddle, even once, sell it or send it to a trainer. You just can't teach a horse much while lying in the dirt or the hospital. Your trainer can determine whether you might have caused the bucking by improper saddling or handling, or whether the horse has a hearty way of showing its enthusiasm, is actually broke to ride, or is just downright nasty and untrustworthy. From there you can make choices as to what you want to do with it.

Playfulness and lack of exercise are the most common reasons a horse will buck under saddle, but there are several other reasons. The horse may not be broke and may be reacting to an alien creature on its back. You should certainly know whether your horse is broke before you ride it. If you don't, or were deceived by a previous owner, you should be able to tell by the time you've tightened your horse's girth, as the horse likely will react strongly and in a negative fashion to the unusual proceedings.

Some horses buck when they spook. They see something frightening, they react by spooking or propping, then they buck. The bucking is usually because they've become excited and is not a real reaction to fear since bucking would not be an effective method of protection against something threatening in a real-life situation.

A horse will buck at times if it's been improperly saddled, the most common reason being a cinch jerked up too tight and too fast by an impatient rider. The horse will be painfully pinched and might decide to get rid of the whole rig, rider and all.

You can antagonize a horse into bucking by kicking, spurring, or whipping it, or by surprising it with a sharp kick or slap. If you try to force a horse to do something it doesn't want to do, such as cross a river, it may buck out of frustration and to get you to leave it alone.

Other horses buck simply because they want you to fall off and have found out this is a pretty good way to get you to do so. Whatever the reason, bucking, even cute little play hopping, is unacceptable. Your horse needs to know bucking is not allowed.

As usual, prevention is the best method of dealing with bucking. If you know your horse is a feel-good, playful bucker, increase its level of exercise until it is not so frisky. Turn the horse out more where it can play on its own, ride it regularly and on longer, more strenuous rides. Walk your horse or lunge it before riding or give it some small circle warm-ups in an arena.

Once you've mounted, if your horse feels stiff legged or humpbacked, twitchy or tense, or splay-legged frozen, you can guess it's going to try to buck. You can either get off and lunge the horse until the kinks are out of its system or you can ride the bucks out gradually. This does not mean you should sit and endure while your horse bucks itself out, but rather that you get it moving slowly and keep it moving (not bucking) until it relaxes.

When working with a potential bucker, use an enclosed area no larger than an arena. Start at a walk, then ease the horse into a slow trot. Ride in very small

The action of a bucking horse is unpredictable and violent. Let your horse get the urge out of its system by allowing free play. Keep a no-tolerance attitude when the horse is under saddle.

circles and figure-eight patterns so the horse is constantly under rein control and must pay attention to your commands. Use a corner area for your circles so you can force your horse's head into a wall if it starts to buck. Almost all bucking is in a forward motion, so the mere presence of a wall or fence to block its path may be enough to deter a horse from further bucking.

Most horses lower their heads to buck so they can lift their rear ends and kick out. By preventing your horse from dropping its head, you can often stop an attempt to buck before it's carried out. The moment your horse begins to drop its head, snatch it back up with the reins and yell sharply. If you can't get the horse's head up with the first snatch, stand up, lean back, and really yank on the reins while yelling sharply at the horse to get its attention on you instead of on playing. When its head comes up, stop the horse and start out again at a slower, more controlled pace and with a firmer grip on the reins to prevent the horse from dropping its head again.

Enlarge your circles gradually until you've moved your horse up to a brisk trot, then keep it going at this pace until you can feel the tension leave the horse's body. Its steps will feel less jerky, its back will feel smooth instead of raised and stiff, its head will be steady instead of tossing, twitching, or pulled down low. Even its tail will be lower and not swishing or twitching. If your horse decides to take advantage of the quicker pace and larger space to attempt to buck, stop and start over.

If your horse is persistent in its attempts to buck, you need to get after it, but only if you have control over its head and a decent sense of balance. When the horse starts to buck, pull its head up and tighten your grip so you have a short, firm hold. Turn the horse so it is near and facing a wall or fence, then kick it and bat it on the rump with a whip. This should all be done immediately and quickly to be effective.

If you are not confident of your abilities to deal with a habitual bucker, don't try. Hire a trainer to work with your horse. If you can't afford to do so, it may be necessary to sell the horse and find one that is more docile and obedient.

Even the nicest, most predictable horse can buck at one time or another. Perhaps it was stung by a bee or was startled. Maybe it hasn't been ridden for months and is excited and tense. For whatever reason, you need to know how to stay on if your horse starts bucking.

The most common bucking motion is with the head down and the rump up. The horse will usually look and feel as if it is jumping imaginary fences, but with its head lowered. To sit this out you can do one of two things. The first would be to stand up in the stirrups, grip hard with your knees, and balance yourself with a hand on the mane, allowing the horse to move under you. Although normally a big no-no, in the case of a bucking horse you can also use the reins to hold yourself up and maintain your balance because the harder you pull on the reins, the quicker you'll get your horse to raise its head and stop. Bend your knees to absorb the shock and you will hardly feel the bucking. This method is most effective with light, straightforward bucking.

If your horse bucks hard, with stiff-legged forward plunges or twisty kicks, use the second method. Lean back and get your feet far forward, as far as you can push them. Press down hard in the stirrups and push your bottom deep into the seat of the saddle, gripping hard with your thighs. Bend your knees and grind your pelvis with the motion of the horse so your rump never lifts up in the saddle. Keep your feet out and forward to brace against any sideways motion. This is basically the position you see rodeo bronc riders take. Your upper body will get the most abuse in this position because as your lower body is held pretty rigid, your trunk will be tossed back and forth. You can control this somewhat by leaning back against the reins and tucking your chin to lessen the whiplash effect.

If your horse does not buck in a straight line, but turns or takes a dive to the side, do what you would any other time a horse makes an unexpected move. Brace your weight against the offside stirrup and ease off on the inside stirrup, squeezing hard with your inside leg. Keep those feet out in front of you as much as possible on both sides and use your hips and hands to keep your trunk centered, but make sure you don't let go of the reins with either hand or let them fall slack.

I know it's hard when you are concentrating on staying on, but don't forget to try to stop the horse by yanking its head up and harshly voicing your displeasure. Don't whip the horse or kick it if you're riding in an open area or have not gained sufficient control over the horse's head. The horse will react by bucking harder and possibly running off. Try not to panic when your horse starts bucking. Panicked people react poorly and do stupid things like try to wrap themselves around the horse's neck or cling to the horse by squeezing its sides with their legs. This will trash your balance, sacrifice any control you might have had, urge the horse to buck more or run—and *guarantee* you will fall off.

This is perhaps the most difficult rule to get through people's heads: you must keep your hands off the saddle horn or pommel when you're sitting on a hard bucking horse. It may look like a good survival handle, but it will get you in trouble. Not only will your upper body be pulled too far forward when hanging on to the horn, but you will have given up at least part of your hold on the reins, which is your chief device for stopping the bucker. On top of that, the motion of the saddle is exaggerated at the pommel and the horn or pommel will jerk you around violently.

After prevention, the best way to stop a horse from bucking is by catching it on the first step. This is why I will stress again that you must always ride in control, with both hands on the reins, both feet set firmly in the stirrups, a firm knee and thigh grip, and at a pace you feel you can maintain your balance and stop the horse if necessary.

You must also be mentally alert to signals your horse is sending you that warn of an upcoming bucking event. Again, the most common signals to watch for in a potential bucker are increased body tension, a splay-legged frozen stance, a raised, stiffened spine (humped up), and the horse moving in short jerky steps, twitching its tail and lowering or shaking its head.

Rearing and Flipping

Rearing is the action of a horse standing or walking on its hind legs with its upper body raised in the air. A horse can be trained to rear for show purposes. We've all seen rearing horses in circuses and on the screen, as well as in the highly disciplined Royal Lipizzaner shows. For the everyday rider, though, there's no reason to teach a horse to rear and a lot of reasons to teach it not to.

Besides the obvious fact that rearing can turn into a nasty habit, one of the major reasons you want to keep your horse's front end down is that rearing can lead to flipping or falling over. Flipping is when a horse rears and throws itself all the way over backward. Flipping can be fatal for both you and your horse.

Too often, rearing is the fault of the rider. Leaning hard or jerking on the reins can cause a horse to rear. A poorly fitted bridle, a painful sore in the horse's mouth or under its chin strap, or a tongue over the bit can irritate a horse enough to make it rear. Hitting the horse on the head may make it rear. Surprising a horse with a sudden slap or sharp spur can cause it to rise up. Trying to force your horse to do something it really doesn't want to do, such as cross a bridge or go past something very frightening, can cause your horse to rear in desperation, especially if you are whipping or spurring it. Teasing or antagonizing your horse by signaling it to go, then restraining it or forcing it to stay behind while other horses go ahead may cause a horse to rear.

A horse will sometimes rear without good reason—either because it is excited, anxious, aggressive, or has learned it can intimidate and possibly remove the rider by rearing. I have to say I can't stand these horses. I have no use for habitual rearers. They are dangerous and foolish animals. Plenty of horses are available that don't rear and are much more worthy of your time, effort, and money.

If your horse rears, you need to find out why, but first you need to stay on and get the horse back on the ground. If you are not prepared, you will probably fall back when the horse rears, pulling the reins back with you. This is the worst thing you can do because you are pulling back on a horse that's already going back fast and can overbalance the horse and cause it to fall backward or to the side.

The moment you feel your horse's front end rising, stand in the stirrups, throw your weight forward, and lean over the neck. Let the reins drop slack and grab the pommel, horn, or a handful of mane to hold yourself forward. This will not only help prevent you from falling off the back of the horse, your forward weight will help push the horse's front end back down.

If the horse rises high, get off its back fast, remembering to kick both feet free of the stirrups before swinging off. Never take a chance of having a horse fall over on you if you can possibly help it.

Don't correct your horse unless you are sure you're not responsible for causing the horse to rear. Are you certain your bridle is well fitted? Did you pull on the reins too hard? Have you been teasing or tormenting the horse? If you feel you are guiltless, you need to reprimand the horse. This will prove very difficult because the horse will likely react negatively to your reprimand, especially if it was already excited, upset, or anxious.

Do not hit your horse over the head to correct it. Many people do this, feeling that since the horse rose up in the front end it should be hit over the head to discourage it from lifting its head and rising up again. The problem with this is that there is a high probability the horse will react by rearing again. When you hit a horse over the head, you are hitting it blind. A blind spot behind the ears prevents the horse from seeing any blow coming from that direction, so a horse smacked like this will be predictably startled or shocked into a dangerous reaction. If your horse already had a tendency to rear, it may rear again, more violently. In addition to startling the horse, the poll area is very sensitive and the pain experienced when you lob it there might be enough to cause it to flip.

I was once taught to reprimand a rearer by lobbing it over the head with a raw egg or water balloon. The idea behind this is that you can't hurt the horse and the unexpected wet or gooey sensation is a good deterrent. I will stand behind my advice that you should not hit a horse over the head *with anything* when it rears, not only for the previously stated reasons, but because it is ludicrous to think you can ride properly and keep control of a potential rearer with a raw egg or water balloon in one hand. Trust me when I say that if you carry any such thing in your pocket, you won't be able to get to it at the critical moment, even if it hasn't already broken.

The best way to reprimand a rearer is to yell at it sharply, boot it in the ribs, and whack it on the rump. Kicking the horse and hitting it on the rump will cause it to jump forward, which puts its weight on the front end and makes it less likely to rise up again. This method is only marginally effective on a serious, habitual rearer but works well for a horse that is just testing rearing.

If you have a horse that rears time and again, even after you've reprimanded it, get rid of it. You can have a trainer work with the horse, but I can almost guarantee that in any future stressful situation your horse will resort to its original habit of rearing.

Furthermore, if you have a horse that has deliberately flipped over, even once, and you know the horse is broke and are certain you did not cause it to do so, shoot the horse or send it to the canners. I am serious. You cannot react fast enough to get out of the way if you are riding a horse when it flips, and there are no graver injuries sustained than those caused by a horse flipping over and crushing the rider underneath it. The horse is not worth your life or someone else's.

Kicking

When I refer to kicking under saddle, I am generally talking about a horse that kicks other horses. It is bad enough that a horse might injure another, but I have also seen riders injured, even fracturing ankles, when one horse kicks at another and hits the rider instead. You might never ride in company with another, but I would be surprised if this is the case. Most riders, at least on occasion, go out on group trail rides, and many riders show or school their horses in an arena shared with other horses. It is foolish to believe your horse will never be exposed to others while under saddle.

The most common kickers are fillies and mares. They just seem feistier and more apt to protect themselves, perhaps as a natural instinct to avoid being bred indiscriminately or at an untimely moment. Although you may be more wary when riding a mare, don't assume a gelding or stallion won't kick.

Often a horse will give warning of its intention to kick by sidling its rear end toward another horse or swishing its tail and pinning its ears. Sometimes there is no warning whatsoever, especially if a horse is suddenly bumped or crowded by another. The moment you sense your horse is going to kick, wheel it sharply so its rear end is pushed away from its intended target. Yell "NO!" in a harsh tone and bat or slap it on the rump on the side it meant to kick from. This is the best you can do, but it will probably not leave a permanent impression on your horse.

Once your horse has attempted to kick, or worse, has delivered a blow, you must assume it will kick again. Be prepared to discipline your horse at any attempt, but this is not enough to protect other horses or riders. It is your responsibility to keep others safe by warning them verbally or by tying a red ribbon in your horse's tail. In addition, you must take precautions not to set anyone up. When riding beside another, keep your horse's head level with the other's shoulder so it can't easily aim. Jerk the horse up or turn it sideways if it attempts to move forward or position itself to kick. When your horse is being followed or passed, don't assume the other rider will avoid you, even with ample warning. Move your horse forward or away or whatever it takes so as not to give your horse even the slightest chance to kick. The less successful your horse is at kicking, the less likely it will be to try in the future.

At times, you and your horse are going to be the victims of a kicker or an attempt at kicking. Again, ride defensively. Expect any horse at any time to try to kick at you or your mount. Unless your horse is itself a kicker, stay just forward of a companion horse when riding side by side. Give plenty of space when passing or following and never position your horse directly behind or at the flank of another.

Stumbling

I hesitate to call stumbling a behavior problem of the horse, but once in a while it is. Certain horses stumble habitually and should be corrected since there is always a chance that a stumble will turn into a fall.

The most common habitual stumbler is a lazy horse. The horse drags its toes to the extent of catching one, even on firm, level ground, and will stumble time and again. The best way to prevent this is to urge the lazy horse to collect itself by using extra leg pressure and intermittent pressure on the reins. The higher step and better head set of a collected animal will greatly reduce toe-drag stumbling.

Another type of stumbler is one that cannot keep its attention focused. Horses that are busy looking here and there tend to wander and lose track of what they are doing and often stumble over any little object in the path. You can correct this by maintaining good hand-mouth contact and constant leg signals so the horse's attention must remain at least partially on you. When riding a horse such as this, it is also up to you to steer the clearest course possible.

Horses that carry their heads low tend to stumble more. Not only do they not pick their feet up well, but they rely too much on their front ends for balance and not enough on their rear ends. Any misstep can cause the horse to fall forward or down in front due to the extra front-end weight caused by the lowered head.

In truth, most horses are not at fault for their own stumbling; their owners or handlers are usually responsible and can prevent most stumbling.

Two common reasons a horse may stumble are overgrown and unshod hooves. Long toes tend to catch easily and trip up a horse. Bare feet are often tender. When a horse with bare feet steps on something sharp or hard, it will stumble to get the weight off the affected foot.

Another human error is to ride a horse past its point of fatigue. Tired horses stumble, just as tired toddlers fall down more often than usual. In addition, riding your horse on rough, steep, uneven, deep, or slippery terrain, especially at a fast pace, can cause your horse to stumble and possibly fall.

Don't take stumbling lightly; do everything you can to prevent your horse from stumbling because the possibility that your horse may fall is very real.

Falling Off

Falling off is not itself a misbehavior of the horse, and for that matter, is not often caused by the misbehavior of the rider. Falling off could more reasonably be considered a misadventure for both the rider and mount. I chose to include the section on falling off in this chapter rather than the chapter on riding because it is so often *caused* by a horse's misbehavior.

As much as we all try to avoid it, I have yet to meet a rider who has spent any significant amount of time on a horse and hasn't fallen off. I have given many pointers for staying on a horse in most situations, but it is naive to think you will be successful in doing so 100 percent of the time. It is wise to prepare yourself by knowing how best to fall off and by taking preventive and protective measures.

Protection and Prevention

To protect yourself, wear a helmet at all times. They don't look silly anymore; almost everyone is wearing one. Choose a well-fitted English or racing helmet with a secure chin strap if possible, but a bicycle or motorcycle helmet will work in a pinch.

Make sure the helmet has a nonelastic chin strap and make sure the chin strap is secured and tight enough that you can't lift the helmet off your head.

The force of falling can knock an even slightly loose helmet off your head before you ever hit the ground.

Wear long pants to protect your legs, long sleeves for your arms, and gloves for your hands, as these areas are often where you will land and skid. A safety vest made especially for riding can protect your fragile ribs, collarbones, and tailbone in a fall. Wear boots with low heels and narrow toes that won't get caught easily in a stirrup. Avoid shirts or jackets that could catch over a saddle horn during a fall and trap you.

To prevent yourself from falling, do what I have been preaching all this time: ride a horse you trust, check your tack and equipment before every ride, ride at a controlled pace, and don't get lazy about maintaining good posture, balance, and a firm hold on the reins.

Falling Techniques

So, say you've done everything right and you still find yourself falling off. If you are catapulted without warning, you'll have little time to think, so it's necessary to practice your falling techniques in your mind over and over beforehand. You can also practice falling by diving off a platform or a hay pile onto something cushiony, but don't get carried away and hurt yourself.

When you are falling, loosen your limbs. The less tense you are, the better chance you have of not getting injured. Don't try to break your fall with a straight arm, as this is how most people break their arms and collarbones or dislocate their shoulders.

If you can land on your feet, don't land straight legged; let your knees buckle and fall to your knees. If you are falling feet first with your momentum behind you, let yourself fall back, catching yourself with your elbows. If you are falling feet first with forward momentum, immediately buckle your knees, tuck your chin, bring your arms in close to your body and roll.

If you are falling head first, try to tuck your head and roll into a somersault. If you are going more at a face-first or belly-flop angle, bend your arms and knees and try to land on your forearms and shins, rolling to the side.

Often you are not thrown clear of a horse but find yourself sliding off the side or hanging on haphazardly. Make a quick effort to pull yourself back on the horse, but don't keep trying if you really know you won't make it; your scrambling and clawing at the horse can cause the horse to react more violently to get away from you. As soon as you know you're going off, kick your feet out of the stirrups if either foot is still in one. Untangle your hands from the reins. Don't worry about letting the horse go; you don't want to be attached to that horse in any way during or after a fall.

You will be very near the horse when you land if you have been falling gradually. This puts you in danger of being kicked or stepped on. When you hit the ground, roll away from the horse if at all possible. Crawl or get up and get away from the horse quickly. If you can't move away from the horse, curl up and roll to your stomach, tucking your head so only the helmet and your back are exposed. Don't move until you sense the horse is out of your way.

If you think that you have been injured in a fall, don't move at all. If there was no one present to witness the event and provide aid, yell for help. If the horse is still running around loose and upset, yell at it sharply so it remains aware of your presence and avoids stepping on you.

Hang Ups

I wish I had some infallibly sound advice on what to do if you become tangled in the reins or hung up in a stirrup when you fall, but this is a nasty situation that often has no happy ending. Sometimes you will get lucky and the horse will just stop and wait for you to free yourself, but don't count on this. It's more natural for a horse to fight against you or try to run away from you because of the scramble.

If the horse does stop, remain as quiet and calm as possible and try to free yourself. Use soothing voice commands of "No" or "Whoa" to encourage the horse to keep still (this is where previous voice-command training will come in handy). Keep in mind that any sudden move you make might cause the horse to take off.

If you are lying on the ground with a foot raised in the stirrup, you may not be able to reach your boot. Hope like hell there's someone nearby that can come and free you. If you do receive help, make sure the person approaches the horse very slowly and quietly so as not to set it off. Have your helper take a good hold of the horse's head before attempting to free you. If the horse tries to take off, the person helping should not let go at any costs, but rather should force the horse to turn in tight circles around him or her. This is not great for you but beats being dragged at a full gallop.

Sometimes the force of being dragged is enough to pull a boot off or break a rein or stirrup leather and you will be freed this way, unfortunately, not necessarily before you've been injured. In addition, if you find yourself dragged by a hand caught in the reins, you do have a chance at stopping the horse by yanking hard on the rein your hand is tangled in. If you're dragged by a leg, however, you will be on the ground and pretty helpless. The best you can do in this situation is protect your head and face with your arms.

After the Fall

If you survived your fall without getting hurt, catch your horse as soon as possible. Be cautious and gentle, as a horse is often as traumatized as the rider after a fall. Check the horse for any injuries and remove or reset any messed-up tack. If all looks well with the horse, you must decide if you want to get back on and try it again.

There's an adage I suspect you've heard concerning getting right back on after you've fallen. That's a great concept but may not work for everybody. Don't feel you must be noble or macho and jump right back up there if you are shaken or frightened. If you are trembling or tense, you will do a poorer job of riding than before and be more likely to fall again. I know for myself that I tremble so hard after a fall I feel weak-kneed, even when I've landed safely on my feet.

Take whatever time you feel is necessary to recover. If your confidence is blown, forget riding for the day but don't feel you must pack your saddle up to the attic.

To regain confidence after a fall, spend some time just working with your horse on the ground. Brush it, take it for a walk, tack and untack it. Get on and off in the stall (if the ceiling is high enough) or have someone hold the horse while you mount and dismount.

When you resume riding, make it a short, slow ride in an enclosed area. Just walk your horse and talk to it. Wait until you are bored and relaxed before you venture into more challenging riding, and do this as gradually as you feel necessary.

The whole key to your confidence is control. When you feel you have total control over your horse in whatever situation may arise, you will feel you can advance to any level of riding you wish.

If you've become afraid to get back on your own horse, supervised riding lessons on a tame schooling horse can give you some relatively risk-free riding practice and at the same time help you determine whether you or your horse is the problem.

Once you've built some confidence on a schooling horse, you can graduate to taking lessons on your own horse under the watchful eye of your instructor. By this time, if you two still aren't getting along and you feel you can no longer trust your horse for whatever reason, you must decide what to do with it. I hope you will recognize that not all horses are untrustworthy and even this horse may have had a justifiable reason for getting you off its back, whether or not you agree with the reason.

Your decision may be to sell your horse and get a gentler one or you may decide to hire a trainer to work with your horse. If you choose to keep your horse for a while and send it to a trainer, take time to go and watch your trainer work with the horse to find out what it, or you, did wrong and how the problem is being corrected. Don't take your horse home until you have ridden it several times in the trainer's presence so he or she can show you how to signal and correct the horse more effectively and can point out any problems in communication between you and your horse.

Be careful about asking your buddy or neighbor to ride your horse for you, rather than hiring a trainer. Make sure the person you choose to help out is qualified and very experienced with horses. Watch this person ride and work with other horses before turning him or her loose with your own. Inept people, especially those that believe they know what they're doing when they don't, can cause a lot more harm than good.

Keep in mind that the whole purpose of riding and being around horses is to have fun. I urge you not to give up on horses over one bad experience, but if you've put in the effort to become a capable horseperson and you're just not having fun, please walk away from it. Sell your horse and take up a hobby that doesn't require daily maintenance. Too many horses fall victim to neglect and abuse due to the lack of interest and disillusionment of their owners.

13

Saying Good-Bye

Facing Up to Selling, Giving Away,
or Euthanizing a Friend

Although it may not be imaginable to you today, there is a point in time in which your horse will no longer be part of your life. The day the two of you part ways could be joyful, heart wrenching, or the cause of any number of emotions in between. Although the reasons you get rid of or lose a horse will have a great impact on the way you feel about the experience, the way in which you deal with the matter from start to finish will also influence the intensity of your sense of well-being or grief. If you act with thought and care throughout the experience, you can later look back without the hindrance of regrets, shame, or guilt.

The Unwanted Horse

By following my guidelines on how to choose a horse and by enlisting the help and advice of a veterinarian and professional horseperson, you probably brought home a decent, manageable horse—one that suits your needs and skills. Sometimes a person can goof, though, or be tricked into buying the wrong horse. Other times you may find you cannot get along with the horse you've chosen, even though it performs well for others.

The horse you've chosen may not be a mistake at all. Perhaps you've outgrown your first horse, not necessarily in a physical sense, but in the challenge the horse provides you. Your beginning mount may have been all you could handle at one time, but proves itself too slow, lazy, or athletically inept as your skills increase and your goals are heightened.

Perhaps your horse is showing real signs of aging, has failing health, or has developed a soundness problem. You may not be able or willing to deal with the time and expense necessary for your horse's health maintenance or rehabilitation, not to mention the grief if you happen to lose the horse or are forced to euthanize.

There is always the possibility the horse experience didn't pan out for you. There are so many factors that can take the fun out of horsemanship. Maybe you were thrown and hurt or frightened by the experience. Perhaps your finances are too tight to make horse ownership comfortable and enjoyable. A new marriage, child, career, or other hobby might have taken your interest and spare time away from the horse. And of course you might have figured out how much work and dedication is involved in properly caring for a horse and decided it wasn't worth it for you.

No matter what reasons you have for no longer wanting your horse, the situation must be dealt with. That sounds obvious; who wouldn't deal with the problem of an unwanted horse? But I've witnessed too often the fact that some people do not face the issue of getting rid of an unwanted horse. The horse simply gets put on the back burner, sometimes entirely forgotten. I picked up a horse once at a boarding stable for a woman who'd gotten it in trade from the stable owner. It took me the better part of a day to get the horse out of the stall where it had been kept four months on the previous owner's orders. For reasons unknown, the owner never came to visit the horse, never changed his orders, and eventually quit paying the boarding bill. The stable owner, reluctant to take responsibility, left the horse in the stall but provided adequate care until the bills ran too high, then ordered his help to stop cleaning and bedding the stall and to give the horse minimal rations. By the time I showed up the horse was in wretched condition—its coat was matted with filth, its stall was mounded in black muck, and the horse had become stall bound—terrified to leave its windowless cell after such lengthy confinement. Although this is an outrageous case, it is not an isolated event; neglect and abuse are more common than necessary and horses are likely victims because of their great need for care and attention, both financial and physical.

Selling a Horse

I believe it is your responsibility, when selling a horse, to ensure the animal receives a good home. Many people will disagree with me. The argument is that anyone willing to pay good money has the right to do with the horse what he or she pleases. Besides that, it is not always possible to check up on a horse after it is sold, and it is pretty much impossible to do anything about the horse's circumstances even if you can manage to check on it. I will not dispute these arguments, but I will stand by my contention that you still have the moral obligation to help choose a responsible, caring home for your horse and the power to meet your obligation through your methods of selling.

The Auction

The quickest, most effective method of selling a horse is to send it through auction. You show up with the horse, hand it to the auction yard's handlers, sign some papers, and go home with a check at the end of the day. The check may not be very impressive, but the horse is sold and gone—out of your life.

Since the money you'll receive for your horse through an auction sale is generally less than the horse's market value, you must have a reason to sell this way. Perhaps you've found the horse unmanageable or the horse is chronically lame or very old. The auction is a great dumping spot for such an animal. But guess what? The new owner is either going to be a canner, who knows what he or she is buying and doesn't give a hoot, a horse trader who will pawn the horse off at a profit to an unsuspecting green horseperson, or an unsuspecting green horseperson with high hopes. In any case, your horse is likely to end up packed in a can of dog food, run through another auction, abused, neglected, or the cause of someone's injuries. The best and luckiest scenario would be for an unmanageable horse to find a home with a skilled trainer willing to put in the time to reform it. Unfortunately, auctioned horses usually aren't found to be worth that kind of effort and money.

The Unusable Horse

There are responsible, guilt-free ways to sell an undesirable horse besides the auction. If the horse is extremely old or has a chronic lameness or health problem, evaluate the situation honestly. Could the horse be of use to anyone? If so, consider giving the horse away or selling it very cheaply on the contingency that the new owner understands the horse's condition and is willing to provide a good home. If the horse is truly no good to anyone and is uncomfortable in its pain, you can sell the horse to the canners—*not* by sending it to the auction (this is a dreadfully slow and usually painful journey for the horse), but by taking it yourself to a knacker, stockyard, or canning facility. Your veterinarian will likely be able to tell you where to find such a facility. You can make an appointment, show up with the horse, accept your money, and actually watch the horse being humanely destroyed before you leave. Although this may sound dreadful, and you may swear you could never do such a thing, please think about it. You will know exactly what happened to your horse. You will know it never stood for days without food or shelter waiting its turn under the hammer, or that it was shipped overseas or cross-country under despicable conditions to be killed fresh as some gourmet treat.

The Unmanageable Horse

If you believe your horse will be hard to sell because of its temperament and bad habits, consider sending the horse to a trainer first. Depending on the quality of the horse, this may not be worth your money; training bills could easily exceed the money you can get for your horse. If it's even a remote possibility, though, you will be rewarded with the peace of mind that you can present a safe, trained horse for sale. You may even change your mind and keep the horse when you see the results of some professional training.

If you cannot afford to hire a trainer and don't want to spend any more time with the rogue, try first to sell the horse to a trainer, revealing the horse's bad traits when you approach the trainer. You will probably not fetch a decent price for the horse, but again you can expect the horse to profit with the training it will receive in its new home, and you can feel fairly assured it will end up in a decent home, as most trainers look to turn out good stock in order to build or fortify a good reputation.

If you must sell your rank horse on the open market, sell it as greenbroke, unbroke, or in need of further training or an experienced rider. Be up-front about the horse's problems and be flexible in your price. An experienced horseperson might get along just fine with your horse or your buyer might have the skills or finances you lacked with which to correct the problems.

Going for Top Dollar

If you have a decent horse you would like to sell, you have every right to seek the highest price possible. Whether you've simply outgrown your beginner horse or are lacking in interest, time, or money, there is someone somewhere that will find your horse perfectly suited to his or her needs.

Your horse should be in top condition before you put it on the market. This should not take much catch-up work if you've practiced responsible horsemanship. Your horse's weight should be within its ideal guidelines, its coat should be kept fairly clean and its mane and tail tangle free. The horse's hoof care and veterinary work should be up to date and documented. The first impression is always the strongest, so if your horse appears vibrant and healthy, it is more likely to be remembered by potential buyers as they make their rounds.

I am amazed at how many people will put a horse up for sale and pull it out of the back forty to demonstrate and show, even though it hasn't been ridden or handled for months. Your nicest, most mannerly horse will not perform at its best if it is rusty, too fresh, or out of condition. Start riding or working with your horse or have someone else do so weeks before you put it on the market. The horse will perform more reliably and show as a stronger, healthier, more coordinated animal. One word of caution: don't overdo your riding with hard, fast, strenuous exercise, especially if the horse is in poor physical condition. You can cause muscle or leg injuries this way, which will delay or destroy your plans to sell the horse.

When wording your ad, stick to the facts and stay honest. A good horseperson will recognize lies or half-truths the first time he or she comes to look at your horse. I have wasted a lot of time driving to look at young horses listed as sixteen or so hands, only to find they stand thirteen or fourteen hands and are old enough to drink in a bar. Honesty does not mean you must be tight-lipped, though; go ahead and present an eye-catching ad. Brag about all the wonderful things your horse can do and about its brilliant coloring and awesome breeding. If your horse is too lazy for you, you can truthfully state the wonders of your horse's easygoing, docile nature. If your horse is a bit of a hyper handful, you can boast about how an experienced rider is going to love the spirited, go-all-day nature of this special animal. What hasn't worked for you is not necessarily bad; the horse might be just what someone else has been looking for.

A conscientious buyer is going to look at a number of horses before making a decision. This is often a slow process and can take weeks, even months. It is vital that your potential buyer remember your horse down to the last detail so it does not get overlooked when the buyer narrows his or her choices. The best memory jogger is a printed flyer listing all the facts and details concerning your horse. You should include a copy of the registration papers and at least one color photograph with your flyer. Hand a flyer to every person that comes out to see your horse, even if the person doesn't seem all that interested. You can also hand out flyers at stables, horse shows, and horse clubs. Not only can you attract buyers directly in this way, but sometimes a disinterested person will know someone who's in the market for a horse and will pass on the flyer.

If your horse fits into the high end of the marketplace, you may want to prepare a video. The video should primarily show your horse performing under saddle, but should also show the horse unsaddled and in hand, at a stand from all angles, and at a walk and trot, showing the front-view approach, side view, and rear-view retreat. Your trainer or riding instructor can help you find a source to distribute your video, or you can look through horse magazines for businesses that specialize in helping you sell your horse through video marketing. Have several copies of the video on hand to send to prospective buyers and present to anyone that takes the time to come see your horse. Simply allowing them to view the video on your television will leave only a vague, forgettable impression.

Ensuring a Good Home

When you've found someone interested enough in your horse to make an offer, it is your right to question that person's capability in providing the horse a new home. Obviously you want to sell the horse and if you haven't had many (or any) offers, you might be justifiably afraid of scaring off a buyer with an interview. Still, I tend to find that people willing to provide a good home have no trouble answering questions and are usually proud enough of the home they've prepared for the horse to invite you out for an inspection.

Try to find out why the person wants the horse. Does the horse's experience and training suit the buyer's needs? Does the buyer have the experience necessary to handle your horse? Will the horse be handled and ridden by children or other green riders? This may not seem like your business, but if a bad match is made and the horse injures a person, it could wind up abused or sold at auction.

Ask the name of the veterinarian the buyer plans to use. A blank stare probably means the buyer didn't intend to spend much time or money on a vet. Insist on visiting the horse's new home. While there, look at the condition of the fences and facilities, the riding area, and any other horses kept on the grounds.

Be very conservative when considering a buyer that wants to make installments on the purchase or wants a rock-bottom price to fit a tight budget. If the buyer can hardly afford the horse in the first place, can you expect your horse to receive proper hoof care, decent food, and veterinary care? Will your horse live in squalor or end up sold after it has lost condition? I may sound very judgmental, but if you've read the rest of this book you know I am adamant on the subject of responsibility and proper care for horses. I don't think anyone *needs* to have a horse; it is a privilege to own one, and a costly one at that. Lack of understanding on this subject invariably leads to neglect and abuse of the horse.

Donating a Horse

If you really care for a horse that has declined in performance or health, selling could be unthinkable, as you give up control of your horse's destiny. Keeping the horse may also be unrealistic. The horse could take up the space and time you have to spend on a more useful animal and will incur ongoing expenses as long as it is around. If you do have time and space and can afford to keep the horse, I applaud you, but many cannot realistically manage this.

I mentioned earlier in this chapter the possibility of giving away a horse of limited use. I have given several horses away that were perfectly usable but no longer suited my needs. These were horses that had a chronic unsoundness that couldn't hold up to hard working conditions or were older, but not aged, and had earned retirement. I gave them to people I knew well and trusted to provide a good home. Each horse did indeed receive good care, and some are still with the people I gave them to, many years later.

One of the best ways to donate your horse is to give it to someone you know and trust. You will be able to check on the horse whenever you want or at least call and ask about it. You can also help that person deal with the horse when it is no longer useful or he or she can no longer care for the horse.

You can spread the word that you have a limited-use horse available through horse clubs or your trainer or instructor. If you find a home with someone you don't know, you may want to put a contract together that states the horse must receive adequate care and cannot be sold or otherwise disposed of without your permission. You can even stipulate the right to take back the horse if care is not adequate or disposal of the horse is planned, but it would be unfair to expect the new owner or ward to agree to return the horse without good reason. If your horse is registered, it might be a good idea to hold back the papers to make any future transaction more difficult. This happens frequently with donated racehorses to prevent the new owner from trying to race the horse or sell it as raceable.

There are some nonprofit organizations that depend on donated, older, docile horses. Some of these horses are used as schooling animals for handicapped riders. They are treated wonderfully and are used lightly, rarely ridden faster than a walk. Others, particularly ponies and donkeys, end up in petting zoos. This is not an exciting life, but it can work well for a quiet, aged, or unsound animal.

Some universities will take donated, unsound horses. Although the horses are used to help train veterinary students, they are generally treated exceedingly well and are sometimes rehabilitated to full usefulness. If rehabilitation is carried out, don't expect to be offered the horse back; it most likely will be sold to help finance the school's program.

A few penitentiaries also have horse management programs which rely on donations. They use horses to teach inmates skills in handling and training horses. Some unsound or aged horses are accepted to teach grooming skills; other unbroke or poorly broke horses are needed to teach breaking and training skills.

Death

A stark reality is that few horses will outlive their owners. With care and planning, you can often successfully avoid facing the death of a horse. This is frequently the only reason an older horse is sold or given away and I will admit to having done this myself, although I didn't wait until the horses were decrepit and always took care to arrange a happy home for them.

Sometimes the death of a horse is a shocking and unexpected event; it can come by way of severe colic, heart attack, a fatal or debilitating injury, accidental poisoning, or some other tragedy. You might find your horse dead in the morning or at feed time, or be faced with an emergency medical situation that requires a quick decision to end the horse's suffering.

More commonly death creeps up slowly. You may discover your aged horse gradually declining in health. A horse with a serious illness may fail to respond to treatment. A horse with a chronic lameness may become so uncomfortable it not only loses its usefulness, it gives up its will to survive.

The Ultimate Decision

At one time, I lived in desert country. In the summer it was unbearably hot during the day, so I rode in the evenings around dusk. One evening, I stayed out too late and was forced to return in the dark along the shoulder of a busy highway. My little mare was hit by a car, right out from under me, and lost pretty much all of one of her hind legs. Being within city limits, I had to wait for a vet to arrive to have the mare euthanized, but if I had had access to a gun I would have shot her on the spot.

There are times when you don't have to think at all to decide on euthanization. Whether your horse has suffered a major fracture or been impaled on a fence rail, or whether the vet has concluded your horse has no chance of surviving an agonizing colon impaction, I believe an instinct is present in any conscientious horseperson to ease a horse's suffering by providing a quick and easy death.

It is more difficult to decide what to do with a horse that is on a gradual decline. Euthanizing such an animal is such a personal decision it is hard to give advice. The most important thing to keep in mind is that your decision should reflect what is best for the horse and not be confused with what is best for you.

I once saw a stallion that hopped around on three legs because of an improperly healed fractured ankle. His hooves were in an atrocious state because he could not set the bad foot down on the ground to allow a horseshoer to trim his other hooves. He could not graze or lie down without considerable effort. The owners insisted on keeping him around because he could still serve to mount a mare and they made a bit of money every season breeding him. Every year they swore they'd put him down after the last mare was bred. I heard this four years in a row before I purposely lost track of the people. Those folks didn't have their stallion's best interests in mind; his physical suffering was insignificant since they could still make some money off him.

I also knew of a pony well into its thirties that was blind, foundered, and had such poor teeth it had to be fed thin cooked mashes to prevent starvation. Still the pony was frightfully underweight. The owner bragged about how she'd ridden the pony as a child herself and how she loved it so much she just could not bear to see it go. The pony was surly and depressed and never moved more than necessary because of its weakened state and painfully foundered hooves. They found him dead one miserable winter morning, frozen to death.

These stories are not terribly common, but they are certainly not unheard of. It is very easy to put greed above humanity or to put personal feelings above the well-being of an animal. As a mature and responsible horse owner, you must resist these weaknesses. Death does not have to be a bad thing; it only becomes bad when much suffering is involved. Judgments should be based on the state of the animal, not the state of your emotions. If an impartial opinion is necessary to aid in a decision, call in your veterinarian to evaluate your horse.

On the other end of the spectrum are those that hasten to destroy a horse without due cause. There are many reasons for doing so. A person may not understand the horse's symptoms and may mistakenly believe the horse has an incurable condition when in fact the horse would do well with treatment. Sometimes a veterinarian is mistaken in his or her diagnosis or overestimates the severity of the problem; a second opinion from a qualified vet is never a bad idea.

Some people have no qualms about destroying a horse that might otherwise cost them money. They head to the canners the moment a horse starts to fail in health, knowing that the longer they wait, the less the horse will likely weigh and the less money they will get for the animal. Canners' per-pound prices often exceed the market value of a horse that is aged, in poor health, or unsound.

A trainer I once worked for saved her pet Arabian after his jaw was shattered by a kick to the face. The injury took extensive surgery to repair, and the horse needed round-the-clock care for quite a while. I admire what she did but am aware she spent far more money than the horse's actual worth—more than most people could or would be willing to spend. In a case such as this, it would be reasonable and understandable if a person chose to put the horse down rather than spend the exorbitant amounts of money and effort necessary to repair the horse's jaw and keep it alive during the time it was unable to eat.

I can only ask that you be fair to your horse when deciding its fate. This is not to say you should martyr yourself for a lost cause or exhaust your resources in an attempt to "do the right thing." Use your veterinarian's diagnosis and advice as a basis for your decision. If there's a chance your horse might be useful to someone other than yourself or that it might be worth rehabilitating by someone more financially able than you, please consider donating or selling the horse cheap.

When the decision to euthanize is confirmed, it should be carried out as quickly as possible to prevent further suffering, financial loss, and the chance you might weaken and change your mind. The ideal method is to have your veterinarian perform the act. A lethal injection will drop the horse on the spot, the only pain being the prick of the needle.

If the decision is one based on an emergency situation where no veterinarian is readily available, you may have to do the deed yourself. This may seem unthinkable, but I have heard of such cases. A horse may fall down an embankment on an isolated trail and break a leg. With no way to transport the horse, the choice is either to kill the horse with whatever means possible or to abandon it.

I mentioned earlier that canning is a possibility in selling a debilitated horse. This may be absolutely unacceptable to you and I respect that, as it does seem harsh, but canning is a humane method of destroying a horse if done properly under the right circumstances.

First, determine whether your horse is fit to make the trip to the canners. If the horse is suffering to the extent that traveling by trailer or van would be dangerous or painful for it, you would do better to have the horse euthanized without moving it. If the horse can handle the trip, you or someone you trust must personally transport the horse. The appointment should be prearranged and scheduled so there is minimal waiting time for your horse after its arrival. You should stay to confirm the horse's death, even if you can't actually watch. If done this way, your horse will be unaware of what is happening to it and will suffer no more than bewilderment over its strange, new surroundings. It will receive one quick, fatal blow to the poll that will end its life, and its remains will be put to good use.

If the idea of your horse used as pet food, glue, or something else is distasteful to you, please be aware that if you have your horse euthanized at your barn, it will still probably end up at a rendering plant. This is where all dead-animal removal services take carcasses and is truly the most sanitary, efficient method of disposal.

Disposing of the remains of an animal the size of a horse or pony must be done properly to prevent creation of a health hazard, and I believe rendering or canning the remains are the only decent methods. I know some people bury horses, especially if they've become family pets. A few famous horses have even been publicly buried, entombed in concrete containers. If you bury your horse uncontained in the backyard or pasture, you are risking contamination of underground water sources or ground water. If you live in a remote area, you also risk having your horse's remains dug up by coyotes or wolves. Many areas have ordinances that prevent the burial of animals of such size, so you could be breaking the law by doing so. The only alternatives I can think of for self-disposal of the body of a horse are butchering for self-consumption and burning the carcass, which I must say I can't imagine doing.

Recovery

I am not a grief counselor and won't pretend to be one. Every one of you is going to grieve over the death of your horse in a unique and personal way. Some won't really grieve at all, but will feel relief; others will have mixed feelings of grief and relief.

There is a retired widower that lives in my neighborhood. He often shows up at the local park when I take my dogs to play; he knows my dogs by name and loves to pet and play fetch with them. The man has a wonderful fenced yard, perfect for a dog. One day I asked him why he had no dog of his own. He told me his dog died two years ago and he suffered so much in his grief that he'd decided never to have another dog, thus never to experience that sort of grief again. That man had lived with his dog for fourteen good years and grieved for several months. His decision was, of course, a personal one but I believe fourteen happy years might have been worth the grieving. I also believe a new dog would more than make up for any future grief with the day-to-day pleasure it could provide.

After the death of your horse, you will also have to think about replacing it. Maybe this is a given and you've got your shopping list out already; maybe you still own one or several other horses and don't need to replace the one you've lost. Whatever the case, I strongly encourage you to go on with it—find yourself another horse and give it a chance to become a part of your life, just like the last one you loved and lost. Don't expect a carbon-copy replacement—why would you want one? Every horse has its own personality and characteristics. The ability to recognize and interpret the individual traits of a new horse will only increase your pleasure and skills as a horseperson. Getting to know and learning to get along with each particular horse is one of the greatest joys of horsemanship.

Conclusion

Owning Up to Your Responsibilities

Throughout this book I have mentioned the importance of responsible behavior when working around horses. This is the key to getting along with horses. Your safety, as well as the safety of the horse and others around you, depends upon your behavior.

As owner or keeper of a horse, you have placed yourself in the position of caregiver. Even if you hire others to do your daily chores or work with your horse, you are ultimately responsible for the treatment your horse receives.

Your horse depends on you to create a comfortable environment for it, provide it with adequate nutritious food and ample water, watch over and tend to the condition of its health, and act rationally and fairly when handling it. Your horse relies on you to learn its limitations and heed your own, to keep your head in panic situations, and to hold your temper during moments of frustration.

Be realistic about the amount of time you are truly willing to invest in a horse. The more time you spend with your horse, the better you will communicate with each other, the more skilled you will become, and the more fun you will have.

Be realistic about the money necessary for horse ownership. Horses are high-maintenance creatures to be sure, but a willingness to provide for your horse's needs will be paid back by a happier, healthier, sounder animal—one more willing and able to serve your needs.

Owning a horse is not a necessity, it is a choice. Those of us who choose to take on this tremendous responsibility do so for a reason. We are irresistibly attracted to these grand creatures. We savor the musky smell and velvety smooth feel of a clean coat. We cherish the sounds of creaking leather, clopping hooves, and a welcoming nicker. We thrill at the sight of a horse running freely and the sensation of sitting astride, as if sitting on top of the world. We stand in awe of the immense strength of the horse and our own ability to capture and contain such power.

We take on the grand responsibility for the privilege of keeping company with these majestic beasts; we do it because we love horses and the endless joy they bring.

Glossary

barrel: Trunk of a horse extending from shoulders to flank, not including the back or spine.

billet: Strap attached to a saddle underneath the stirrup flap; used to attach a girth.

bit: The mouthpiece of a bridle; used as a control device during riding.

bit shank: Bar attached at the end of the mouthpiece bar of a bit; used to increase stopping leverage of the mouthpiece bar.

blaze: Wide strip of white hairs on the face of a horse.

bosal hackamore: Teardrop-shaped nosepiece of a bridle on which both the reins and headstall attach; used as a control device during riding.

bot blade: Single-edged razor blade set into a handle; used for removing botfly eggs from horsehair.

bridle: Complete bitted or hackamored head harness and reins; used to guide and control a horse during riding.

bridlepath: Shaved or cut area of mane behind the ears of a horse; used for cosmetic purposes and to keep mane hair from tangling in crownpiece straps.

browband: Strap attached to the headstall of a bridle horizontally across the forehead of a horse just below the ears; used to stabilize the headstall.

butt strap: Chain or strap fitted across the back of a horse trailer or van stall; used to prevent a horse from backing out.

cannon bone: Bone on the leg of a horse that extends from the knee joint to the ankle joint or from the hock joint to the ankle joint.

canter: Gait of a horse, a slow gallop (term commonly used by English-style riders).

cantle: Upward-curving rear piece of the seat of a saddle; used to prevent the rider from sliding back.

cast: Position of a horse when it rolls too close to a wall or fence and becomes stuck.

cavesson: Nosepiece used with a bridle to prevent a horse from opening its mouth while being ridden.

chin strap: Strap attached to the bit of a bridle against the chin or jaw of a horse; used as additional leverage to the bit or hackamore to help stop or slow a horse while riding.

cinch: Band that lays against the girth area of a horse, attached by rings and latigo straps to each side of a Western saddle; used to hold the saddle in place.

colic: Stomach disturbance or intestinal discomfort.

colt: Male horse under five years of age.

conformation: Particular way a horse is physically put together.

cooler: Light, thin blanket that covers the body of a horse from neck to tail, commonly attached by straps at the girth and chest.

coronet band: Band of tough, hairless flesh abutting the top of a horse's hoof.

cow kick: Type kick in which a horse swings a hind leg forward and out to the side.

cribbing: Action in which the horse anchors its teeth on an object and sucks air into its stomach.

cross-firing: Action during the canter in which a horse takes opposing leads on the front and hind legs.

crownpiece: Part of a bridle headstall or halter that lays behind a horse's ears.

curb bit: Bit that consists of a bar mouthpiece raised in the center and bit shanks attached to each end of the mouthpiece.

curb strap: See **chin strap**.

curry: (1) Act of brushing a horse using a circular motion. (2) Grooming tool used to remove or loosen dirt or to detangle the tail and mane of a horse.

dam: Female parent horse.

dorsal line: Line of dark or black hairs running the length of a horse's spine from withers to tail.

ear shy: Aversion of a horse to having its ears or area near the ears touched.

electrified tape: Narrow nylon tape woven with wire that is electrified by way of a battery connection; used as fencing material that will deliver a mild electrical shock when touched.

farrier: Person that shapes, sets, and applies shoes to horses' hooves.

fender: Flap of a Western saddle that lays under the rider's leg and attaches the stirrup.

fetlock: Tuft of hair that grows from the hind point of the ankle of a horse, designating the ankle area.

filly: Immature female horse under five years of age.

flipping: The action of a horse in which it deliberately rears up and throws itself backward until it falls.

float: To rasp smooth the edges of a horse's molars.

foal: Horse of either gender under one year of age.

forelock: Part of a horse's mane that covers the poll and forehead.

founder (laminitis): Affliction of the hooves and neck of a horse characterized by excessive heat, swelling, and disfiguration.

freezing up: The action of a horse in which it becomes rigid and refuses to move.

frog: Spongy heart-shaped protrusion on the underside of a horse's hoof.

gallop: Fastest gait of a horse.

gelding: Castrated male horse or colt.

girth: (1) Area of a horse's barrel behind the shoulders and elbows and in front of the belly. (2) Band that lays on the girth area of a horse and is buckled to billet straps on each side of a saddle; used to hold the saddle in place.

girth channel: Neoprene or foam-rubber band that lays under the girth of a saddle against the girth of a horse.

hackamore: Bitless head harness equipped with a nosepiece; used for control during riding.

halter: Head harness used for leading and tying a horse.

head shy: Aversion of a horse to having its head or ears touched.

headstall: The straps of a bridle that are used to hold the bit, hackamore nosepiece, or cavesson in place on a horse's head.

heat (in heat): Hormonal cycle of a filly or mare in which she can become pregnant; see **horsing**.

hock: Middle joint of a horse's hind leg.

hog fuel: Ground-covering material consisting of large, coarse wood chips and strips of bark.

horse hand (hh): Unit of height in which a horse is measured; equals four linear inches.

horsing: State of a mare during the time she is ovulating and can become pregnant.

hotwalking machine (hotwalker): Machine consisting of a center base motor and attached overhead metal arms with tie lines at the ends of the arms; used to walk horses in a continuous circle for exercise.

hot wire: Wire fencing material connected to a battery; will deliver a mild electrical shock when touched.

in foal: State of a pregnant mare.

in season: See **horsing**.

jipping: See **lunging**.

laminitis: Disease of the hooves; see **founder**.

latigo: Nylon or leather strap used to attach a cinch to each side of a Western saddle.

lead: (1) Rope or strap used to lead a horse. (2) Furthermost extended leg in a cantering stride.

lead shank: Lead line with a chain attached at one end; used for increased control while leading and handling a horse.

loafing shed: Sheltering structure with at least one open door or side in which a horse can enter and exit at will.

lope: Word commonly used by Western-style riders; see **canter**.

lunging: (1) Action of a horse that suddenly leaps forward. (2) The act of exercising a horse by moving it on a long lead line in a circle around the handler.

mane: Line of long, coarse hairs that runs the length of a horse's neck along the crest.

mare: Female horse over age five.

martingale: Piece of tack used to keep the reins low and help set a horse's head during riding.

muzzle: (1) Lower part of a horse's head, including all of the nose and mouth area. (2) Plastic, wire-mesh, or leather device that fits around the muzzle of a horse and is held in place by attaching to the halter nosepiece rings; used to prevent the horse from eating or biting.

neck-reining: Method of steering a horse during riding in which the rider presses a rein against the horse's neck in order to push it into a turn.

overgirth: Band that fits around the horse over the saddle and girth or cinch; used to stabilize the saddle.

overreaching: Action of a horse in which it nicks or steps on a front heel or leg with a hind toe during a stride.

paddock: Fenced outdoor enclosure for containing horses.

pastern: Area on a horse's leg between the ankle joint and the hoof.

pasture: Fenced outdoor enclosure; can be identical to a paddock but commonly considered a larger, grass-covered area.

pecking order: Order in a herd of horses; ranging from the most dominant members to the most passive.

pelham bit: Bit used for English-style riding, similar to a **curb bit** but made to be used with two sets of reins.

plow-reining: Method of steering a horse in which the horse's head is pulled around in the desired direction of the turn by pressure on the rein.

poll: Area of a horse's skull between its ears.

pommel: Raised front part of a saddle that rests over a horse's withers and in front of the rider's seat.

posting: Action of a rider at the trotting gait of a horse in which the rider rises up from the seat of the saddle on one step and sits during the alternate step.

propping: Action of a horse in which it abruptly stops or ducks to the side.

proud flesh: Granular flesh that grows over the opening of a wound.

pulling (hairs): Act of thinning and shortening a mane or tail by pulling some of the hairs out by the roots.

rearing: Action of a horse in which it stands with its front legs raised off the ground.

reins: The lines attached to the bit or hackamore nosepiece of a bridle and held by the rider; used to steer, slow, and stop a horse.

roaching: Act of shaving or cutting short the hairs of a horse's mane.

sheet: See **cooler.**

shedding blade: Grooming tool consisting of a flexible metal band with one dull serrated edge and two handles; used to remove loose hair from a horse's coat.

shedrow: Aisle or walkway of a barn or stable, commonly in front of or between a row of stalls.

sire: Male parent horse.

snaffle: Type of bar-bit mouthpiece with a joint or multiple joints in the center of the bar.

snip: Strip of white hairs on the muzzle of a horse.

sock: White marking (hairs) below the knees and hocks of a horse.

spade bit: Type of bar and shank bit with a high spoon or spade-shaped extension on the center of the bar; used for extreme stopping control.

speedy cut: (1) Action of a horse in which it hits one leg with another during a stride. (2) Injury caused by aforementioned action.

spooking: Action of a horse in which it reacts in any manner out of fright.

stallion: Male horse over age five.

star: Spot of white hairs on the forehead of a horse.

stifle: First joint of a horse's hind leg just below the flank.

stirrup: Flat-bottomed metal or wooden ring attached to a saddle in which the foot of a rider is held.

stocking: White marking (hairs) that covers a horse's lower leg and extends to or past the knee or hock.

striking: The action of a horse in which it throws out a front leg.

surcingle: Band that encircles the girth area of a horse; most commonly used to attach drive lines.

sweat scraper: Metal or plastic-coated, dull-edged blade used to scrape sweat or water from a horse's coat.

tack: (1) Any equipment used to handle or ride a horse. (2) The act of placing tack on a horse.

teaser: Stallion or hormone-induced gelding used to entice a mare to accept a breeding stallion.

throatlatch: Strap attached to the headstall of a bridle that runs from temple to temple under a horse's throat; used to hold the headstall in place.

thrush: Fungal growth found on the bottom of a horse's hoof.

tie down: Piece of tack used to keep a horse from raising its head high during riding.

trot: Gait of a horse in which two feet hit the ground simultaneously, one front foot and one hind foot of opposite sides.

Vetwrap: Bandaging product made of thin, stretchy, gauze-like material that adheres to itself.

washrack: Area designed and used for bathing horses.

weanling: Foal that has been weaned, commonly six months to one year of age.

weaving: Action of a horse in which it steps side to side with its front legs, swinging its head, while its hind legs remain nearly motionless.

webbings: Nylon or plastic woven straps that stretch over the opening of a stall to act as a gate.

withers: Raised portion of a horse's spine at the junction of the neck and back.

yearling: Horse between the ages of one and two years.

Index

References to photographs are in italic type.